ROCHE
versus
ADAMS

ROCHE
versus
ADAMS

Stanley Adams

JONATHAN CAPE
THIRTY BEDFORD SQUARE LONDON

First published 1984
Copyright © 1984 by Stanley Adams

British Library Cataloguing in Publication Data
Adams, Stanley
Roche versus Adams.
1. Hoffmann-La Roche   2. Drug trade – European
Community countries
I. Title
338.4'76151'0924   RS68.H/

ISBN 0–224–02180–X

Photoset in Great Britain by
Rowland Phototypesetting Ltd, Bury St Edmunds, Suffolk
Printed by St Edmundsbury Press
Bury St Edmunds, Suffolk

For my dear daughters
Nathalie, Alexandra and Stephanie
with my love

Contents

Illustrations

The author and publisher are grateful to the following for permission to reproduce illustrations: Granada Television Company Ltd for nos 1, 5, 6 and 7; E.E.C. London office for nos 8–13; and the European Parliament London office for nos 14–18.

Introduction

This intriguing and moving account of an individual's fight for justice in a situation where national and international law have clashed violently, is both unique and extraordinary.

For the man who acted in accordance with his conscience and with no thought of personal gain it has had tragic consequences, not only for him but for his family, and certainly cries out to be resolved. Whether it will ever *be* resolved is a matter of real concern to Stanley Adams, and for anyone else coming after him who feels impelled to act in a similar way.

Unless the law is clarified, people in future will be disinclined to bring to public notice any irregularities or peculiar dealings they have observed in the conduct of companies which might affect people's health and financial well-being, wherever they might be. Big business has long tentacles and wields immense power in order to increase profits. Individuals will hardly risk being penalized for what they consider to be a moral gesture, and will prefer to retreat into the safety of silence.

A Commission setting out to examine the effect of cartels on the body politic is in an admirable position, being able to report without fear or favour on its findings, but a single individual, not having the protection of numbers, is at a perilous disadvantage and is liable to suffer cruelly through his isolation.

For anyone who is interested in justice and the complexities of international law versus national domestic law, and who would like to see it simplified and strengthened in all countries, this book is a must. It lays bare the plight of an individual in a dangerous and sinister situation besides revealing the weaknesses and ambiguities a Commission has to deal with when it attempts to bring to heel recalcitrant nations who seek to circumvent the law and fudge the issue.

The issue which gave rise to this intensely human story, the agonizing dilemma in which Stanley Adams found himself and which drove him to seek refuge in this country, still remains to be dealt with. A final judgment deserves to be set plainly before the public so that it may have an opportunity to know that justice has been done and been seen to be done. Unfinished business is unfair to all concerned. Not only must money be made available in order to set the wheels in motion, but good will exerted by everyone involved to ensure a satisfactory conclusion, otherwise the 'Stanley Adams Affair' could turn out to be as harmful internationally as if the famous Dreyfus case had been allowed to languish unresolved.

A man naturally wishes to clear his name and have the stigma of a prison sentence removed if that is possible, but without substantial help, he has little chance of achieving this and is left feeling deeply frustrated and helpless. That is what Stanley Adams wants to do – clear his name.

RT HON THE LORD GARDINER P.C., C.H.
LORD CHANCELLOR 1964–70

1 Formative Years

'Let conscience be your guide,' the proverb says, but the proverb doesn't live in the twentieth century. This is the story of what happened when I followed my conscience, and of where it led me. It is a story of intrigue and ruthlessness, of betrayal and imprisonment, a story of politics and politicians, and of justice and injustice. Like many such stories it has no beginning and no end. If I was forced to choose a date, then I would say it began in March 1972, the month in which I was promoted to being a World Product Manager for the giant pharmaceutical company Hoffmann-La Roche, and in which I started to see for the first time how big business really operates. But the roots of what happened stretch back through the time I spent working for Roche, between 1964 and 1973, through my working life before ever I joined Roche, through the poverty I saw in Africa and South America, and through my adolescence and childhood in Malta.

I was born in Malta in 1927 into an ordinary, middle-class family. We had a town house and a summer house, and were relatively well off. I was brought up to look on Britain as my true home, and I was proud of the fact that I was a British citizen and that I spoke English as my first language. As the eldest son in a family of five children, I spent a lot of time with my maternal grandparents who instilled into me a strong sense of honour and duty. During the war Churchill was my great hero. Even as I took refuge in the shelters from the daily and nightly bombing raids, I was sure he was infallible and that right must eventually triumph over might. For a young man growing up, Malta was too small and too confining. I was determined to leave as soon as possible, and set my sights on Britain. I wanted to travel as widely as I could and from quite an early age had decided to go into business as the best means of fulfilling that ambition. I was a good linguist, and by the time I was eighteen I spoke English, Maltese and Italian. By the age of twenty-three I also spoke French, Spanish and Arabic. When the war ended I took my chance and went to Tripoli to join the British Military Administration as a translator and interpreter. I worked first for the Road Transport department, and then for the Police and Prisons department. In the afternoons, after work, I used to study Arabic. Sometimes I would accompany my boss to a house to find that all the inhabitants, whole families, had been slaughtered. It was a brutal education and I grew up quickly in the two years that I was there.

From Tripoli I went to England to study economics, first in London and then in Oxford. I rarely missed a debate at the Oxford Union and I became fascinated by politics and the art of government. Churchill's defeat in the general election that followed the war had left a lasting impression on me of the way that true democracy works. Despite all that he had done during the war, and the power that he had held, the British voters had quickly rejected him and his government when peace came, in favour of the socialist administration of Clement Attlee. I met Clement Attlee and his wife later over a drink after a Union debate and was very impressed by his simplicity. Even as a young boy I had sometimes thought that Churchill was rather dictatorial in his attitude and had excused it as perhaps being necessary in wartime, but gradually I began to realize that men of peace can do as much for the general good as men of war, and this belief was reinforced in me as I watched the way in which India gained independence under Clement Attlee's government, and Aneurin Bevan began his monumental work which eventually became law as the National Health Service, a service which is still the envy of many countries today.

Churchill may have been my childhood hero, but as I grew into a young man Aneurin Bevan replaced him as the man for whom I had enormous admiration and respect.

I spent my long summer holidays mainly with companies in London and abroad, learning business administration and practice. So when I left Oxford I was well prepared for work. My first job was with a British import–export firm based in Liverpool, and I worked for them in Lagos and then in Accra. I managed branches in both places.

I travelled extensively all over Africa. However, my ideology never permitted me to visit South Africa, either on business or on holiday, though I had many opportunities.

From Africa I moved to South America to the port of Santa Marta, in Magdalena Province, Colombia, where I worked as a shipping insurance agent for Lloyd's of London. I was appointed as the British Vice-Consul for the Province, and later as full Consul, and served the interests of the British community for five years. I spent the little spare time I had at weekends trying to build up a small banana plantation, buying up minute plots of adjoining land and spending hours in negotiations to produce twenty-five acres of forest, which I then had cleared and planted. By the time I left Santa Marta, when the British government decided to close their consulate down, my little plantation was producing regular crops of fruit and I sold it for a profit as a going concern. Deep down I have always had a passion for agriculture and farming, and this experience only whetted my appetite. I decided to do the job properly and moved to Kenya to study agriculture at Egerton College in Njoro with the aim of eventually going into farming as a full-time business.

All this time I had been living extremely well. I had had big houses, good cars, servants, the comfortable lifestyle of the expatriate who could rely on cheap labour and on high business expenses. I didn't experience the unease that some expatriates did at being away from home and in a foreign culture. I felt comfortable and at home. I loved working with different people, learning their language, learning the way they worked, exploring new cultures. It didn't occur to me to question any of it until the Mau Mau activities started up in Kenya. That forced me to think deeply. I do not, and cannot, condone indiscriminate violence which hurts the innocent as well as the guilty, but when I saw what was happening around me I had to ask myself, why? Why such anger? And I began to realize how much had been taken out of these countries, and in comparison how little had been given back. I had seen a lot of poverty in Africa and South America and now it was beginning to dawn on me that the responsibility for it did not lie solely with the Africans or the South Americans. Not, I have to admit, like many others, that that realization made any difference to the way I lived. I liked living abroad, I liked the comfort of big houses, and the possibility of employing maids and chauffeurs and gardeners if I could afford it. The lifestyle was very seductive.

Because of the Mau Mau activities I was persuaded by friends that this was not a wise time to be buying property or starting to farm in Kenya, so when I had finished my year's agricultural training I returned to Europe to go back into business once more. First I worked for A.E.I. in Rugby. Then I landed up working for an American company in Belgium, the Outboard Marine Corporation, as Assistant Commercial Manager. It was a good life. I enjoyed the fun, the sport, the prestige, the status of fast luxury boats. I had everything a young man of my age could want. But I was ambitious. After three years I was looking for an industry where I could develop and move ahead fast, and where there was an opportunity for travelling. I chose the pharmaceutical industry deliberately, because it was growing, and because it was the highest paying industry at the time, higher even than oil.

In 1962 I joined Sterling-Winthrop, the American drug multinational, and my career in pharmaceuticals began. This job took me to Manila in the Philippines. Two years later I found myself holding a letter from Hoffmann-La Roche of Basle, inviting me to go for interview. They were poaching, as companies do all the time. They had heard that a placement I had expected in Sterling-Winthrop had not materialized, and I might possibly be looking for somewhere else. I went for the interview. The Roche grapevine was very extensive. They had a complete dossier on me and seemed to know more about me than I did myself, but they offered me a very good salary and I accepted the job.

In the summer of 1964 I became a Roche employee. I was delighted. I thought that now I was really on my way up. A job with Hoffmann-La Roche was a job to be proud of. They were a Swiss multinational, and were known to favour Swiss nationals for their senior positions, so to be hired by them in a managerial capacity was quite an achievement. My contract stated that I would spend three months in Basle, learning my way round the Roche empire, and then would be sent overseas as a manager in one of their branches. My salary was to be 4,500 Swiss francs a month (Sfr. 59,000 a year, nearly £30,000 at an exchange rate of Sfr. 2 to £1) which, considering I was still in my thirties, was not a salary I felt like refusing.

It soon became clear that I was going to spend more than three months in Basle. I had had a lot of experience working for other firms, and this was considered unusual in a Swiss firm where the tendency is for an employee to spend most of his life with the same company. I got on extremely well with my immediate boss, who found it stimulating to have someone around him who could look at things with fresh eyes, and because I had knowledge of different management systems, and in particular the American management system, it was not difficult for me to pinpoint areas where traditional methods could be improved in ways that had not been thought of before, or to solve problems by finding a new way round them (which I had seen in operation elsewhere). When my three months' basic training was up, it was decided not to send me abroad, but to take me right through Roche, training me in every department. This was a very unusual procedure, and I don't know anyone else, Swiss or non-Swiss, who was put through all the departments in the way that I was. Normally when a person came into the firm they were trained only in the area in which they were going to work, in Finance, for instance, or Medicine. I had been assigned to the division dealing with Bulk Vitamins and Chemicals, but I was trained in all the other departments. Finance, Ethical department (medicines), Manufacturing, the Analytical department, Packing, Shipping, I went through every one of them, and all that time I was learning about the way Roche operated. If I could do anything to help, then I did, but basically I was there to learn, not simply to earn money for Roche. I have never had such a thorough training in anything. Even today, after everything that has happened, I am grateful to the company for that.

I rented a beautiful house with gardens in an elegant suburb of Basle and made myself comfortable. I was single and I led an active social life, entertaining and being entertained, playing tennis, spending weekends in the mountains. I even started taking flying lessons at the Basle flying school with a chemist colleague of mine. From time to time I reminded Roche that they were supposed to be sending me abroad, but each time they found something to hold my interest a little longer and increased my salary so that I wouldn't get discontented.

Although I trained in all departments I only ever worked in the Bulk Vitamins and Chemicals division. This division was made up of three sectors: the pharmaceutical sector, the human nutrition sector, and the animal nutrition sector. It sold bulk. In other words, we didn't sell tablets, but tons of vitamins and chemicals to Roche branches and outside customers to make up the tablets, or tons of vitamins A, D and E to go into flour or margarine, vitamin C to go into soft drinks, beer or wine (where it has a stabilizing effect) or into tinned and fresh meats, or most of the vitamins together to go into animal feed. (Animal feed was a most important area, particularly in intensive farming.) There is a very comprehensive list of uses for the different vitamins and alone amongst its competitors Roche sold the complete range.

After a couple of years I began to get restless, despite my salary increases, and urged Roche to find me a position abroad. Instead, in 1967, they asked me to do a complete survey of the Latin American market in Bulk Vitamins and Chemicals. Spanish was one of my languages, and I had been dealing with Latin America from headquarters, so I was a logical choice. The survey took nine months and I travelled to Brazil, Paraguay, Argentina, Uruguay, Chile, Bolivia, Peru, Colombia, Venezuela, Panama, Costa Rica, Nicaragua, Salvador, Honduras, Guatemala, Mexico and the U.S.A. I visited all the Roche branches and agents, and assessed the potential for future development. I had full authority to draw on the Roche branches out there for whatever I needed in terms of money, cars, drivers and accommodation, and I set out on my journey with a huge wad of airline tickets. It was a fascinating exercise and when I finally returned to Basle to draft my report it ran to a hundred and fifty pages of analysis, recommendations and suggestions. I was called to a meeting with the President of Roche and his senior managers, and they went through the report in detail with me. One of my recommendations had been that Roche should open a new Bulk Vitamins and Chemicals branch in Venezuela, and shortly after that meeting I was called back and asked whether I would like the job of setting it up.

It was just the kind of business challenge that I enjoyed most, but I deferred my answer until I had spoken to someone else. Her name was Mariléne Morandi, she was Swiss-French, and I had fallen deeply in love with her. She had originally come to work for me as my secretary but had then moved to another post in Roche and, when we knew that we were seriously interested in each other, to another job altogether outside Roche, to prevent any hint of the careless gossip at work that can be so damaging to people.

Mariléne was in her early twenties. She was an accomplished linguist, very intelligent, and highly educated in schools in Switzerland, Germany, France, and England. Her first language was French and she had been brought up in Lausanne as the daughter of an entrepreneur who owned a medium-sized road-building company and worked mainly for the Lausanne local authority. Later on I was to discover that she was not ignorant of the way that business works in Switzerland, and the way money controls most aspects of it, but now all I knew was that I loved her. She was at times quiet and serious and at other times lighthearted and gay, and fun to be with. She could be very intense, she was artistic, a good painter, a good musician. (I used to spend hours listening to her playing the classical guitar.) But she was also an excellent skier and tennis player, and generally very athletic. We had been seeing each other for some time, long before my trip to Latin America, and I thought the moment had now come to ask her if she would marry me and come to Venezuela so we could set up home together there. She agreed. I accepted the post as manager in Venezuela, and we were married on September 9th, 1967 at St George's Roman Catholic Chapel in Castagnola, a picturesque village in the mountains overlooking Lake Lugano. (Mariléne was a devout and practising Catholic.) It was a beautiful setting for a wedding, and the hotel where we had the reception was equally lovely. We spent our honeymoon in Florence, where Mariléne satisfied her love for art by visiting every museum and art gallery she could find, and we spent many happy hours as well exploring the Tuscan countryside together. We returned to Switzerland only to pack our belongings in readiness for the departure to Venezuela. In December we flew via Paris to New York, spending ten days as a final extended honeymoon in a luxury Manhattan hotel, before flying on to Caracas, where we were going to live for the next three years.

After three months in Caracas we bought a penthouse on the seventeenth floor of a very grand, German-built apartment block, the 'Residencías Parqué Sebucan'. The fact that it was German and solidly built was important. Caracas was occasionally subject to earthquakes and anything that was not properly built was liable to disintegrate. The front windows of our flat looked out over the main national park in Caracas, on Avenida Miranda, and from the back we had glorious views over the Avila mountains. We had three bedrooms, two lounges, three bathrooms, a maid's room, a maid's bathroom, a kitchen and two lifts which came directly into the flat. Many of the other owner-residents were foreign diplomats from the American, French and German embassies, and others were businessmen like myself. Soon all of them were our friends. Mariléne and I furnished the flat ourselves, buying from a furniture store, 'Capuy', which was so exclusive you had to ring the door and be checked through a spyhole before they'd let you in to shop. Mariléne loved beautiful things, and I had earned more money in Roche than I could spend, so now we bought whatever we wanted to. We had servants too, a cook called Isabella, and later, when our first daughter, Nathalie, was born, a nurse called June. Isabella was Colombian and June was Jamaican. The city of Caracas is high up, but the sea is a twenty-minute drive away and every Saturday morning, early, Mariléne and I used to get into my yellow Mustang (I've always been a lover of good cars – this one had a black vinyl sun-roof, I remember) and drive down to the beach to bathe.

On June 21st, 1968 Nathalie was born, and on May 29th, 1970 Alexandra, 'Sandy', followed. They gave us enormous pleasure. Mariléne was one of those women who revelled in motherhood, and of course being able to afford help in the house meant that both of us could enjoy the children more, without too much of the hard work associated with looking after them. We were a very happy family.

Our well-being depended on accepting the system we were in and at the time I didn't question it too closely. My salary, for instance, had gone on increasing steadily while I worked for Roche. Roche operated a scheme whereby they paid the agreed monthly rate for the job but they could vary the number of payments. I started on thirteen payments a year and by the time I left Roche I was getting fifteen payments a year (double salary in June and treble salary in December). The scheme was used to reward people without other colleagues on the same level finding out about it. Everyone knew officially that the salary for this level of management was so much a month, but no one knew how many monthly payments were being made to anyone else. The same kind of principle was applied when paying managers abroad, but the main purpose then was to keep wages down in developing countries. Once Roche and I had agreed the level of salary I was to earn as manager in Venezuela, then Roche would decide how much they would actually pay me in Venezuela, and how much extra they would pay into my Swiss bank account in Basle. Then they would notify the Venezuelan accountant only of the amount I was paid in Venezuela, so that in Venezuela that was the amount I declared and paid tax on. The amount in the Swiss account would not normally be declared in Switzerland, and would not be caught for tax in either place. Although there were obvious tax advantages for overseas managers paid in this way, it was not done for that reason. What Roche wanted to do was prevent the local people who worked for them in other countries from realizing how much money those on foreign contracts were earning. As far as the Venezuelans who worked for Roche were concerned the differential between the money I earned and, say, the money of a qualified Venezuelan chemist who worked for me, appeared to be only the normal differential between that job and a manager's job. If they had realized that in fact I was earning perhaps double that amount, and that was the Western market value of the job, then there would have been an uproar because they were equally well educated and qualified. A Venezuelan manager would be paid only at the Venezuelan rate, without benefit of extra payments to other bank accounts.

As in all multinationals, in Roche the overseas manager is the servant of the parent company. Quite how much this was true I didn't realize until I returned later to Basle to work in a senior management capacity and saw how tightly regulated the overseas manager is, even in terms of the information that the parent company chooses to give him, or not give him. I enjoyed the challenge of building up a branch from nothing, of finding office staff and salesmen and training them from scratch, of teaching them the business of vitamins and chemicals, and at the same time of going out myself to drum up orders to get things started. Venezuela is a vast country, but it only had a population then of around ten million and of that ten million approximately nine million had little or no economic power and were on the breadline or below it. The buying market was effectively restricted to around a million people. Nevertheless, in three years from a starting point of near zero we had built the Bulk Vitamins and Chemicals turnover of the company up to 6 million Swiss francs, and had a total staff of about a hundred and twenty. Nearly a

hundred of those were women working in the packing department, but we had a sales team of around twenty-five in all.

It was when it came to the payment of wages that the restriction
on overseas managers was most obvious. We could not pay people
the wage which we personally might think they deserved. The
limits were set for us and worked out in Basle by people who sat all
day looking at the world market place and making theoretical
decisions, which I and other managers then had to put into
practice. We would be given some room for manoeuvre – a
bottom price and a top price and a scale in between on which to
place employees, depending on how much we valued them, and
on how tender our consciences were – but there were definite
limits we could not cross.

The women who worked in the packing department in Roche
Venezuela were paid less than my maids for a long, eight-to-five
day with only a short break for lunch. I could never pay them what
I wanted to because their wages were fixed, though I and other
foreign managerial staff were getting regular increases in our pay
packets. So I did the next best thing. I picked three or four of the
most intelligent employees and suggested to them that they
should form a savings association, with a lawyer and a treasurer
and a secretary, and start putting aside a little bit each week. On
the money they were paid it was virtually impossible for them to
save anything, but without that I couldn't help them. They did as I
advised and I helped them draw up the papers. Then they came to
me, following my instructions, and told me they wanted to put
their money in the company and they wanted to know what the
company would give them for it as an inducement to saving. I, as I
had promised, recommended the scheme to Roche headquarters,
suggesting that the company meet their savings penny for penny.
(We had already set a maximum amount of savings each week,
otherwise Roche would never have accepted the scheme.) At first
Roche only offered a half to one, but within a year they met the
sums deposited with an equal amount, and all the employees who
could afford it were saving the maximum weekly amount. It was a
very roundabout way of increasing their earnings, but there was
no other way of doing it and it was the best I could think of.

In October 1970, towards the end of my contract in Venezuela,
the president of Roche, Dr Adolf Jann, wrote to me. He thanked
me for all I had done and suggested that, knowing the way I was,

and that the Bulk Vitamins business of the branch was now running smoothly, I might like to move on to a bigger challenge. He wanted me to move to Mexico and manage the Bulk Vitamins and Chemicals business there. If I agreed, he said, he would suggest that when Mariléne and the children and I returned to Switzerland for the long holiday that was due to us, we should leave behind in Caracas all our belongings packed up and ready to be shipped from there to Mexico. I agreed. I also recommended that a local man, Juan Carlos Silva, who I had been training up, should take over the management when I left. I saw no reason why local people should not take the top positions and Roche also had their reasons for accepting my recommendation. On December 19th I handed the branch over to Juan Carlos and flew back to Europe with my family.

We were met at Malpensa airport near Milan by Mariléne's parents, who had retired and moved from Lausanne to a village not far away on the Swiss–Italian border, and with whom we were going to spend Christmas and the New Year. We were also met by my Christmas present to the family, a new Jaguar 4.2 litre automatic which I had ordered the year before, direct from the British Leyland factory. It was already paid for, and I had had it specially adapted to my specifications with electric windows, drinks cabinet, a radio cassette player and special sun-tinted glass so I could drive it in hot countries. The car was a distinctive colour, one I particularly like, a metallic willow green which was not part of the normal Jaguar colour range. I had cabled the factory and British Leyland had sent the car with a driver to meet us at the airport, complete with drinks in the drink cabinet and flowers for Mariléne.

I had four months' leave, which I took with my family, relaxing and enjoying having time to be with my wife and play with my children. Most of the time we stayed in a flat set in the top of the villa belonging to Mariléne's parents. They had built it for Mariléne when she was single, but had had the foresight to make it big enough to cope with a husband and children, if she ever married. The villa was in a beautiful setting, on the top of a hill, with gardens and a small pond with a fountain playing. Mariléne's parents were delighted with their two new 'Venezuelan' grand-daughters, and when in April 1971 I went back to Basle to start studying the Mexican operations in preparation for our move there, Mariléne and my two children stayed with her parents rather than move to Basle for the couple of months it would take before we all set off again for Mexico.

At least, we thought we were going to Mexico, but one afternoon in June 1971 I was summoned to the President's office and told that, although I had been studying the situation in Mexico for two months by then, I was not after all going to be posted there. I was given no reason but I was assured it had nothing to do with my capabilities and that the real reason could not be told me. (I later discovered that they had tried to shift someone to make room for me and had lost a battle at board level because the person in question had influential connections. In Switzerland nepotism was an occupational hazard. Who you knew was usually more important than what you knew, and Roche was no exception.) Instead of Mexico I was offered a posting to Montevideo in Uruguay, Managua in Nicaragua, or Manila in the Philippines, or, if I preferred, I was given the option of remaining in Basle at headquarters. Mariléne and I discussed it and decided to remain in Basle, partly because the children were small and it would be nice to be near the grandparents for a while, and partly because none of the three postings offered was as big or as important as the Mexican operation. They were about on the same level as the Venezuelan posting, and I was eager for something a little more challenging. So I told Roche I would stay in Basle but would be happy to be considered if a different posting came up. They were very pleased, and after some consideration made me a Regional Manager, in control of selling operations on the American continent covering Canada and Latin America.

The Bulk Vitamins and Chemicals division had three regional managers, each controlling a zone of the world. The other two managers were Swiss and controlled Europe and the Far East respectively. I was given what the Swiss call in German the 'Prokura'. It's the power of attorney and in Switzerland is considered very important. It meant that I had the right to sign Roche letters, and anything I signed was binding on Roche. Without that power any letters or contracts signed would not be considered legally binding. It is an indication that you have reached a certain level of authority in a company. Big decisions, small decisions, increased prices, reduced prices, discounts to win new business, everything in my zone came through me. If the letters were addressed to the president, I answered them on presidential notepaper and sent them to him for his signature. If they weren't addressed to the president I signed them myself and they were countersigned by another signatory. (Roche had a two-signatory system.) Most of my time I spent dealing with other Roche companies, because outside customers in Canada and Latin America tended to write to the Roche companies on the spot there, who in turn sought advice from me on how to respond. Occasionally I dealt with outside customers direct, but not very often.

But in March 1972 all that changed. Roche altered their system. The three regional managers were promoted to World Product Managers, and instead of splitting the world into three zones, they split the Vitamins and Chemicals range into three, with each World Product Manager taking responsibility for a certain number of products and extending that responsibility to sales worldwide. It didn't seem so significant at the time. I was paid more, for which I was grateful, and I had new areas of responsibility which I thought would be interesting, but it never crossed my mind that this innocuous change would start the chain of circumstances that finally ended in the destruction of my wife and family.

2 Disillusion

The change in system was significant because it meant that for the first time I was dealing not only with the American continent, but with the Far East and Europe as well, and as Europe was the base of many of Roche's biggest customers and competitors, that meant I now dealt far more directly with outside customers as well as with Roche branches. Many of the companies that Roche Basle dealt with were as big as Roche itself and, as multinationals, did not buy for just one company, but for all their world needs. The business from one company alone could be worth many millions of pounds. If I was not actually present at meetings between company presidents, because they were happening at the very highest level, I was often asked to be in the room next door, ready to receive the minutes after the meeting finished so I could brief myself on what was happening and could put into practice policy decisions affecting my area.

Roche produced almost the entire range of over twenty vitamins. If a manufacturer was making perhaps just one or two of the vitamin range, then since vitamin making is a costly business, they would be much better off if another company were to provide them at very low prices with vitamins which they could package and sell as their own. Then economic logic would persuade them to close their manufacturing processes down and save themselves money. During my time with the company at least five firms closed down factories and bought their vitamins from Roche, which in the long term only served to increase Roche's monopoly of the market.

The next move was to get together the major vitamin and chemical producers and talk prices with them. Meetings were held, often in Basle. The manufacturers discussed world prices for the different vitamins and chemicals, and set a price which they all agreed to keep, thereby removing the main element of competition between them.

From long experience I know that using all sorts of factors it is possible to estimate more or less accurately what world demand for a product is likely to be in the coming years. Once this is estimated a level of production is set, always slightly below world needs in order to keep demand and therefore prices high, even if it means factories not producing at full capacity. Roche and the major vitamin producers control the market completely. The consumer has no choice but to pay the asking price. If a small company was foolhardy enough to challenge the major manufacturers, then it could be commercially killed by cutting prices to a level that made it bankrupt, when prices could go up again.

The practices were illegal, but the advantages of eliminating competition were such that Roche did not appear unduly bothered by scruples. Where making money was concerned Roche was unscrupulous. Roche would instruct Product managers to make contact with the most important customers and suggest that if they were to buy their needs exclusively from Roche, or a set level of their needs (usually between 90 per cent and 95 per cent) then at the end of the year, at Christmas, Roche would estimate how much their business was worth and give them a rebate of 5 or 6 or 10 per cent depending on how much business they did. The agreement, of course, was to be a purely private one between the customer and Roche, and was a 'reward for loyalty'. The rebates were called fidelity rebates. Customers were invoiced and paid at the full amount (which meant that the competitors would not know that Roche was undercutting them) and given the rebate by cheque at the end of each year.

A circular issued to Roche management in December 1970 explained fidelity contracts and their advantages as follows:

Fidelity contracts
According to the experience of various Roche companies, fidelity contracts provide a very efficient protection against competition, especially as far as BASF* are concerned. In our today's Management Information we have therefore made a special provision for such contracts and would like to give you a brief definition of their content and short description of their

---

* The largest German multinational chemical company.

advantages. A fidelity contract should cover the following points:

– The customer undertakes to purchase at least 90% of his total requirements of vitamins from Roche.

– Roche applies automatically to all purchases of customers their best price for the quantity involved. Should the customer receive a lower quotation from another vitamin manufacturer, he will give Roche the possibility to meet this quotation before he places the order with the competitor in question. Should Roche not be willing to meet the price submitted to them, the customer is free with regard to this particular purchase without losing his fidelity status. The same principle applies if Roche are unable to cover the entire requirements of the customer due to a shortage.

– At the end of the year the customer receives a fidelity rebate on his overall purchases during the year. This rebate will be cancelled entirely if the customer has not complied with the above principle for any single vitamin required by him and manufactured by Roche. Since the fidelity rebate is being paid at the end of the year, there is no need for a written contract in cases where customers are not favourable to such a formal way of negotiating [or don't want anyone to know what they are doing . . .].

The advantages of such agreements are obvious. If a feed mill for instance is purchasing Vitamins A, E, B2, Carophyll etc., even the most tempting offer from a competitor like BASF for Vitamin A and E alone cannot induce the customer to change his supplier, because he would otherwise lose the fidelity rebate for Carophyll and for the vitamins BASF are not manufacturing. For the same reason it is in many cases possible to make the customer accept somewhat higher prices for individual items than the one offered by the competition, because the overall deal is still favourable for him.

I myself negotiated a number of these contracts, and because contracts were generally drawn up in English, and that was my native language, I was usually called on to help in the drafting of others even if I hadn't negotiated them myself. One clause in several of the fidelity contracts I had drawn up according to instructions tied buyers to informing Roche if they were offered a better price by any other reputable manufacturer. In theory the object of this was to guarantee customers that if Roche did not meet that price, they could go elsewhere without losing their rebate. In practice this clause provided Roche with an exclusive, private, market intelligence service, for which they paid nothing, and which enabled them to hang on to their customers and undercut their competitors.

Roche provided an added incentive for customers to stay with them. As they produced an almost complete vitamin range, and on certain vitamins had a virtual monopoly, it was easy for people like myself to suggest to customers that if they didn't want to buy everything from us, then it would really be very awkward for us to sell just one or two vitamins to them, and perhaps they should go elsewhere for their supplies, knowing all the time that the customers knew there was nowhere else that could sell them the quantities they needed of that particular vitamin. Shortages of vitamins were used as another way of persuading customers to accept fidelity contracts, since the customer with a fidelity contract could be sure of getting first priority on the vitamin he needed (which meant that those without fidelity contracts might find themselves without the vitamins they needed). In August 1971 Roche issued an internal circular containing the following comment,

... precarious Vitamin C situation, of which customers will soon become aware, provides an excellent opportunity – and possibly the last one for a long time – to convince even the most reluctant firm of the advantage of such a 'partnership' between manufacturers and users of the goods. Fidelity contracts, which are in the first place designed to give security to the customer, may therefore help you to penetrate the market . . . without a collapse of the present price levels.

This judicious blend of persuasion and reward proved very effective for Roche. They finally had fidelity contracts with twenty-two separate companies, and some of those were multi-nationals buying world wide. The object was never to compete, but rather to eliminate competition.

During my business career I had travelled extensively all over the world and particularly in poor countries. I had seen the effects of the drug companies' policies. I had seen so much poverty in the world and seen people unable to buy medicines and vitamins because of the price. I had also seen that within Roche, when news came of an influenza epidemic in, for instance, India, instead of putting vitamin C out in greater quantities and reducing the price, we would control the quantities going out to the market and usually increase the price. I thought that somebody more powerful than industrial companies should be able to control the situation.

To me this was a callous abuse of power. It made me angry, and uneasy. As I looked around I became more and more aware of the arrogance of Roche, of its impertinence in believing that it could do what it liked, break its competitors commercially if they got in the way, destroy as it liked because it had power and money and wanted more of both.

There was a feeling about Roche that was both aggressive and grandiose at the same time. In my imagination, then, even the building echoed it – a giant glass and marble skyscraper towering twenty-eight storeys high, and dwarfing the people beneath. Inside it was an auditorium, capable of seating nearly two thousand people. From time to time, Dr Jann, Roche's president, would send a circular round top management, down to about my level, summoning us all to a presidential 'talk'. These always took place in the auditorium. It was circular, with a raised podium in the centre and seats going up in tiers all round. The stairs were built from Siena marble, the walls were panelled in beautiful woodwork, the seats all covered in Roche's colour, a plush sea-green. When you arrived for the talk you might have been arriving in a ballroom, the place was so brilliantly lit, but then the lights would dim, the president would take his place on the stage, and by the time he had started talking you would be sitting in darkness while he stood alone in a pool of light shining down from the spotlights above. I don't know what role he thought he was playing, but the script was always the same. Make more money for Roche. We haven't invented anything new for a long time. We need more products. We need new ways of making money and increasing our turnover.

I used to think, during these lectures, and wonder what I was doing there. I didn't particularly like the message that was coming over, but then Roche was a large multinational firm, and most such firms exist to make money first and foremost. I had a job to do, I was paid to do it, perhaps I should just get on with it and stop worrying. Besides which, as far as I could see, there was nothing I could do. There was nobody I could report Roche to who could take action. Switzerland does have competition laws, but they would scarcely take any notice of a single individual complaining against one of their biggest companies. And Roche was a great patron, a great benefactor of the arts and music, a great donator to good causes. The city of Basle in particular had good reason to be grateful to Roche. Roche imported orchestras to play to the citizens of Basle. (Roche employees were admitted free.) Roche loaned or donated paintings and works of art to Basle Art Gallery. Roche employed thousands of people living in Basle. Basle was definitely not the place to be critical of Roche, as I discovered later to my cost. I could, I suppose, as a former British citizen, have reported them to the British, but the Government would only be able to take action over any dealings Roche had with British firms and that was only a small part of the whole.

Besides which, I had my family to consider. By now Stephanie, my third daughter, had been born (on March 4th, 1972) and I had no wish, I confess, to be a martyr and find myself out of work with no means of supporting my wife and three children. We lived well on the salary I earned, and managed to save a substantial amount which we hoped in time to put into a business of our own. So I said nothing, but continued working, like many others before me. After all, I reasoned with myself, there was no point in making hopeless gestures, and personally I had always been treated extremely well by Roche. I had no reason to complain. But it was becoming increasingly difficult to live with the knowledge that I was doing nothing while the power of the company continued unchecked. 'What kind of a man am I,' I thought, 'to be part of these things and say nothing?' And I had seen enough poverty and distress in other countries to know the effect that some of Roche's decisions could have.

Human nature being what it is, I don't think, looking back, that I ever questioned the level of my own salary, or thought that I shouldn't have been earning so much, but I knew how low the wages were in the developing world, compared with what we paid in Switzerland and Europe, and I knew there was little difference in the work done, and I saw the injustice of it. And I saw the ability of the big multinationals to ignore national frontiers, manipulate prices, create demand for a product and fill or not fill that demand, just as they pleased, without any outside controls, and that was beginning to frighten me.

I have always been an avid reader of newspapers and magazines. It was useful for me in my job to know what was going on in the world, but I was interested politically as well. I liked to know everything that was happening, and why. In the middle of 1972, therefore, I realized that Switzerland was debating with the Common Market the possibility of signing a Free Trade Agreement governing trade between Switzerland and the E.E.C. countries. If the Agreement were signed it would mean that any Swiss company trading in the E.E.C. would be bound by the E.E.C. rules of competition, contained in the Rome Treaty, and restated in the Agreement.

On December 20th, 1972 the Agreement was ratified.

For a month I considered the position and read as widely as possible, looking at the implications of the Agreement for Roche. Article 86 of the Treaty of Rome, the document governing the setting up of the Common Market, forbids any firm to 'abuse a dominant position' in the market. And the Swiss Agreement with the Common Market tied them to keeping that part of the Rome Treaty. From any angle that I looked at it, it seemed that 'abusing a dominant position in the market' was exactly what Roche were doing. At the time, too, I was naive enough to think the E.E.C., governed by the European Commission, would stand a better chance of controlling a multinational, since their jurisdiction stretched over the nine member countries.

Mariléne and I spent many hours discussing what I should do. She knew already that I was unhappy with what was happening in Roche, and agreed with me that if there was a chance to do something about it then I should take it. We had already decided that it would be a good thing for me to leave Roche and for us to set up a business of our own when the children reached school age, because we didn't want to interrupt their education with changes of posting from one country to another. Nathalie, our eldest daughter, was now four so we had already put in train the long process that leads to starting up a business and had begun selecting which country we would like to live in and investigating possibilities of land and government aid.

1 The Hoffmann-La Roche headquarters in Basle. In the centre is the 28-storey skyscraper where the mass of office personnel work. Behind it is an older, much lower building, which houses the President, the Board of Directors and all the senior executives. Stanley Adams' office was always in this building. To the right of the skyscraper are some of the chemical factories of Roche.

2 *Above*, the wedding of Stanley Adams and Mariléne Morandi, Lugano, September 9th, 1967.

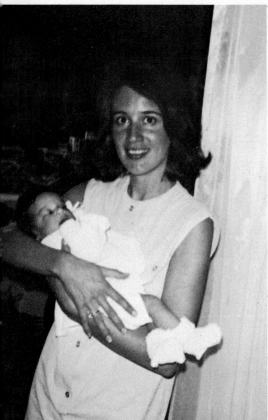

3 *Left*, Mariléne with the 5-week-old Nathalie, Caracas, November 1968

So it was that on the evening of February 25th, 1973, at home in our flat in Basle, I sat down with Mariléne and typed a letter to Mr Albert Borschette, Commissioner for Competition at the E.E.C. Commission in Brussels. We stamped it, put it in the mail, and went to bed. The letter read as follows:

Dear Sir

Re: Offences against Article 86
in the sale of Bulk Vitamins
and Chemicals in Europe

I am writing this letter out of a sense of duty, and I trust that you will be able to take some action in the matter. I am not after any position in the EEC institutions, nor am I in any way interested in compensation of any kind. I am a British citizen,* economist by training, and for the last ten years employed in the International business division of F. Hoffmann-La Roche and Co Ltd of Basle, Switzerland, dealing exclusively in the Bulk Vitamins and Chemicals pricing and marketing. I am still with the named company, however I plan to leave around July 1973 and start my own meat industry near Rome, Italy.

As you are probably aware, Roche is the largest world producer of bulk vitamins for the Pharmaceutical, Human Nutrition and Animal Nutrition sectors. Roche's own production of all vitamins on its own is more than sufficient for the present demand of the entire world. It has production facilities in Switzerland, the U.S.A., Germany and U.K., France, Italy and Japan. Its headquarters are of course in Basle, Switzerland. In addition it has branches all over the world.

With its expanded production all over the world, and the consequent reduction of costs of production, Roche could see a price-fight coming some years ago. Thus Roche first embarked on persuading the smaller producers to close down their production facilities and purchase bulk vitamins from Roche, at specially reduced prices . . . These com-

---

* Technically speaking, I had allowed my British citizenship to lapse. That did not mean I felt any *less* of a British citizen than previously.

panies at the same time agreed to sell at the same prices as Roche at all costs.

Then those manufacturing companies which could not be persuaded to stop production of bulk vitamins, were eventually persuaded to agree to selling prices identical to Roche's own, world wide. Furthermore, when one or other of these producers started cutting into the market share of Roche, they were persuaded to agree to fixed market shares for each individual vitamin for each individual market . . .

Among the production companies situated in Europe, there is complete control of selling prices, and regular meetings take place . . . As far as Roche's own subsidiaries are concerned (all over Europe and all round the globe) strict price control is maintained by the issue of price lists from Basle at regular intervals. The prices are known and called by Roche 'Personal Limits'.

Now we have the situation where world production of all bulk vitamins and fine chemicals is far greater than world demand, yet selling prices are now in 1973 far higher than they were ten years or even three years ago. On the other hand, increased and modernized production facilities have reduced costs of all producers very considerably. Such examples can be mentioned as, for example, *d-Biotin* (vitamin H) costs 0.56 US dollars per gram to produce, yet it is marketed at 10 dollars a gram. Vitamin B2 (*Riboflavin*): cost of production around 6 dollars per kilo and now selling at 33 dollars per kilo. *Ascorbic acid* (vitamin C): costs one dollar per kilo, sells at 5.50 dollars per kilo outside the U.S.A.; yet in the U.S.A. this same vitamin C sells for 3.80 dollars per kilo, since the Price Commission intervened there.

It is clear that Roche has eliminated fair competition; and that where competition could not be eliminated, Roche . . . has distorted competition completely.

Around 75% of all sales of bulk vitamins go for Animal Nutrition, thus they have a direct bearing on food costs (such as meat in the E.E.C.). Since the annual market for bulk vitamins has a value of over 700 million dollars outside the U.S.A. alone, and since Europe consumes the major part of this total, you will readily see the importance of lack of competitive prices.

I request you not to let my name be connected with this matter. However, I remain at your entire disposal for further information as well as documentary evidence about every point which I have raised in this letter. Furthermore I am prepared to discuss any point with your assistants or yourself at any time, and if necessary I am prepared to fly to Belgium or Rome for this purpose. Additionally, after I leave Roche round July 1973 I would be prepared even to appear before any Court to give sworn evidence on my statements.

I trust to hear from you soon to know in what direction I can be of further help, and in the meantime I remain, dear sir,

Yours faithfully,

Stanley Adams

A month later, on March 26th, I received a reply from Mr Willi Schlieder, Director-General for Competition and second in command to Albert Borschette who was the Commissioner. Mr Schlieder suggested that I should contact Mr Carisi (Director of Inspection) or his assistant Mr Rihoux and fix a time to go and talk to them. On the evening of Friday, April 5th I flew to Brussels for my first meeting with the Commission.

We spent most of Saturday in the big conference room attached to Schlieder's office in the Commission, going through the papers that I had brought to illustrate what I was saying, and discussing the policies of Roche and the other multinationals working alongside Roche. I met Mr Borschette, the Commissioner, briefly, but the main business of the day was done with Willi Schlieder and his assistants. Carisi and Rihoux were the ones with whom I had the most contact in the months to come. I think in all there were five or six of us round the table that day. From time to time Schlieder would leave the room to inform

Borschette of what was happening, and then return to the conference table.

Eventually, when we had gone through everything, Schlieder said to me that he thought there was a case, and that Mr Borschette was prepared to go ahead and investigate, but they could only do that if they had my co-operation. It wasn't enough simply to have told them what was happening, if they were going to build a case then they would need a lot more inside information. I told them I would be quite happy to co-operate, but they must remember that I was still working at Roche, that I had a wife and three children to look after, and therefore they must be extremely discreet and make sure that nobody ever knew where their information was coming from. They agreed that the matter would be treated in the utmost confidence, and from then on I said they were free to write to me, to phone me, or to meet me and I did my best to give them whatever they needed.

In the months that followed we exchanged several letters and phone calls. My main contact was with the Director of Inspection, Aldo Carisi, an Italian lawyer. On July 21st I wrote him the following letter:

Dear Mr Carisi,
With reference to my letter of April 15th, 1973 I am sending you some additional information about Roche's doings in the Bulk Chemicals and Vitamins division.

1) As I have already explained to you, the pressure placed by Roche on other producers of vitamins and chemicals in Europe has obliged the following companies to stop production . . .

After stopping production each of these companies signed a contract with Roche (a co-manufacturer's agreement) to buy from Roche all the vitamins and chemicals which they needed both for internal consumption and for re-sale on the international market. Obviously, this co-manufacturer's agreement means that these companies are buying their products from Roche at a secret and very low price. As they are selling Roche products under their own labels it is clear that competition has been eliminated.

2) Besides that, the following companies, which are the most important consumers of chemicals and vitamins in the areas of animal nutrition, human nutrition and pharmaceuticals, have signed fidelity contracts to buy everything they need exclusively from Roche . . .

I am sending you as an example a copy of the contract between ——— and Roche dated August 5th, 1968, accompanied by a letter changing certain clauses, dated July 8th, 1970. I attach as well a copy of a letter of 30th May, 1973 which will give you an idea of the extent of the rebate and a list of all ——— subsidiaries in the whole world.

3) The photocopies of a letter written by the president of Roche on June 25th, 1973 and of a customer profile concerning ——— will give you additional information. This letter, and its annex, has been sent to the managing director of each Roche branch in every country where ——— has a branch. (See page 3 of the annex.)

In fact Roche Basle is in the process of preparing a customer profile about each company mentioned under no. 2 in this letter. When these customer profiles have been drawn up an example will be sent to every Roche branch.

4) The conversations and secret arrangements between Roche [and other vitamin producers] continue regularly. In fact they are in the process of agreeing to a general increase of price for vitamins A, E, B2 and C. This increase will be announced shortly to customers from all the European markets.

I'm taking this opportunity to tell you that I will be at Roche Basle until the end of October 1973.

I remain willingly at your disposal, and send you my regards and best wishes . . .

Please pass my regards on to M. Rihoux.

Drawing up customer profiles was one of my functions. Using Roche's substantial information network I would explore all the strengths and weaknesses of prospective customers and competitors, detailing their profitability, their turnover, their branch structure, their selling powers, their market share and so on. Any information that would be useful in selling to them, or competing with them.

In addition to writing letters and sending information I was asked on occasions to meet members of the Commission's legal department who wanted to ask me specific questions. These meetings never took place in Switzerland, although I stated that I would have been happy to entertain them there. I always had to go to them. They never came to me, although sometimes we split the journey and I met them in Milan or somewhere like that. At the time I just thought I was dealing with a busy bureaucracy and that I must wait on their convenience, which I confess irritated me on more than one occasion. It never occurred to me, until much later, that they were actually frightened of crossing the border into Switzerland. Although the Commission can accept complaints and information, it may not solicit them and its officers were afraid that any attempt to see me in Switzerland might be interpreted as soliciting information. Knowing the way the Swiss worked, the E.E.C. officials were afraid they might be arrested. I, of course, had no idea there was any such danger. I lived in a free country, so I thought, and no one troubled to inform me that I was doing anything that could be considered dangerous. So we went on meeting in Italy or elsewhere and I continued willingly giving the information they asked me for, without once giving a thought as to why we were not meeting in Switzerland.

At the end of October 1973, when the Commission had all the information that I could supply them with, I finally left Roche and began preparations to set up my own business in Italy. Roche were totally unaware that I had been discussing them with anybody outside, and my departure was cordial. I resigned and they wished me well in my new career. I had no further contact with the Commission. I had done what I could and my energies were now concentrated on getting a new business together. For the next few months I stayed in southern Switzerland with my family, making frequent trips to Rome to fix up the details of the business we hoped to start there. On April 1st, 1974 we moved to Latina, a small town on the Mediterranean about seventy miles south of Rome, and were all set to start our new life together as a family, away from Roche, or any thought of Roche.

3 Roche and the Monopolies Commission

Roche, meanwhile, had problems of their own. Like most pharmaceutical companies they worked from a very narrow base. About 80 per cent of their turnover came from just ten products, and two of those products, real money-spinners for Roche, were under attack in Europe. They were the tranquillizers Librium and Valium. Librium had been introduced into the United Kingdom in 1960 and Valium in 1963. Up till then barbiturates had been widely used but the number of fatalities from overdose or suicide had worried the medical profession who turned with relief to a 'safe' tranquillizer. And Valium and Librium had sold widely, not only in the U.K. but across the world. In Britain 60 per cent of National Health Service demand for tranquillizers was met by the use of Valium and Librium, and 90 per cent of Roche's business was with the N.H.S. Roche held the patent in both Librium and Valium. The patents were due to expire in Britain in May 1975 and December 1976, so Roche were determined to maximize their profits while they had time.

Because of the patents Roche had the monopoly of supply in Britain until 1968 when a small firm called D.D.S.A. was granted a compulsory licence to manufacture or supply chlordiazepoxide (the generic name for Librium) and 1971 when D.D.S.A. and a second firm, called Berk Pharmaceuticals, were granted a compulsory licence to manufacture or supply diazepam (the generic name for Valium). Compulsory licences were issued by the British Comptroller of Patents in an attempt to bring competition into the market and remove the total monopoly from one supplier, in this case Roche. Both D.D.S.A. and Berk Pharmaceuticals, along with seven other firms, had applied previously to Roche for voluntary licences to supply the generic forms of Valium and Librium. All had been turned down. This was Roche policy.

They argued, along with many other major drug manufacturers, that since the costs of developing a new drug were so high, and since the patent at that time only lasted sixteen years, they should be allowed the period of the patent to recover the high costs invested in the drug. They considered that anyone else coming into the market with the same drug was 'stealing' their product.

Roche fought the applications for compulsory licences in court but they lost and the licences were granted. Roche subsequently took action against both D.D.S.A. and Berk Pharmaceuticals on the colouring of their pills, alleging that they were attempting to pass them off as Roche's products. In one case Roche were granted an injunction against the company and in the other they lost. Despite Roche's disapproval both companies remained in the market but they made little impact on Roche's dominant position, capturing less than one per cent each of potential sales. Prices of Librium and Valium remained high and on September 14th, 1971 the Department of Health and Social Security referred the matter to the Monopolies Commission.

On April 11, 1973 the British Monopolies Commission presented its report. On April 12th Sir Geoffrey Howe, then Minister for Trade and Consumer Affairs, accepted the report's recommendations and issued an order compelling Roche to cut the price of Librium by 60 per cent and the price of Valium by 75 per cent. Prices were to be set at 40 per cent and 25 per cent respectively of the 1970 prices. Roche were stunned.

When I first read the Monopolies Commission report I was fascinated. It was detailed, and damning, and very dangerous to Roche in several ways. It threatened profits in the U.K. It threatened profits in other countries where there was bound to be follow-on reaction. And, as I recognized immediately from my own experience, it highlighted the way in which Roche worked. I had never actually worked in the ethical (medicines) department, although I had trained there, but I recognized all the manoeuvres that were being described. They were familiar Roche practice.

Roche had not gone willingly to the slaughter. They had a reputation for being a very secretive company and they fulfilled this reputation in the way they dealt with the Monopolies Commission. Sir Geoffrey Howe commented in the House of Commons 'The task of the Monopolies Commission was complicated by the refusal of the Roche group to supply certain information about its costs and sales.'

The Commission itself was more specific:

The Basle company, through Roche Products Ltd (the U.K. subsidiary) has supplied certain information we asked for, but some additional information which we considered necessary to support the Group's claims as to the proper charge for research expenditure was refused. The published accounts in this case are exceptionally uninformative and the limited information we have been able to obtain about the world-wide trading and costs of the Group has not been such as could be verified or reconciled with any published accounts, as would normally be the case with a United Kingdom company.

The main basis for the case against Roche was that they were charging their British subsidiary, Roche Products Ltd, £370 a kilo for the raw powder ingredients of Librium, which could be bought in Italy for just £9. The charge for Valium was £922 a kilo, as opposed to £20 a kilo in Italy. (There was no patent protection in Italy and so no means of keeping the prices high. Prices represented just the manufacturing cost with some added profit.) Not surprisingly, therefore, the Monopolies Commission argued that although in the yearly accounts Roche Products Ltd showed they were only making a small profit on Librium and Valium, the real profit to Roche as a whole was quite different. The Monopolies Commission estimated that in 1971 alone Roche Products had made a profit of £4.8 million just on Librium and Valium and their derivatives. But the accounts stated that Roche Products Ltd had showed an overall profit of only £886,000 in 1970, and in 1971 and 1972, according to a survey of the drug industry by I.C.C. business ratios, Roche Products Ltd had actually shown a loss. (And this was before the price-cutting order.)

The key to this anomaly was a system known as 'transfer pricing'. It was a system I knew well when I worked for Roche and it applied of course to all Roche products, not just to tranquillizers. Transfer pricing had two advantages. It enabled the company to avoid a large amount of taxation, and it allowed them to overcharge without appearing to do so. It worked like this. If a Roche manufacturing company needed to buy raw material from the parent company in Basle to make the finished article, then the raw material was not, as you might think, provided at cost or cost plus a certain fixed level of profit. No. First Roche headquarters had to decide what the world market price of that product was, or in other words just how much they could sell it for and still be sure of having buyers. Then they had to look at the different levels of taxation in the various countries, and then they had to decide, bearing that in mind, just how much profit they wanted each individual company to show, if any. Once they had made that decision, which obviously depended on how high or low the taxes on profit were, and on the political situation in any given country at the given time, then, and only then, Roche headquarters set the price the subsidiary had to pay them for the material they wanted. The price bore no relationship to manufacturing costs at all. Of course, each Roche company was given a margin between the price at which they had to buy from the parent company, and the price at which they could sell the finished product on their home market. If they hadn't had that margin the situation would not have been credible and governments might have begun to ask why the company was in business at all. Roche were, after all, in the business of selling. The Monopolies Commission inconveniently pointed out this way of doing business:

> Roche Products agreed that in fixing selling prices no particular system . . . was used by the Group. Price fixing was largely a commercial operation in which 'price' was broadly what the market would bear. When the price had been set an allowance to cover United Kingdom operations and contributions to group research and overheads was deducted, and the residue was called the 'transfer price' i.e. the amount payable to the Group. In the company's words, the 'reasonableness of the price (transfer price) is tested by what is reasonable for taxation purposes'.

While a company appeared to be making only a small profit then it was difficult for a host nation to accuse it of overcharging. According to the books it was only meeting costs and making a modest profit on top. (Or loss, as the case may be.) However, if those costs contained large amounts of 'transfer pricing' then there was a hidden profit going back to the parent company. If that hidden profit was added in, then they could be accused of considerable overcharging. The Monopolies Commission concluded that, at a very conservative estimate, Roche had made £24 million profit on Valium and Librium alone in the United Kingdom between 1966 and 1972. Of that they estimated £19 million had crossed back into Switzerland through transfer pricing. The excess profit was such that in addition to recommending a drastic price cut they also recommended that Roche should repay the National Health Service a specific sum, to be decided by the D.H.S.S. (This was later set at £12 million.) They did not mince their words in declaring their final decision:

> No future price which it is practicable to recommend for the reference drugs (Valium, Librium, and their derivatives) could take full account of the excessive profits which have been made on them at the expense of the N.H.S. in the past and will continue to be made until the prices are reduced . . . We certainly see no room for argument that in recommending what may appear to be drastic reductions we are being unduly severe.

The Monopolies Commission only had a brief to examine the prices of Librium and Valium in Britain. If they had moved further afield they would have seen how transfer pricing worked in Roche as a whole, and was a fundamental part of its profit-making policy. If the Roche headquarters in Basle didn't want their subsidiaries to pay too much tax, then they certainly didn't want to pay too much themselves either. To this end, they had set up a company in Montevideo, Uruguay, Roche International Ltd, ('RIL'). Montevideo is a tax haven and any profits made in Montevideo are untaxed. Roche had no manufacturing facilities in Montevideo but customers became customers of RIL rather than of Roche Basle. If the product concerned cost, for instance, £8 a kilo to make, and the world selling price was £20 a kilo, then the customer would pay the £20 to RIL: and if Roche Basle then invoiced RIL at £8.50 a kilo, just over cost price, that meant that Basle would have made a profit of only £0.50 a kilo, while RIL made the main profit of £11.50.

This system applied equally to Roche subsidiaries. When I was the manager of Roche in Venezuela I ordered all my materials through RIL, Montevideo, whether they were for use in producing Roche's own drugs, or for reselling in bulk to outside customers. Of course, when Roche were dealing with their own companies, the price they charged from themselves to RIL was always just above cost, but from RIL to Venezuela (or wherever) was a flexible amount depending on the local taxation and political situation. More than half the material exported and manufactured by Roche Switzerland and other major Roche companies in Europe is invoiced through Roche International Limited, Montevideo.

In the British Monopolies Commission report Roche argued that the profit they made through devices such as transfer pricing was necessary to enable them to put sufficient money into research and development of new products, and in the ensuing argument with the British Government they constantly referred to this need to have adequate money for research. Research was expensive, they argued, and without the profitable drugs subsidizing the less profitable and life-saving ones, there would be no advances in finding cures for many diseases. Yet Roche refused to let the Monopolies Commission see detailed figures for research expenditure, though they told the commission that they 'expected to recover their current research costs out of their current sales'.

From all that I saw and heard when I worked at Roche, Roche worked on the premise that, once overheads and so on were met, the profits that didn't go to the shareholders mainly went back into research. Research for Roche was an investment and while it was extensive, it was primarily concerned with finding new 'winners', drugs with a high market potential, and the most effort was expended in that direction. Drugs which had a smaller specialist market were seen as being good for Roche's image, but a great deal less money was spent overall on their development.

The Monopolies Commission disagreed with Roche that such high levels of expenditure on research were sufficient reason for charging high prices on Librium and Valium.

Where a company in a science-based industry exercises considerable market power without self-restraint, that power may therefore be manifested in either excessive profits or excessive research expenditure, or a combination of the two, depending upon the preferences and policies of the management. In the present case . . . the current cost of research is higher than it would otherwise have been as a direct result of the high prices charged for the drugs currently marketed. We do not accept that, in the virtual absence of price competition, there is no limit to the price and profit levels a manufacturer is justified in setting himself, as long as he uses the proceeds to expand his research.

The Monopolies Commission report was interesting to me in another way. I had reported Roche to the E.E.C. Commission largely because of their activities within the Bulk Vitamins and Chemicals field in reducing competition and keeping prices high. Reading the report I could see that the same kind of philosophy prevailed in other divisions as well. Roche had no time for competitors. In Britain there were two other firms competing in the tranquillizer market, one selling Tropium, a brand name equivalent to Roche's Librium, and one selling Atensine, a brand name equivalent to Roche's Valium. Both firms were the subject of various court actions by Roche seeking to prevent them operating at all. Then they had difficulties in finding sales outlets. One of the firms, D.D.S.A., sold directly to retail pharmacists and doctors, supplying them by post. They told the Monopolies Commission that they didn't use the wholesale outlets because of the difficulties they had encountered there. They suggested that the small impact they had on the market, amongst other things, could be due to the fact that:

1   The large pharmaceutical manufacturers can exercise considerable direct and indirect pressure upon the wholesale chemists, who derive a substantial part of their income from the margins on those manufacturers' products (these include not only their high volume and sometimes expensive prescription drugs but also their over-the-counter medicines and cosmetics).

2   Wholesalers have varying methods of discouraging retailers from ordering low-priced drugs competing with large manufacturers' products. Thus such doctors as prescribe D.D.S.A.'s version of chlordiazepoxide (Librium) may be told that it is 'not available' for one reason or another and cease prescribing it.

Roche were under pressure from the D.H.S.S. to reduce prices from 1967 on, but rather than reduce prices and risk affecting their prices in other countries they offered the D.H.S.S. cash rebates instead. In 1967 they paid £200,000, in 1968 they paid £500,000 and in 1969 £900,000. But when D.D.S.A. came into the market they changed their tactics. They refused to give any further rebates and offered instead to give the N.H.S. hospitals and military hospitals free supplies of Librium. In 1971 when Berk Pharmaceuticals started up with their version of Valium, Roche gave the same hospitals free supplies of Valium. This made it virtually impossible for either D.D.S.A. or Berk to compete in the hospital market which, as D.D.S.A. pointed out to the Monopolies Commission, not only 'denied [them] access to the hospital market but also made it likely that general practition-ers would continue to prescribe Librium rather than any other version or the generic form for patients whose treatment has commenced in hospital.'

Roche also cut the price of Valium substantially in response to Berk's challenge knowing that Berk also had to take into consid-eration the payment of a high licence royalty to Roche for the right to sell the product in the first place. The Monopolies Commis-sion commented:

Roche Products may have had other motives in mind when it decided to reduce its selling prices for diazepam (Valium). It may have seen this as a deterrent not only to Berk Phar-maceuticals but to any others who might contemplate applying for compulsory licences; and it may have hoped to restore the former price level after driving Berk Pharmaceuticals out of the market . . .

They went on to state

We note also that, in supplying reference products (tranquilliz-ers) to N.H.S. hospitals and the armed forces at low price (or, for some time, free of charge,) it was deliberately differentiat-ing in terms of supply to keep competitors as far as possible out of that part of the market and that in the view of at least one of the competitors concerned as well as of the D.H.S.S. this in turn makes access to the rest of the market much more difficult.

The strategy for keeping competitors out of the market was working in one place and was likely to work in another. At the same time as they were dishing out great quantities of free tranquillizers to hospitals in Britain, they were doing the same in Canada. Government legislation there had removed most of their patent protection in 1969 and allowed other companies to manufacture and sell the same drugs. Roche felt that what was rightly theirs had been taken away from them, and they were forced to battle fiercely to protect their market against the newcomers. The hospital market was the most crucial because they believed that doctors and interns who had prescribed Librium and Valium when they were in hospital would continue to prescribe them when they went into general or private practice. Their first move, therefore, was to give away one free Valium with every two bought. When their main competitor answered with give-aways of their own, Roche decided to give all Valium away free to hospitals for a six-month period. They subsequently extended this offer by a further six months. All in all they gave away 141 million capsules and sold only 41 million. The result was that their rival, a firm called Frank Horner, withdrew from the hospital market. On July 2nd, 1970 Horner wrote to the hospital pharmacists:

While we have succeeded in effecting a lowering of diazepam prices, we feel we are not now in a position to offer it free in hospitals. In the event that you receive any such offer, we will not be able to meet this competition.

Ten years later, on February 5th, 1980, in the Ontario High Court of Justice, Roche was found guilty of unfair competition through predatory pricing in a case brought by the Government under Canada's Combines Investigation Act. The judgment referred to the tone of a number of letters and internal memoranda demonstrating Roche's state of mind. One letter read: 'It is our feeling that this tactic will not only abort Horner's efforts but serve as a warning to others who seem to be showing an interest in the product.'

Other memoranda referred to 'plugging' the Valium market, as they did with Librium, and 'filling the pipelines, which will serve notice to all present and future parasites that we mean business'.

The judge thought this was 'reflective of an unacceptable state of mind'. He pointed out,

> Just as in self-defence from physical attacks, a person can use only a reasonable force, so too, in defending one's market, a person must use reasonable methods. If someone slaps you, you cannot shoot him. Similarly, if your competitor cuts prices, you may decrease yours too, but you cannot reduce them to zero for six months and expect a court to find that your intention is other than to eliminate competitors or substantially lessen competition . . . In seeking to discover the true intent of Roche during the year of free Valium it should be noted that Roche was prepared to lose, and did lose, 2,600,000 dollars worth of Valium sales to prevent a forecast loss of only 600,000 dollars in sales to Horner in that year. This manifests to me that Roche was interested not in competing with Horner, but in preventing Horner from competing.

The Canadian Government, incidentally, encountered the same difficulties as the British Monopolies Commission in assessing the real financial position of Roche in Canada. The Government lawyer told the judge,

> It is difficult to assess accurately the company's financial status. The Canadian company . . . shows small profits, although the books also reveal that large transfer payments are made to the Swiss parent company for research.

But in 1973 Roche were not concerned about a possible Canadian court case that would not be heard for many years ahead. Their immediate concern was the Monopolies Commission Report, in Britain. It was vitally important to them that they refuted the report and got the price-cutting order cancelled before repercussions started in other countries. On the day the report was published, they fired their first shot in the newspapers. 'Does the public want to opt for some price savings on existing drugs in the short term, or does it prefer to obtain substantially larger long-term savings in better health and longer life due to the discovery of new breakthrough drugs?' On April 13th, two days later, they held a board meeting to discuss how they should react to the report. They came out fighting. The cuts were unfair and punitive, they said. They were being singled out because they were not a British company. The Government was attempting to take away their patent protection. They were levying what amounted to punitive tax on supposedly excess profits. 'Roche', they said, 'has always contended that profit restrictions of this kind are a form of excess profits tax in which there are no rules for precise assessment nor for equal application to all others supplying drugs to the National Health Service.' They warned that their company in the U.K., Roche Products Ltd could become loss-making if it continued to send its 'fair share' of research funds to the Group. If they had anticipated that, they would never have invested in Britain the way they had. At a press conference, on April 27th, 1973, held at the Basle headquarters, Roche president Dr Jann stated: 'If we have to sell at the prices ordered by the British Government we will be in the red.' Roche would have to reconsider its position in Britain.

'If the English Health Service refuses to contribute, there are a number of countries which would be very glad to have a Roche research centre,' threatened the vice-president, Dr Hartmann, adding that Roche had intended to expand their vitamin production centre in Dalry, Scotland (an area of high unemployment).

'But we have other centres, and we have to reconsider where we are putting our next vitamin plant.' Roche had no intention of paying any money back to the Health Service.

'We consider the profit we made was a hundred per cent justified,' stated Dr Jann. Paying back would amount to an admission of immoral profits. (Two years later he was to regret that statement – Roche repaid the British Government a large sum of money as part of an overall settlement.)

Roche, Dr Hartmann said, was considering the possibility of taking the British Government to the European Court of Justice in Luxembourg under Article 86 of the Treaty of Rome governing competition. This was the Article that I had, two months before, reported Roche to the E.E.C. for breaking! Only Roche were now accusing the British Government of forming a *buyers'* cartel and abusing their monopoly buying power. They were unaware that I had just reported them for forming a sellers' cartel in Bulk Vitamins and Chemicals.

Roche turned to British law in the hope of overturning the

order to cut prices. First of all they were given leave to present a petition to the House of Lords Special Orders Committee, asking them to appoint a select committee to review the Government order to cut prices. This was a little-used process of law designed to aid individuals who felt they were being discriminated against by Government rulings. It was also a way of having the Monopolies Commission report reviewed, this time giving Roche a chance to fight back publicly. When the petition was presented Roche again emphasized the importance of research spending.

'If every country in the world took the same attitude and allowed us to charge only half our research costs, how could we carry on our research?' argued their Q.C., who likened the behaviour of the Monopolies Commission to the Russian purges of the 1930s. 'An empty file arrived on the desk of a prosecutor saying that comrade so and so is guilty of crimes against the State – prove it. Having got that, they got the evidence.'

On June 8th, 1973 the House of Lords Special Orders Committee ruled in Roche's favour that a select committee should be appointed to enquire into the price-cutting order. But the appointment of the committee had to go for approval to the full House of Lords, who promptly rejected it on an amendment by forty-three votes to twenty-three. Roche changed tack. On June 25th, 1973 they took out a writ against the Secretary of State for Trade and Industry, then Peter Walker, seeking to have the order declared invalid, and on the same day they challenged the Government. Sir Geoffrey Howe reported in Parliament:

I have to tell the House that the company through their solicitors have given notice to the Government that unless the Government agree to certain conditions in connection with the possible repayments of monies representing the difference between the pre-order and post-order prices Roche intends to disregard the order and raise prices to pre-order levels tomorrow at noon.

This was a deliberate challenge to the Government's authority (a Conservative government) and was a move intended to provoke the Government into going to court to get an injunction to prevent Roche disobeying the order. Once in court, Roche would argue that the Government must give undertakings to repay them the money they lost by keeping prices down if the main court hearing eventually found in their favour and cancelled the price-cutting order. The debate following Sir Geoffrey's announcement was highly critical of Roche, and of their 'refusal to provide information which almost any other company in any other part of the world would regard as perfectly reasonable to be published in any newspaper or given to any journalist'. Sir Geoffrey agreed that 'the behaviour of Roche causes, and has caused disquiet to many other companies, not only in this industry. It is unrepresentative of companies whose conduct is investigated by the Monopolies Commission.'

The Government went to the High Court for its injunction to prevent Roche raising their prices. The High Court agreed with Roche that the Government should give compensation undertakings. The Government refused and the injunction was refused. The Government went to the Appeal Court, who agreed with them and ordered Roche not to increase its prices. Roche appealed to the House of Lords.

But by now the damage was done for Roche and they were in serious difficulties. The Monopolies Commission report and their reaction to it had been widely publicized. In August of 1973 the West German Cartel office announced they were looking at the prices of Valium and Librium, following the Monopolies Commission report in Britain, and the Dutch government announced a similar investigation. The D.H.S.S. rubbed salt into the wound by awarding the N.H.S. contract for the Librium equivalent, Tropium, to D.D.S.A., Roche's competitor (since most of Roche's business with the N.H.S. was not done under contract). This particular contract would only have been worth £10,000 to Roche, the amount the D.H.S.S. claimed they were saving *daily* since Roche's price cuts, but the snub still hurt. (It hurt the more because Roche knew they had submitted the lower tender.) They claimed that the D.H.S.S. was taking revenge on them for their opposition to the Monopolies Commission report. The D.H.S.S. of course denied this. But D.D.S.A. had the contract and the world-wide repercussions continued.

Germany asked for cuts of 40 per cent in the price of Valium and 35 per cent in the price of Librium. Denmark asked for an overall 20 per cent cut. The Americans suddenly discovered they were paying three times as much for Librium and Valium as the

British had before the price cuts. One senator pointed out that the American people were paying 1,000 per cent more for Valium and 700 per cent more for Librium than the price considered fair by the British Government.

In July 1974 Roche lost their appeal for compensation undertakings in the House of Lords. Their main writ against the Secretary of State for Trade and Industry, calling for a cancellation of the price-cutting order, was still outstanding, but in November 1975 Roche finally gave up the fight and reached an out of court settlement with the British (Labour) Government. They withdrew their writ, paid the D.H.S.S. £3.75 million (instead of the £12 million set by the previous Conservative Government – see page 31), agreed to invest heavily in new plant, and joined the Voluntary Price Regulating Scheme which the D.H.S.S. ran with other drug firms, and which Roche had always in the past firmly refused to join. In return the price-cutting order was withdrawn and Roche were allowed to increase their prices of Valium and Librium to around half of what the 1970 prices had been before the price-cutting order. Roche's president, Dr Jann, made the best of it. 'Now we are happy,' he said. 'Everybody will gain from this settlement.'

But he was left with the legacy of long and wearisome court battles still to be fought in other countries to prevent price cutting, or at least to delay it until patents ran out and new competition forced Roche to cut their prices anyway. And Roche were now embarked on another battle. This time it was with the E.E.C., and it was provoked by the information I had given them, back in the beginning of 1973.

4 The E.E.C. Investigation and My Arrest

Throughout 1973 and 1974 the E.E.C. Competition department, DG4, had been steadily building their case against Roche. In October 1974 they took action. Armed with an 'authorization to investigate', signed by Willi Schlieder, the Director-General, on October 22nd Inspectors Pappalardo, Rihoux and Cappi, accompanied by M. Sogno, an official from the French Ministry of Finance, raided Roche premises in Paris. And on October 29th, while Inspectors Pappalardo and Rihoux raided Roche premises in Brussels another inspector, Guerrin, made a second visit to Roche in Paris. The Inspectorate concentrates on anti-trust activities and has specific police powers laid down in Article 14 of the E.E.C.'s Competition Law. They have the right to look at books, papers and company records, to ask questions on the spot, to copy papers if they wish, and to enter premises, land, or cars and trucks belonging to any E.E.C. company under investigation. The national agents of the country where the company is based are obliged to give them help if they ask for it. And in October 1974 DG4 had gone into the E.E.C. companies, asking very specific questions and demanding to see certain documents and company circulars which they knew existed from talking to me. Their raids were successful, and they found the evidence they needed to confirm that the information I had given them was correct, but at the same time Roche were alerted to the fact that they were being investigated.

Roche immediately sent a lawyer to the European Commission to find out what was going on. Instead of sending one of their house lawyers, and they have several, they chose instead a Swiss M.P., Claudius Alder, to represent their interests. He argued with the Competition department that there was no case to answer, and demanded to know where the information was coming from. The European Commission say they refused to tell him, and continued their investigations, despite the pressure from Roche.

I did not know, because nobody told me, that the European Commission had taken action against Roche, or that Roche had sent a lawyer to Brussels to complain. As far as I was concerned, my part in the case was over. I had left Roche, I had done what I felt was right, and I had no further involvement. In the spring of 1974 my family and I had left Switzerland and moved to Italy, to a town called Latina. Mariléne and I had found a house to live in, furnished it with all our Swiss and South American possessions, and made ourselves comfortable. My three daughters had settled in quickly and were busy making new friends in the neighbourhood, and I was immersed in the practicalities of developing a large industrial pig farm.

Latina itself was a small, new, industrial town, not particularly attractive, but our house was only five miles from the sea. We used to go down to the beach regularly with the children in the hot Italian summer. It was not far from the sea that I'd found the land I needed to build the farm on, and that was the reason we settled in Latina. Because it was in the Mezzogiorno (the middle), the area qualified as a development zone, and anyone planning to set up an industry there was welcomed with open arms by the Italian government. Italy had a chronic meat shortage. At the time they produced only 45 per cent of their meat requirements and the rest had to be imported. The scheme I had in mind, prompted by market surveys I had commissioned while I was still at Roche, was a large, intensive pig-rearing and fattening unit.

I aimed to have 500 sows and 25 boars, from which the turnover would have been 10,000 fattened pigs a year. Meat was big business and very profitable and this particular scheme had the advantage of the fact that full production was reached within less than a year of the breeding pigs arriving. First sales could be expected after a further few months and then sales of slaughter-weight pigs would follow at constant intervals all the year round. A British firm of consultants had carried out a feasibility study for me and they reported that the ideas were good and the business should come quickly into profit if it was well managed. And for me it had the added advantage that I would be able to use the experience that I'd gained with Roche on animal nutrition and

THE
STANLEY ADAMS
APPEAL
COMMITTEE

The Rt Hon. Peter Archer QC MP
Arthur Davidson QC
Sir Charles Fletcher-Cooke MP
Graham C. Greene
Edward Holloway
Jennifer Horne
Professor A.R. Ilersic
Michael Ivens CBE
John Lyle
Eric Moonman
Peter Paterson
John Torode
Ivor Walker

Readers of *Roche versus Adams* will be interested to know that in 1980 the Stanley Adams Appeal Committee was formed so that lack of money would not inhibit Stanley Adams in his struggle against huge organizations with unlimited funds to cover *their* legal costs.

Donations should be sent to:
The Stanley Adams Appeal Committee
40 Doughty Street
London W1

foodstuffs, one of the main sales areas of the Bulk Vitamins and Chemicals division. I planned to buy my own feed mill and prepare the foodstuffs from raw material bought outside. The mill I had in mind was capable of producing two tons of feed an hour, and I hoped to sell off the surplus to local farmers for extra income. The actual practice of breeding and rearing pigs I intended to assign to a general manager and I had already spoken to a major English pig-breeding consortium who had promised to supply not only the pure-bred pigs when the time came to start production but also to supply a highly qualified manager, and a special consultant for the first two months to oversee the start. On paper I was all ready to go. But first I had to arrange finance. I had a considerable amount of capital of my own, but I would need more than that to take me into the production stage. I talked to representatives of the Italian government about the possibility of aid and low-interest finance. They were enthusiastic about the project and said they could help. I had a promise from the owner of the land I needed that he would sell to me if and when the necessary finance for the farm was forthcoming. Finally, after much to-ing and fro-ing, the Government grant agency, the Cassa per il Mezzogiorno (of which more later) agreed to give me a grant of 403 million lire (in those days around £300,000), and one of the Government finance agencies, the Mediocredito Regionale del Lazio of Rome, agreed to make me a loan of 400 million lire at an interest rate of only 5.3 per cent per annum, repayable over twelve years. The agreements they gave were verbal. Once they had agreed, they told me to go and buy the land and bring the deeds back to them to show them it was mine and free from mortgages and on receipt of the deeds they would sign the necessary papers and I would be able to start building.

My next port of call was a commercial bank, to seek a bridging loan. The Government grant and loan would only be paid out in instalments as building progressed, and in Italy such payments could come anything between four and six months late, long after it was necessary to pay the builder. But with the guarantee of Government finance to come there was no problem in finding a commercial bank willing to make money available. My bank agreed that as soon as I had presented them with completed signed Government papers they would advance me the loan I needed at the current commercial rates of interest.

Mariléne and I were delighted. By the time I'd finished all the negotiations it was nearly Christmas. We bought the land, complete with stables and farmhouse, which we intended to renovate for the manager and his family to live in, and were all ready in the new year to start building as soon as the contracts were signed. In the meantime we had decided to spend Christmas and New Year with Mariléne's sister and parents near Luino, in a small town that straddled the Swiss–Italian border, not far from Lugano. On Christmas Eve we set off. We never ever gave Roche or the E.E.C. a thought.

Mariléne's parents lived just on the Italian side of the border. And we had a happy Christmas with them. The children were excited by their presents and by waking up to find themselves staying in a house they remembered from previous visits. They rushed round noisily, laughing and shouting and tumbling about, stopping only to eat the huge Christmas dinner that was waiting for them. Mariléne and I sat and talked with her parents, swapping family news and bringing them up to date with our plans for the pig farm, telling them how well everything was going, how we were about to start building, what the farm would be like, what the house in Latina was like now it was all furnished, how the children were settling in . . . all the normal sort of family gossip. We made plans for New Year's Eve. We decided that we'd go and spend the day with Mariléne's sister Yvonne and her husband Osvaldo Tomasina, who lived in Astano on the Swiss side of the border, and they would then come back with us and we'd all celebrate the coming of the New Year together.

So on the morning of December 31st, 1974 we all piled into the car and set off for the short drive that would take us to their house. The route took us into Switzerland through the small customs post of Palone. It was a journey we had made hundreds of times before over the years, and we'd been through several times in the last few days. Our car was well known locally with its English number plates and distinctive willow-green colour and normally the customs men just waved us through. This time they stopped me and asked for our passports. I handed the guard the five passports and sat there expecting him to hand them back and wave us through. Instead he told me to wait and went back into the customs house. Through the window I saw him pick up the phone and dial a number. He said something briefly, listened for a couple of minutes, and then hung up. He came out without the passports. 'I'm afraid you'll have to wait.' I asked him what it was all about, but he either couldn't or wouldn't tell me. I shrugged my shoulders and parked the car against the wall where he indicated.

It was a bright sunny morning, still quite early. One of those crisp, frosty days that make you feel glad to be alive. After about twenty minutes I went back to find out what was happening. They told me they were expecting someone to come from Lugano, and I must wait a bit longer. We waited another half hour. The morning was passing. It was now nearly eleven o'clock. Mariléne had a hair appointment to go to and the children were getting bored and restless. I wasn't unduly worried, but it was irritating. Mariléne and I discussed which particular piece of Swiss bureaucracy I might in the past have forgotten, or which dangerous criminal I was being mistaken for, although she destroyed that particular fantasy by pointing out the customs guard had known us for ten years or more and wasn't likely to make a mistake. When eleven o'clock had come and gone with no sign of our being able to move I went back to the customs house and asked if Mariléne and the children could go on. The guard telephoned for instructions and told me they could but they must not take the car. Heaven knows what the police expected to find in it. I telephoned Yvonne and she came and picked them up. We joked about the situation and I said a casual goodbye to Mariléne and the children, expecting to be with them that afternoon. Half an hour later a police car, with two plainclothes officers inside, arrived. The men introduced themselves, checked the passports and handed Mariléne's and the children's back to the guard for collection later. Mine they kept. They told me to get in my car and drive to Lugano police headquarters. One of them would ride with me, and the other would follow behind. I protested. I wanted to know if they were arresting me, what I was supposed to have done, why they wanted me to go to the headquarters. They answered quite frankly that they didn't know what it was all about. They had been instructed by the federal police authority in Berne to stop me when I crossed the border into Switzerland. I wasn't being arrested, I was just needed to help the police with certain enquiries.

By midday I was at the police headquarters in Lugano drinking coffee and leafing through newspapers, and wondering what the hell it was all about. I'd been told that there were two officers coming down from Berne to interview me, and they had just got on the train. Berne to Lugano is a six-hour journey, so I knew I had a long wait ahead. At one o'clock I went to a nearby hotel for lunch with one officer and I thought I'd see if I was really under arrest or not. I said I needed to go to the bathroom. Police Superintendent Parsani didn't follow me but stayed at the table, so I took the opportunity of sneaking a quick phone call to Mariléne without his knowing. Osvaldo, my brother-in-law, answered and I told him that I was in Lugano, I was waiting for the police from Berne, and I would obviously be there some time so it would be late that night before I was home. I couldn't tell him any more, because I didn't know any more.

After lunch we went back to the police headquarters and I sat there all afternoon with nothing to do wondering what it was about. I finally decided that probably I had forgotten to pay some tax or other. The Swiss have a number of specific taxes. You pay a church tax, a military tax, taxes of all kinds. Perhaps, I thought, there is a particular tax you have to pay when you leave the country and I didn't know about it. Perhaps I'd completed some paper-work incorrectly. After all, I'm not Swiss, I'm a foreigner, it's quite possible there is something I haven't done that I should have. Having settled this in my mind, I went back to reading the newspapers for the fifth time, wishing that the Swiss had been a little less efficient and had not stopped me on New Year's Eve of all days when I wanted to be celebrating with my family.

At seven o'clock the two men from Berne finally arrived. They were members of the political police, the Swiss special branch. The man in charge was an elderly, white-haired superintendent called Hofer, Commissioner Hofer. He was friendly and cour-teous and apologized for the fact that it was New Year's Eve. I'd been waiting a long time, he said, and obviously wanted to get back to my family. He and his assistant also wanted to get home again as quickly as possible, so if I would just co-operate he was sure we could all be finished in an hour or so. At all times there was a third police officer present, Superintendent Parsani. Could I raise any bail money if necessary? I told him that I had in-laws near by so I was sure we could manage whatever might be necessary to get me home again. He seemed relieved and said he just wanted to ask me a few questions, and he'd be as quick as possible. 'Ask what you like,' I said, 'and I'll answer if I can.'

'Mr Adams,' he said, 'did you give the E.E.C. any information about Hoffmann-La Roche?' 'Yes,' I replied, 'I did.' If I was surprised by the question, he was surprised by the promptness of my answer. But I didn't see any reason to conceal anything. I had done nothing illegal and I no longer worked for Roche. If the police wanted to know about it, I would tell them. Hofer was pleased. 'Good', he said. 'We'll just take a statement and then see what we can do about getting home.' Then the questioning began in earnest. Why had I done it? Did I have a grudge against anyone at Roche? Was I happy in my job? Where did I get the information from? Had I approached the Commission, or had they approached me? How many meetings had we had? Hofer spoke English and I answered the questions in English, but his assistant busily typed down all the questions and answers in German. It was a slow process and it was midnight before they had finished. Hofer telexed Berne, asking for instructions. They telexed back that they had not yet decided whether to charge me or release me. Lugano police headquarters had no accommodation so I was taken to Lugano's 'La Stampa' prison for the night. Commissioner Hofer explained to me that it was just for convenience, that I wasn't under arrest, but just being held for questioning. It was unfortunate, but there was no other accommodation. They would come and pick me up first thing in the morning. I was too tired to argue. And I still didn't really think it was that serious. Apart from anything else I couldn't think what I could possibly be charged with. To the best of my knowledge I had committed no crime, and there was nothing the police could do to me, even if Roche were getting annoyed and shouting a bit. I suspected that this was merely a way of showing Roche that they had taken action, and that was where the matter would stop. I was allowed to make a quick phone call to Mariléne, to tell her that I would be staying in Lugano overnight, and would be back home the next day. I was not allowed to say anything else. They warned me that if I mentioned Roche, or said anything about the questioning, then they would cut me off. It seemed pointless to play games so despite Mariléne's distress on the phone I simply told her what I had agreed I would say and reassured her that everything would be all right in the morning.

I can't begin to describe my feelings when I was taken through the prison gates. I knew, or I thought I knew, that everything would be sorted out in the morning, and that this was just a temporary inconvenience, but I had never in my life before been near a prison, not even to visit anyone, and it was a terrible shock. The New Year, which I thought held out so much promise for us as a family, had arrived and instead of celebrating it with them I was by myself, locked in a prison cell. I confess I cried myself to sleep that night, from sheer exhaustion and bewilderment.

I woke in the morning feeling grubby, uncomfortable and depressed. I was still in my dirty clothes, and I hadn't been able to shave. The political police picked me up at about half past ten and we returned to police headquarters, to the private office that had been set aside for my interrogation. The door was closed and the questioning started again. It continued all day, with a break for lunch. Finally, at four o'clock, Commissioner Hofer called a halt. He had been in contact with Berne again to see if he could release me, or let me go on payment of a surety and had just received the reply. He was instructed to charge me and there would be no question of release. I was officially arrested.

I demanded to see a lawyer. I said they had had no right to detain me the previous night. I said I would not allow them to charge me unless I had a lawyer present. I quoted Habeas Corpus at them. I lost my temper and shouted. They pointed out that I was not in Britain now, I was in Switzerland, and I was being held under Swiss law. I had no right to have a lawyer present. In fact, they told me, Swiss law states that from the time of arrest, which was now, the suspect may be held incommunicado for fifteen days while enquiries are made. He is not entitled to see anyone in case the enquiries are prejudiced. Switzerland has no Habeas Corpus law, and, the police informed me, they were acting quite correctly in behaving as they did.

I was presented with a transcript of the interrogation, running to dozens of sheets of paper, all in German, and asked to sign it as a true record of the proceedings. I refused. I did not understand German and by law there should have been an official interpreter present. Hofer insisted. Finally I signed with a written protest that I was signing without understanding the contents. Then they charged me. I was charged under Articles 162 and 273 of the Swiss penal code. Article 162 covered breach of trade secrets. It dated back to 1935 and protection against the economic espionage of Hitler's Germany. If you had stolen a secret formula from one company and then sold it to another, then you would be charged under article 162. But Article 273 (promulgated during August 1914) covered crimes against the State. I was being accused of taking economic information and giving it to a foreign power. Only two other countries have a similar law, South Korea and South Africa. I had reported Roche to the E.E.C. for illegal activities. Now I discovered that in Switzerland whatever affects big business affects the State, and I was the one being treated like a criminal. Under Swiss law I was charged as a spy and a traitor.

Later I learnt that it was Roche who had initiated my arrest. On December 18th, shortly after his meeting with the E.E.C. officials in Brussels, Dr Claudius Alder, working on Roche's instructions, had lodged a denunciation with the police against person or persons unknown for breach of articles 162 and 273. I was named as first suspect.

I was taken back to Lugano prison, but before that I was allowed to make one phone call to Mariléne. This was for purely practical reasons. I had been nearly two days now without changing my clothes or shaving, and I had no clean clothes at all. I was told to tell her to bring wash things, shaving kit and a suitcase of clean clothes. I was forbidden to tell her anything else, either on the phone or when she arrived with my things. I was told I must speak in English, so our conversation could be understood. I must not mention Roche. I must not mention the E.E.C. I must not give any indication of why I had been arrested.

She brought me my suitcase but we were not given long together. After a few minutes the police separated us. Mariléne left the room in tears, not knowing what I had done, or why I was being arrested. It was New Year's Day, 1975.

I never saw her again.

5 Mariléne, My Wife

In Lugano prison I was put in a cell by myself on the first floor. I was not allowed any contact with my family, nor was I allowed any contact with fellow prisoners. I could only look through my cell window on to the deserted prison yard, the size of a football pitch. I was not allowed out during recreational periods or anything like that. I had no contact with the outside world, and could only hope that Mariléne had found a lawyer and was trying to get me out. I still couldn't believe that this was more than a temporary situation. Every day I expected to be summoned and told that bail had been arranged and I could go. I used to listen to the footsteps echoing along the corridor outside my cell, expecting them each time to stop at my door, unlock it and tell me I could go.

Then on the morning of January 11th, 1975 the footsteps did stop outside. A guard had been sent to collect me and escort me downstairs to the governor's office. I went in and stood in front of the governor's desk. (I had not been there long, but I had already been taught my place as a prisoner.) In front of me were two men, both in their sixties, with greying hair. I was uncertain which was the governor, but settled for the one who told me to sit down. At the same time he asked the guard to go and fetch me some coffee. By now I was sure that Mariléne had finally managed to fix it. Prisoners are usually left standing. I waited for him to say, 'Well, Mr Adams, bail has been arranged for you. You are free to go.'

Instead the other man spoke. 'My name is Dr Clericetti,' he said, 'and I am the lawyer appointed by your wife.' The guard handed me my coffee, and I waited. 'I have come to tell you that your wife is dead.'

I couldn't believe it. I thought I had misheard him, and then that it was some kind of sick joke. Mariléne was only thirty-one, a young woman and I had left her in perfect health. How could she be dead? When it began to sink in that he was serious, I asked what had happened. Had she had an accident? I thought, perhaps she's had a car accident. The Jag was a powerful car and she didn't drive it very often. Perhaps she'd not been thinking and had driven too fast or something. Or perhaps she'd fallen in the lake. I couldn't think what could have happened. My mind was racing over the possibilities so I hardly heard at first what Dr Clericetti was saying. It wasn't an accident. My wife had committed suicide. I don't remember much of what happened after that. I know I broke down completely. I cried and shouted and I remember, I think, that at one stage they had to hold me down. They brought me more coffee and I think they gave me drugs to sedate me. When I finally came to myself the room was empty except for the guard sitting there watching over me. The governor and the lawyer had gone. The guard had been given instructions not to take me back to my cell or leave me alone and for the rest of the day he walked me around downstairs, staying with me in the T.V. room or walking me up and down the corridors, making sure I came to no harm.

It was only after I came out of prison months later that I discovered what had happened. When Marilène had left me on January 1st, knowing that I was being taken to prison, she had lost no time in appointing a lawyer to act for me. He was Dr Dario Clericetti, a criminal lawyer with a very good reputation in Lugano, and an ex-military judge. The first thing he did was to contact the Lugano public prosecutor and see if he could get me released on bail, but he was told this was nothing to do with Lugano, it was a federal case and he would have to deal with the State public prosecutor in Berne. In Switzerland all the offices are closed over the New Year until January 5th. It's a public holiday. So there was little he could do apart from mailing the various documents asking for my release on bail, but from January 5th he started telephoning Berne and asking for a decision on my release. Every day Marilène went down to his chambers to see if any progress had been made and every day in her presence he would telephone Berne and ask if they were ready to let me go on bail yet, and every day the answer was 'No, perhaps tomorrow.'

At the same time Marilène herself was put under considerable pressure by the police. They called her for questioning and refused to allow her to take anyone in with her. (They had told her in my presence when we were at the police headquarters together that they would want to ask her a few questions.) Her interrogator was the local representative of the Berne political police, Superintendent Parsani. I don't know how many times she was 'invited' for questioning. In a later reference in a court case, working from confidential court documents, my lawyer stated, 'During the 1st to the 9th of January 1975 the Swiss Federal police and the Cantonal police of the County Ticino subjected the applicant's wife Mariléne . . . to lengthy and repeated "informal interrogations".' All I know is what I was told by Mariléne's sister, who was refused permission to go with her into a police interview. She said that on that occasion Mariléne came out very distressed, crying and saying she had been told that I would be in prison for twenty years.

In the few days that I was locked up my wife lost nearly two stone in weight and friends say she hardly moved for several days, but just cried, saying, 'What shall I do, what shall I do?' On January 9th Mariléne arrived at Dr Clericetti's chambers for the fifth day running, and asked if I was going to be released. The day before she had been told that she could expect a positive decision on my release the next day. Mariléne had driven in to ask where to pick me up from. Clericetti phoned Berne for information. They had made a decision, the public prosecutor's office told him. I was not going to be released. Instead, I was to be transferred to Basle, where the original offence had taken place and could better be investigated. Future enquiries should be directed through the Basle public prosecutor's office. Basle, the lion's den, the city governed by four big drug companies, and the city where Roche had its headquarters. For Mariléne, already pushed to the limit of her endurance, it seemed as if all hope had gone. The police were right. I would never come out and she wouldn't ever be able to see me again. One of the cruellest things about the decision was that they were going to transfer me before the fifteen-day incommunicado period was up, so I couldn't even see Mariléne or reassure her in any way. That night, in the early hours of the morning on January 10th, she got out of the bed where she was sleeping, took a last look at our three little girls, and went upstairs to the empty flat that had been hers and mine. She went into the bathroom,

4 and 5 *Above*, Alexandra (4), Stephanie (2½) and Nathalie (5) with their father, photographed by Mariléne in August 1974; *below*, at Luino station, February 1980

6 and 7 The farm in Latina: *below*, in July 1979 construction came to an end, leaving the pig sheds uncompleted

closed the door behind her, and hanged herself. She was thirty-one years old.

The autopsy estimated the time of death as two a.m. Tucked under the rug in the lounge she left a note. It said simply 'I am sorry for what I am about to do. I love you all very much. I love the children. Please take care of the children. I love you all, but I cannot continue without Stanley.' Nathalie was nearly seven, Alexandra was under five, and Stephanie was not yet three years old.

Thirty-three hours later they broke the news to me about her death. The next day, when I had quietened down, the lawyer came to see me again. He was very gentle, and said he too was a family man, and had children, and he understood how I must be feeling, but now the most important thing for him was to look after my interests, because I was going to be transferred to Basle and I would need another lawyer to represent me there. But first, before we discussed that, did I want to attend my wife's funeral? I said, of course, that I did and he agreed to put the necessary requests through as soon as he left the prison. It was the first I had heard of a transfer to Basle, and I suppose in other circumstances I would have been worried, but now all I could think about was my wife, and my three little daughters who would be looking for me and finding I wasn't there when they most needed me.

My request to attend Mariléne's funeral was referred from the Berne public prosecutor's office to Basle. Basle refused. On the day that my wife was buried I was taken in a prison van from Lugano prison, which is a little way outside the city, to the railway station. There I was taken out of the van and handed over to two plainclothes officers who were to escort me to Basle prison. I didn't want to talk to them, so I asked permission to buy some newspapers for the journey. It was one day before my incommunicado period was up, and I was being transferred away from my family, and from any hope of seeing them. I exchanged a few words with my escorts as the train drew out of the station, and after that I withdrew behind my newspapers and remained silent. I didn't speak for the rest of the five-hour journey.

As the train approached Basle station I saw a friend of mine waiting for me on the platform. Willi and Christine Stücklin were godparents to my youngest daughter Stephanie and had been great friends of ours in Basle. Willi was Swiss. Christine was French and had never lacked initiative. Now she had found out when I was being transferred and come to greet me. She ignored the two officers and as soon as she saw me ran up and threw her arms around me. I embraced her and we started to talk. The officers of course couldn't allow this, but they didn't like to make a scene so as they walked me down towards the end of the platform Christine walked behind me, talking in English, which they couldn't understand. We couldn't say much, but for just a little while the day seemed more bearable.

When we got through the ticket barriers I was taken to a single small room, a kind of mini-police station. There was a policeman sitting behind a large counter, who took my name and relevant details and checked the papers handed him by the escorting officers. I looked round. It was a shabby room, occupied already by about a dozen or so people, vagrants picked up for sleeping rough, drunkards, drug pushers, pickpockets, the usual kind of clientele picked up at large railway stations. Some were sitting on a long bench against the wall. Others stood, aimlessly staring round them. It was a very depressing scene. I felt as if I was caught in some strange nightmare and soon I would wake up and everything would be normal again. But I didn't. We were loaded into a van outside like so many cattle and driven off, to arrive fifteen minutes later in the inner courtyard of Basle prison. The sun was shining as we stood herded together outside the great wooden doors. A guard slid open a small window, swung the main door open and as the last prisoner filed in, clanged it shut behind us.

I'd already been charged in Lugano, so there were few formalities to go through and I was quickly ushered through another door, this time an iron grill, and that was locked behind me too. My belt, my tie, shoe laces, ring, watch and money were all taken from me, my suitcase was rapidly searched and returned to me, and I was given a mattress, two blankets, a pillow and a towel and told to pick them up and follow the guard. I was bewildered and didn't seem to have enough hands to cope. The guard shouted at me and I tried to pick everything up together. Eventually, somehow, I managed and stumbled along the corridor with mattress, suitcase, blankets, towel, pillow, the lot. He shouted again, something, I don't know what, unlocked a door and pushed me in.

After the bright sunshine outside, the cell seemed pitch black. I could just see three pale faces in the gloom. 'Your space is there, by the wall,' they said, and the key turned in the door behind me.

6 Detention in Switzerland

After a few minutes my eyes became accustomed to the darkness and I was able to look around me. I was in a small cell, square, with a very high ceiling. Basle was an old prison, about two hundred years old or more, and the walls were very thick. The only source of natural light was a window set high above our heads, about eleven feet up. I call it a window, because it was made of thinner material than the wall, but it had long since ceased to function as one. It was crusted in the dirt of centuries and no light passed through. A grimy neon tube which burned night and day provided the alternative. On the floor, once my mattress had been added, were four mattresses, side by side. They fitted the space from wall to wall precisely, each mattress touching the other. Between the foot of the mattresses and the door was a handbasin, a W.C. – open, not curtained off – and a small table, about two foot square, with four stools. And that was it.

'La Stampa' prison in Lugano had been new, and the facilities there were good. (I learnt later that 'La Stampa' was referred to by the other prisoners as a 'hotel'.) My cell there had been clean and light. I had had a proper bed, and the W.C. was curtained off, even though it was a single cell, to protect one from the eyes of the guards. If Lugano was a hotel, then Basle was a doss house. I made my bed with the two rough army blankets, no sheets, placed my suitcase on the mattress and lay there without speaking. I couldn't talk. I couldn't face human contact of any kind. I knew Mariléne had just been buried, but I knew too that whatever had happened could not be undone. I could not bring her back again. So my main fear and concern now was for the children. I imagined them asking for their daddy and being told he wasn't there. They were so little it seemed impossibly cruel not to be able to go to them and comfort them, to take them in my arms and reassure them that all would be well. I couldn't get their image out of my mind. I saw them all, Sandy, Stephanie, Nathalie. I saw them playing, I saw them frightened, I saw them bewildered. I couldn't stop myself. My imaginings were brought to an end by the abrupt opening of the grill in the upper half of the cell door. It was the evening meal arriving. One of my cell mates collected the plates and we sat down. We were jammed together so tightly round the table that it was impossible not to respond to the human contact. They asked me why I was in prison and why I was in Basle. They knew I'd been arrested in Lugano, and my transfer to Basle didn't make sense to them. In Switzerland you are normally imprisoned in the canton where you are arrested. So I explained my story to them briefly, that I had worked for Roche, that Roche was based in Basle and that was why I'd been transferred, that I had given information to the Common Market, that I had been arrested in Lugano and my wife had committed suicide . . . and so here I was. They were amazed. They couldn't believe that such a thing had happened. They were all young, in their early and mid-twenties and were there on minor offences only. One was in for possession of drugs, smoking cannabis or something like that, another for non-payment of a road tax, and the third was a conscientious objector who'd refused to do his annual fortnight's military service. They had no experience of the power of big business or how it could affect the way they lived. I was heartened by their sympathy and pleased because although all three of them came from Basle and were Swiss German, they all supported me in what I did. They didn't understand the ins and outs of it, but they accepted what I said and when I asked for help, they gave it me.

I realized that the authorities might have made a mistake in putting me in a cell with other prisoners. I had been kept completely isolated at Lugano and I guessed that sooner or later the prison wardens might realize their mistake and move me back into solitary confinement at Basle. After a day or so I decided I could trust my cell mates so I asked for their help. I explained that the European Commission had no idea that I had been arrested and I had no means of informing them as I had no contact with the outside world and would not have for some time to come. As they were all in on minor offences it seemed likely that they would be released within the next few days, and I wanted whoever got out first to take a message for me. They all agreed to help.

I took one of their shoes and wrote on the inside sole the name Willi Schlieder (the Director-General of DG4), his phone number, and the address. They passed the shoe round and each one copied it into the inside sole of his own shoe. I told them that all they had to do, if they got out, was find a phone, call Schlieder and say 'Stanley Adams is in Basle prison. He was arrested because he gave information to you. His wife has committed suicide. Please help.' If they didn't have the money for a phone then they should take a piece of paper, any piece of paper, even toilet paper, it didn't matter, write the same message, put it in an envelope and post it, with or without a stamp to Schlieder's office. They didn't have to sign it, just send it.

A day or two later I was called out of the cell. 'Adams, get your things, come with me.' There was never any explanation, just the shouted order. I gathered the mattress and sleeping things together, left them outside the door as instructed, said goodbye to the lads in the cell, knowing I would probably never see them again, and followed the guard up the steps to the first floor. A door was unlocked for me and I found myself in a single cell, as I had been in Lugano, only this wasn't Lugano and the cell was small and dirty and depressing. But there was a bed in it, with a mattress on top, and a table and stool to myself. I had no way of knowing whether any of my cell mates had been released. If they had been released, had they been searched and the message found in their shoe? Or had they gone out and in the joy of being out simply forgotten me? Or had they remembered and delivered the message? I could only wait and hope.

I grew used to the routine of prison life. Breakfast at six-thirty – a tin mug of coffee and a roll of dry bread. Dinner at twelve. Supper at six. The food was nearly inedible and prisoners flushed it down the toilet when the guards weren't looking. Potatoes, rice, bits of stewed meat floating in strange coloured water, fish floating in what was meant to be fish sauce, it all went the same way after the first couple of forkfuls. But the arrival of the meal trolleys broke up the day and gave you a sense of time. At night I slept badly. The lights were never turned off. Other prisoners managed to sleep by covering their faces with the blankets, but I couldn't bear the scratchy material near me, either on my face or touching me anywhere. I used to sleep clothed, socks and all, to protect myself. Highlight of the week was shower time. A shouted order, a quick grabbing of the towel and a dash down to the showers. Once my incommunicado period was over, the highlight of the day was a visit to the library. The books were in German, which I couldn't read, but I soon learnt that if I didn't take the opportunity I never left my cell all day. At least for that half hour I could look at papers and see human faces around me, even if I wasn't allowed to talk to them. Apart from this one half hour I was locked up twenty-four hours a day. There was no exercise, no recreation time, no T.V. or association with other prisoners.

Some time shortly after my arrival in Basle prison I had been called downstairs to an office by the guard, presented with a two-page document, all in German, and told to 'sign here'. In prison you do as you're told. You don't stop to ask what it is, or say you want to read the small print, or would the officer please translate it because you don't read German. At least, you don't if you want to stay in one piece. So I signed. I never knew what I signed, but I worked it out years later that it was actually an order extending my incommunicado period for a further fifteen days as 'enquiries were still continuing'. Certainly for the whole of January I received no letters or visits, from family or lawyers, and no news of the children or how they were faring. I was not even allowed to exercise with the other prisoners. I was kept totally in solitary confinement.

My one luxury was reading the morning newspapers. As I had had some money with me when I was admitted to Basle prison I was allowed to order daily papers. I ordered three: *The Times* from England, *Le Monde* from France and *Corriere della Sera* from Italy. All three could be bought from the newsstands on Basle railway station. In happier times, when we lived in Basle, I used to go down every Sunday, taking one of my little girls with me for the ride, and buy the Sunday newspapers in several different languages. I liked to keep up with the news and it kept my languages fluent. I was reading *Corriere della Sera* one morning, about a week after I'd been moved to a single cell, when my eye was caught by a small paragraph on an inside page, headlined STANLEY ADAMS. It was very short – just a couple of inches in a single column, stating that Stanley Adams was in prison in Basle, that he'd been arrested on December 31st in Lugano, transferred to Basle a few days ago, and was facing charges because he had reported Hoffmann-La Roche to the Common Market for monopoly abuses and price fixing. I knew then that my cell mates had kept their word. One of them must have been released and made contact with the Common Market as they had promised. To this day I don't know which one it was but if they ever read this, thank you. One morning Willi Schlieder's secretary had put in front of him an envelope, containing a scrappy piece of paper, unsigned and unaddressed, that merely said, as I had asked them to, 'Stanley Adams is in Basle prison for giving you information about Roche. His wife has committed suicide,' and added that this message was being sent by a fellow prisoner. At first Schlieder thought it was some kind of a joke, that someone was trying to frighten him, but he checked it out through the usual diplomatic channels and discovered it was true and from then on the European Commission started putting pressure on the Swiss government to have me released.

All I knew then, reading those few lines in the newspaper, was that I was no longer alone. The outside world knew where I was. And I had hope. When you're in prison on your own you have no one to share your happiness with, no wife, no children, no girl friend, no friends, nobody. You can't even shout through the wall and share it with another prisoner because the walls are so thick they wouldn't hear you, and if they did, they wouldn't know what you were talking about. So you hug your elation to yourself, talk to the walls, and cry as I did with happiness and relief.

Soon after that I was allowed out to exercise with the other prisoners in the morning, whether because the second period of incommunicado was up, or because the Commission was putting on pressure, or both, I don't know. But I could at least see human faces and the sky again, and breathe fresh air. The exercise yard was tiny. Twenty prisoners circling in line filled it, so the prisoner in front touched the prisoner at the rear. It was a little square yard, with a mass of plants and flowers trying to pretend it was a garden. Compared to the yard at Lugano it was laughable but it was outside, and it was exercise. You could at least stretch your legs and move your body and look up at the sky. Most of the time it was raining, but I always went out. I had an expensive navy-blue cashmere coat, which looked ridiculously out of place, but it was all I had (you didn't wear uniform on remand) and I wore it constantly, collar turned up to keep the rain off so I could get my dose of fresh air. Those who'd been in prison a long time shot inside at the first drop but I was not yet used to being locked up and stayed outside as long as possible.

In February they started my interrogation. I wasn't questioned inside the prison but escorted by a police officer and Alsatian dog to the Basle police headquarters about half a mile away. My interrogating officer was a man called Werner Wick, Commissioner Wick. The first time we met he told me that they were going to scrap the Lugano interrogation and start afresh. I would be brought from prison every morning, interrogated for a couple of hours, returned to the prison for lunch, and then, depending on his work load, I might or might not be questioned in the afternoon. Commissioner Wick took six weeks or more to cover the ground that had been covered in Lugano in ten hours. Every day I would be asked questions, which I answered, and the next day Commissioner Wick would come back with new questions, digging deeper into my answers. It was quite evident to me that he was being fed the new questions from somewhere. A lot of the discussion was highly technical and the knowledge was not such as was usually held by a police superintendent. I can only assume that he took my answers to someone when I had finished and was then instructed on the new questions to ask the next day in response to my answers. Sometimes it was so obvious that I laughed. It had to be my ex-colleagues at Roche who were helping him. No one else had the information. It was a farce, really. Here I was being charged by the State, prosecuted by the State, and questioned by the State, and yet it seemed that the whole affair was being stage-managed by Roche. If I hadn't been caught in the middle of it, I might have found it funny.

Once the questioning had started then my lawyer made contact. When Dr Clericetti and I had discussed lawyers in Basle, I had mentioned the name of a man I knew socially, Dr Georges Bollag, who was the senior partner in a major Basle law firm. Dr Clericetti had phoned him from Lugano prison and Dr Bollag had agreed to accept me as a client. Bollag was not a criminal lawyer, I discovered later, but a commercial one, so my case was mainly given to one of his junior lawyers, Mr Hans Portmann, to handle. Hans Portmann used to visit me once a week, for half an hour, to discuss my case. He didn't visit in the prison, but came to the police headquarters while I was there for interrogation and talked in an office set aside for us. He wasn't of course allowed to be present while I was being questioned. On one of these visits I asked him to get in contact with the European Commission who had offered to pay my defence costs, and Hans Portmann did in fact contact Willi Schlieder, and later visited the Competition and Legal departments in Brussels who gave him a lot of help.

I had other visitors while I was at Basle prison. Christine Stücklin used to visit me regularly once she had been given permission to do so. Again, she was only allowed to visit me in the police headquarters, never in the prison. It was a strange system. There were visiting facilities in the prison, as in all prisons, and other prisoners received visits there. It seemed very odd to me that I was only allowed to see people in this one room in the police headquarters. It wasn't normal practice at all. I suspected that my conversations were being listened to, but it was only a suspicion. Still, I was always very careful what I said, just in case. If I wanted Christine to contact anyone for me I would slip her a small piece of paper with instructions on it just before leaving, but we had to be very careful. Christine told me that on one occasion after leaving the police headquarters she had been followed by plain-clothes policemen in a car for the rest of that evening and all the following day.

The visiting arrangements had an element of absurdity too. There were no laundry facilities in the prison. You either washed your clothes yourself in the handbasin and hung them on the radiator to dry or, if you had willing visitors, they took them for you and returned them clean on their next visit. Christine offered to do my washing for me, so on the days they were going to visit I used to set off for my daily question-and-answer session, clutching my black plastic bag of dirty washing, which would be dutifully searched at the gates by the prison guards. I'd sit in Wick's office answering complex technical questions, prompted by Roche, with my dirty washing at my feet, and swap it when Christine arrived for a returned bag of clean washing. It was very good to see friends though. It was a time when I needed them badly.

When the police had finally asked all the questions they had to ask, in as many different forms as possible, and as many times as possible, and with as many variations as possible, and could find no possible way of detaining me any further they declared they had finished interrogating me. It was my view that the whole charade was merely a means of keeping me in prison as long as possible since they knew that even if I was found guilty when the case came to court I would still only be given a suspended sentence, and if I was to serve as an example to anyone else tempted to reveal the secrets of Swiss business, then it was important that I spent some time in prison.

Once the questioning had stopped my lawyer was in a position to apply for bail for me. There was no possibility of an application being even considered before then, never mind accepted. The Basle public prosecutor, Dr C. Wunderlin, first of all refused the application for bail, then he granted it but set the bail price at an extraordinary 1,000,000 Swiss francs. Finally, after weeks of haggling and delay, he agreed to set bail at 25,000 Swiss francs.

The European Commission had promised to pay my bail and when they were told the amount they said they would send it immediately. I waited and it didn't come. My lawyer phoned them. The cheque had been signed and was on its way. It didn't come. After two or three days, when the money still hadn't arrived, I asked the Stücklins and my sister-in-law to put up the bail money for me as a temporary measure, which they did. The money was paid into Basle court and on March 21st, 1975, three months after I had been arrested, I collected my belongings from the prison office and walked along the corridor to the reception room where Christine Stücklin, my sister-in-law Yvonne and my lawyer Hans Portmann were all waiting to greet me. Together we walked down the stairs to an innocent-looking side door. No bolts, no bars, no clanging keys. I opened the door and stepped outside. I was free.

7 The Aftermath

It's a strange thing, leaving prison. Until you walk outside that door all your energies are concentrated on getting out. You long to see your children, to talk to your friends, to walk in the sun. And then when the moment comes and you stand outside, your happiness at being out evaporates. You feel insecure and frightened, your shelter has gone and now you are forced to get on with living. All the problems you put aside while you were in prison, because there was nothing you could do about them, have now got to be faced. And that's what it was like for me. The minute the prison door closed behind me all my worries crowded in – how am I going to manage to bring up three little girls by myself without my wife? What about the business? What about the house that's been shut up for so long? What about my case which still had to be fought? My happiness was completely dwarfed by the problems I knew I had to face.

We walked slowly across the courtyard, Christine, Yvonne, Hans Portmann and I, towards the great archway that led into the street outside. A group of journalists were waiting beyond the arch. I could see a T.V. film crew with cameras amongst them. I looked round to see who they had come to film, but there was nobody there. One of them advanced and greeted me. 'My name is Anthony Terry,' he said, 'and I'm a journalist from the *Sunday Times*. We know how you must be feeling and that you must want to get back to your children, and we won't detain you long, but if there's time before your train goes, perhaps you'd come and have a cup of coffee with us and we can talk a little.' I was astounded. I had been totally isolated in prison and had no idea that my case had become something of a *cause célèbre* outside. I'd never talked to journalists in my life before, except on the occasional P.R. presentation of boating trophies when I worked for Outboard

Marine in Belgium! I certainly never expected to find a reception party waiting for me outside the prison gates. In the years to come I was to get quite used to it, but the publicity that followed my imprisonment by the Swiss government was not something I ever intended when I gave information to the E.E.C. Commission. In fact, quite the reverse, I had intended that no one should ever know that it was me who had given the information.

Hans Portmann went back to his chambers and I had coffee with the journalists, in a nearby café, and gave them the interview they wanted. Yvonne and I then had about an hour to spare before we caught the train back to Lugano, so we went home with Christine. While she was putting the kettle on for tea I phoned Willi Schlieder at the Commission and told him I had been released. He congratulated me warmly and then advised me to 'get out of Switzerland immediately'. I was surprised. He was a lawyer by trade and lawyers are not generally given to panic. Besides, he knew I was on bail and I didn't yet know whether I would be allowed to leave Switzerland. Yvonne and Osvaldo lived in Astano, on the Swiss side of the border and my children were still with them, so I didn't say much. I wanted to assess the situation for myself. Two weeks later I thought I understood the reason for the panic. The European Commission felt the need to issue a statement in Luxembourg which, amongst other things, said:

> The rumours that the Swiss authorities have issued warrants for the arrest of Mr Borschette, the Commissioner responsible for Competition matters, and two or three members of his staff directly involved in the Hoffmann-La Roche affair have not been confirmed and are probably unfounded.

To me that could only mean one thing. The Commission were under pressure and were disturbed by the possibilities of what might happen under Swiss law. And one of those who 'probably' did not have a warrant issued for his arrest would have been Willi Schlieder. Clearly, rumours or not, the Commission were frightened by the possibility of further retaliation.

Yvonne and I caught the train back to Lugano. It was a five-hour journey and for most of that time we talked about Mariléne. Yvonne was her only sister and very close to her, but she just couldn't imagine why she had committed suicide after such a short time. I couldn't help her. I had been in prison and I had even less idea than she did. It seemed such a terrible waste. Here I was, free after three months, and Mariléne had lost her life. And I had known all the time that they couldn't keep me in for long, three months, six months, ten months perhaps, but certainly no more. It seemed incomprehensible that anyone would kill themselves after just a few days without waiting to see if I would be freed. It wasn't as if Mariléne had been in a motel somewhere, depressed and alone in the early hours of the morning. She had been in her mother's house, sleeping in the same room as her three little daughters, whom she adored, and with her sister only ten minutes' drive away if she needed to talk to someone. Ever since it happened, everyone I have met who knows my story has asked me the same question. 'Why did she do it?' Yvonne and I had no answer on that train journey back to Lugano, and I don't have one today. All I know is that she must have been under extraordinary pressure of some kind or another, and the exact nature of that pressure will always remain a mystery. Did the police push her too hard? Did her parents disapprove too strongly of what I had done? Did she think I was a real spy? Did she think I would never be released? As a Catholic she had very definite views about divorce and would never have contemplated it. She had money, she had the house in Latina, she was well provided for in my absence, and, most important of all, she had the children. But it wasn't enough. Something very fundamental snapped. I tried later to find out what had happened and talked to many people who had known her in the past. I even visited some of her old schools and talked to the people who had taught her, but I never really found out anything, except that she had been happier and more secure married than she had ever been before. Perhaps she just couldn't face losing that.

Yvonne and I were met by Osvaldo at Lugano railway station. It was nearly midnight when we got home. The children were sleeping that night at their grandmother's as Yvonne had been away all day, but they would be over first thing in the morning. They thought I was away on a trip, in France or Germany or somewhere and every day, Yvonne told me, they asked when they got up if Daddy was back, or if Daddy had phoned to say he was coming home. During my last month in prison I had managed to get permission to phone them once a week, with a guard listening in, and tell them I loved them and was thinking of them and would be home soon. I used to pretend that I was abroad somewhere and kept up the pretence with little inventions about where I was staying and what I had been doing. I didn't want them to know where I really was. They were too young to understand what it was all about. In their world only 'bad men' went to prison. The next morning was a grand reunion. Like small children everywhere, when the excitement of seeing me had died down, they wanted to know what presents I had brought them back from my trip. I always used to buy them little souvenirs from the countries I visited. Of course I had nothing, but I promised there would be something later when I unpacked my bags (and after I had made a hurried visit to Lugano!).

It was hard to assess the impact of Mariléne's death on them. They were very young. Later they told me that an angel had come and taken Mummy away in the night to be with Jesus because she was so good. It was what they had been told, and they seemed to accept it, but it's impossible to know with small children what they are really thinking and feeling inside, even when all seems well on the surface.

While I was staying at Yvonne's I had several visits from the press. Italian television, Swiss television and British television all made programmes on me. I was interviewed by *L'Espresso*, a weekly magazine based in Rome, and by *Gente*, a weekly Milan magazine. I became quite adept at telling my story. Sometimes it seemed to me as if I was talking about someone quite different. I felt as if somehow I was living on two separate levels.

In early July the European Commission invited me to go to Brussels at their expense. I had been completely wrapped up in the personal implications of what had happened to me and my family, but it appeared that what had happened had other implications as well. The European Commission, and Members of the European Parliament, were almost sure that by arresting me and charging me with spying the Swiss government had broken the Agreement on Free Trade that they had signed with the E.E.C. in December 1972. If that proved to be the case, then there could be serious repercussions. International agreements are not made to be broken lightly, and there were members of the European Parliament who thought that the E.E.C. should withdraw from the Agreement altogether in protest. As the Free Trade Agreement had proved extremely profitable for both sides, the European Commission did not find this a very welcome suggestion. They were therefore doing their best to establish whether or not Switzerland was actually in breach of the Agreement, and, if so, to decide what diplomatic action should be taken.

The part in the Agreement that was giving the Commission cause for concern was Article 23. It was the Article which described the practices that were not consistent with the principles of Free Trade and which quoted the competition Articles, 85 and 86, of the E.E.C. Treaty of Rome. It was these Articles which I had believed Roche to be breaking, and had quoted when I first wrote to the European Commission. It had been my impression that the Agreement signed between Switzerland and the E.E.C. had tied both Switzerland and the E.E.C. to observing the principles contained in them, and the European Commission shared this interpretation. Article 23 of the Free Trade Agreement stated:

> The following are incompatible with the proper functioning of the Agreement in so far as they may affect trade between the Community and Switzerland.
> i) all agreements between undertakings, decisions by associations of undertakings, and concerted practices between undertakings which have as their object or effect the prevention, restriction or distortion of competition as regards the production of, or trade in, goods. (See Article 85 1. of the E.E.C. Treaty.)
> ii) abuse by one or more undertakings of a dominant position in the territories of the contracting parties as a whole, or in a substantial part thereof.
> (See first para. of Article 86 of the E.E.C. Treaty.)

I had certainly thought that Roche were restricting and distorting competition, and I·was pretty sure that they had been abusing their dominant position as well. After all, I had been involved in selling vitamins for them and I knew what use they made of the fact that they were the world's largest vitamin supplier, and I knew how their fidelity contract system put pressure on buyers to buy exclusively from them or possibly risk supplies of key vitamins that only Roche manufactured in sufficient quantities for their needs. The European Commission's Competition department had thought there might be a case against Roche as well, which had led to their investigation, which in turn had led to my arrest for passing information to the E.E.C. The question to be asked was whether I was legally entitled to pass that information on or not? The E.E.C. said I was. The Swiss government said I wasn't. The E.E.C. said I was because Article 23 of the Agreement stated, 'Should a contracting party (the E.E.C. or Switzerland) consider that a given practice is incompatible with this Article it may take appropriate measures under the conditions and in accordance with the procedures laid down in Article 27.' And Article 27 was the Article which set up the Joint E.E.C./Swiss Committee to monitor the running of the Agreement, and which contained this phrase, 'The Contracting Parties shall provide the Joint Committee with all relevant information and shall give it the assistance it requires in order to examine the case and, where appropriate, to eliminate the practice objected to.'

Under the Agreement, the Commission thought, the Swiss were obliged to tell them of any practices (such as those carried out by Hoffmann-La Roche) which might be breaking Article 23. And I was working in Switzerland, and I had told them. The only problem was that the Swiss had then arrested me and charged me with providing economic information to a foreign power, which had really put the diplomatic cat among the diplomatic pigeons. How could one of the 'contracting parties' to the Agreement be called a foreign power in those circumstances? And how could giving information, which the Swiss were duty-bound to give, be called spying? Just to make matters worse there was another Article in the Agreement, Article 22, which stated, 'The contracting parties shall refrain from any measure likely to jeopardize the fulfilment of the objectives of the Agreement. They shall take any general or specific measures required to fulfil their obligations under the Agreement.'

It seemed to the European Commission (and to me) that throwing people into prison for spying, when they tried to tell the E.E.C. what was going on, might well be thought to 'jeopardize the fulfilment of the objectives of the Agreement'. Certainly it was a strange measure to take when the Swiss were bound by the Agreement to report Hoffmann-La Roche themselves anyway, or at least to put a stop to any activities that might appear to break the Agreement.

When I visited Brussels the diplomats were still trying to work out the logic of it all, without much success. All the Swiss would say (in a press release issued by the Swiss Foreign and Economic Affairs Ministry) was that 'Article 23 of the agreement lays down certain principles as regards competition . . . but . . . the application of these principles must be the responsibility of each of the parties to the agreement in its own territory and on the basis of its own law' which basically meant that the Swiss would decide for themselves what they did about enforcing the competition rules in the Swiss/E.E.C. Agreement, and under their law they had decided to charge me with spying. This response was not calculated to soothe the feelings of the European Commission and the European Parliament. A question was put down in the European Parliament on May 14th by the chairman of the Socialist Group, Mr Ludwig Fellermaier, who wanted to know:

Is the reason for the arrest of a former employee of the Hoffmann-La Roche company by the Swiss authorities the fact that he notified the Commission of an infringement of the rules of competition, or is this case one of industrial espionage?

The Commission confirmed that I had been charged under Swiss law with spying and summed up their confusion on the matter:

It is, however, difficult to believe that the authorities could prosecute anyone for economic espionage simply for voluntarily communicating to the Commission certain information on the practices of the multinational group of companies whose parent company is registered in Basle, particularly as these practices could involve serious infringements to Articles 85 and 86 of the E.E.C. Treaty. It may be added that the Commission frequently receives information, much of which leads to official open procedures . . .

But that is precisely what the Swiss had prosecuted me for, and they showed no signs of dropping the prosecution. The European Commission and the members of the European Parliament were very good to me when I was in Brussels. I was still dazed by my experience and could hardly take in everything that was happening around me. I was astounded that what I had seen as a private tragedy had developed into a major international debate, with far-reaching implications for Switzerland and the E.E.C. Everybody I met in Brussels seemed to know about it. The Commission undertook to pay all my defence costs, and my bail money. They also offered to give any advice necessary to my lawyer, Dr Bollag, in preparing the case and were prepared to send a Commission lawyer to testify on my behalf, if that would be considered useful. (Dr Bollag thought a Commission lawyer would probably not be allowed to testify in a Swiss court. The Swiss were very possessive of their national rights.) The hope was that the courts would find me not guilty, thereby averting any further diplomatic problems, but it was a faint hope.

I was grateful for the Commission's help and sympathy and repressed the thought that if only they had warned me in the first place of the dangers of going into Switzerland when the action against Roche had started, then all this help would now be unnecessary. I also repressed the thought that my bail money, promised in March, had still not arrived, and if I had waited on the promise of the European Commission instead of borrowing from friends and family I would still be in Basle prison now, not talking to the Commission in Brussels. The money, in fact, took forty-five days to arrive from the day on which the Commission were first notified that a price had been set on my bail. If I hadn't had friends and family to help me I would have been in Basle prison for another six-and-a-half weeks.

I stayed in Brussels for about three days. While I was there I received a message in my hotel that John Prescott, M.P. (leader of the British Labour Delegation to the European Parliament) would like to meet me. I agreed to meet him and some of his colleagues for dinner. To be quite truthful I was so tired and confused and bewildered by this stage that I was saying yes to everything. I was just letting things happen to me without asking questions, being picked up and introduced to people, returned to my hotel, taken somewhere else, told to sleep or wake up or eat dinner or discuss my case . . . it was all a blur of different faces and different activities. But I didn't regret meeting John Prescott. It was the beginning of my acquaintance with the Socialist Group of the European Parliament. John Prescott told me they thought the whole affair was outrageous and promised their support. They were determined, he said, to see that I got justice and that the European Parliament acted on my behalf. As a group they were very kind to me, and they kept their word. The Socialist Group have been active on my behalf ever since that day, inside and outside the European Parliament.

When the three days were up I returned home to Yvonne's house and my children. I had no idea then that the arguments and the political repercussions would continue for the next nine years, or become so important. All I knew was that I had my own personal problems to come to grips with, and I was finding it very difficult. The European Parliament and the European Commission could sort theirs out without me. I needed time to think and adjust to life without Mariléne, and to the responsibility of having three small children to bring up on my own.

It was nearly six months before I plucked up the courage to leave Yvonne's, where we had been staying, and brave life on my own with the children. It wasn't so much that I missed Mariléne, although I did, desperately. It was just that there was so much to cope with all at once. I had my three daughters to look after and guide through life without the advice of a mother. I had the business to get going in Latina, which had been left untouched since my arrest. I had the house which had been closed for nearly a year to open up and make habitable again, and then to clean and maintain while we lived there . . . I just wasn't sure I could manage. It wasn't as if there were friendly relatives round the corner to give a helping hand. Latina was 800 kilometres away from Astano. When I moved back, I was going to be very much on my own.

But I couldn't go on staying for ever with Yvonne, so in September I took my eldest daughter Nathalie with me (she was then about seven), and we drove down to Latina to see what the situation was like. Everybody had read about my case in the papers or seen interviews on television, and my neighbours were all very sympathetic. They took us into their homes for meals, offered to help me get the house set up, to look after the children . . . their kindness was very reassuring. Nathalie and I went to the convent school which she had attended before my arrest. The nuns embraced us both and promised they would try and find someone to live with us in the villa in Latina and help with the house and the children. The children, they said, could stay all day in school if it would help (the school, fortunately, had a kindergarten which could take Sandy and Stephanie). Nathalie and I stayed a week in Latina, sorting things out, and then returned to Astano. Ten days later, when the nuns had found someone to help (the first in a succession of maids), I packed up the car with the possessions we had had with us on holiday when I was arrested the previous December, said goodbye to Yvonne and Osvaldo, seated Nathalie, Sandy and Stephanie in the back of the car and set off for the long journey home to Latina.

When the girls were properly settled and had started school again I turned my attention to business and the private company, Zootecnia Anglo Italiana SpA, that Mariléne and I had formed together. (Even in business we had been anxious to keep the English connection open.) Now that Mariléne was dead it was hard to summon up enthusiasm, but I knew that I had to get the business going. So far we had made quite good progress in living together as a family without Mariléne and I was beginning to think that if I persevered life might soon settle down into something like a normal routine for us. It never occurred to me that what I had done in Switzerland would follow me to my new life in Italy. It was now November 1975, more than a year after I had been in contact with the various banks and financial institutes, but I didn't think that would cause much of a problem. Everything had been agreed before I left Italy, and the contracts had been submitted for signature. I assumed that now I was back it would only take my final signature to complete the contracts and then I would be able to start building the farm. I wanted to get the building under way as fast as possible and I was anxious not to waste any more time, so I started on the round of visits to let people know I was back in Latina and ready to start work again.

My first visit was to the commercial bank that had agreed to give me a bridging loan on receipt of the official papers giving me a grant and long-term finance. I called in to say that I had been away, but I was back in Latina and would be calling in shortly with the Government contracts. The bank said they were sorry, but they would have to discuss everything afresh. I was surprised. We had already agreed the loan before I left for Switzerland and it was only awaiting official confirmation. It was clear that they knew about my case and that it disturbed them. Still, I wasn't too worried. If that particular bank had problems, there were still plenty of commercial banks to choose from and Government finance is good security in Italy. I didn't anticipate any problem in finding a substitute bank. Two or three days later I visited the Mediocredito Regionale del Lazio, the semi-Government finance institute that had offered me a low-interest loan, to match my grant. And the same thing happened. The manager said to me, 'Well, I'm sorry, Mr Adams, but we'll have to look at everything again now. We've heard about it, you know.' 'What do you mean, you've heard about "it"?' I replied. 'We've heard about your case,' he said and opening his desk he took out a large file of press cuttings, all about me. He had more information on me than I had. I'd never seen half the items he had in his file. This worried me more. There are only half a dozen or so finance agencies similar to the one I had chosen. If I had to find another one it was likely to prove difficult since they are all partially Government-controlled and likely to have similar attitudes.

My third port of call was the Government agency that was giving me the grant, the Cassa per il Mezzogiorno. The agency is responsible to a Government minister and it's the only one. There is no alternative. Again the story was the same. 'I'm sorry, we'll have to start afresh. We'll have to study everything again.' This meant that they were totally ignoring the verbal agreement which we had had before I was arrested when everything had been agreed and drawn up ready for signing. If it hadn't been for my arrest I would have returned from my Christmas holidays, paid another visit to the agency, and then another, until they finally got round to signing the final contract, which is the way things tend to work in Italy. I had expected everything to be signed and delivered by February or March 1975 when I would have begun building.

I was now in a very awkward situation. When the Government verbally agree to give you a development grant they instruct you to go and buy the land and bring them the deeds showing that you are the true owner and there is no mortgage or other charge on the land. (This is a fixed pre-condition. They then take out a mortgage themselves on the land as security against the grant, or loan, or both.) Until that point all you need is a promissory note from the owner saying he will sell to you when you have the building licence, the grant and the finance approved. Up till that point all you have spent on the land is 10 per cent of its value, which you give to the owner as a deposit with the promissory note. But once the Government has inspected the land, verbally agreed the grant, and told you to buy, you are committed. I had bought the land and the Government already had the deeds among their papers. What's more, because Italian bureaucracy is known to be slow, I had not wasted any time and had invested my own money in preparing the land for building, so that when the contracts were signed I could start straight away. This meant that I had already had the land fenced off all round and completely levelled. What I had bought was agricultural pastureland. What I had now was the ground foundations for a very large industrial pig farm. As such there was no chance of reselling it at the price I'd paid. And I had over £50,000 invested in the land, and more in the work that had been done on it.

I had enough money put by to support myself and my family for one more year, but at the end of that time we would have nothing. It was imperative that the farm should be built and brought into production as fast as possible, but I was trapped. I couldn't move forward and build because I didn't have the finance, and I couldn't move backwards and sell because the land use had already been altered in anticipation of the building.

In February 1973 I had written a letter to the E.E.C. about the activities of Hoffmann-La Roche and other multinationals. Three years later, in February 1976, I was facing the fact that a business I had spent years planning, and in which I had invested large amounts of money, might not even be able to get off the ground. It seemed hard to believe that the two events were connected, but they were.

8 The Swiss Verdict and the European Verdict

On July 1st, 1976, my case was to be heard in the Basle Criminal Court. Three weeks previously, after three years of investigation into Roche's behaviour in the vitamins market, the European Commission issued their decision, which read:

Article 1
The Hoffmann-La Roche company has committed an infringement of Article 86 (of the Treaty of Rome) by concluding agreements which contain an obligation upon purchasers, or by the grant of fidelity rebates offer them an incentive, to buy all, or most of their requirements exclusively, or in preference, from Hoffmann-La Roche.

Article 2
Hoffmann-La Roche is hereby enjoined to terminate above infringement forthwith.

Article 3
A fine of 300,000 units of account (three hundred thousand) being 1,098,000 Deutsche Mark (One million ninety-eight thousand) is hereby imposed on Hoffmann-La Roche. This sum shall be paid within three months of the date of notification of this Decision.

Article 4
This Decision is addressed to Hoffmann-La Roche and Company AG Basle (Switzerland). Done at Brussels, 9 June 1976.

The Commission had based their case entirely on Roche's use of fidelity contracts, although in the first letter that I had written in February 1973 to Albert Borschette, the Commissioner for

Competition (which had produced the invitation to go and talk to DG4 in Brussels), I had not mentioned fidelity contracts at all. (See pages 21–3.)

My accusation then had been that Roche and the other major vitamin manufacturers had formed themselves into an illegal cartel, and were meeting together to fix prices, agree levels of production, and share out the vitamin market between themselves, deciding who should keep what percentage of the market. As far as I was concerned this meant they were breaking E.E.C. competition laws, and it was not only Roche who were involved, but other major non-Swiss companies as well. Roche's use of fidelity contracts was an added twist to the story, in which Roche were trying to tie up what little part of the market was left, and to undercut their competitors (and allies) secretly, by undermining their own price-fixing agreements. It wasn't until six months after I'd written the first letter that I mentioned fidelity contracts in another letter written to Aldo Carisi, Schlieder's number two and Director of Inspection. (See pages 24–5.) For reasons of their own the European Commission decided to concentrate only on Roche's use of fidelity contracts. They told me it was because I couldn't provide them with enough information on the other issues to establish a full case, but I wondered whether there might not also be political considerations involved as it would have meant prosecuting other companies belonging to member countries of the E.E.C. For whatever reason, the case was based on the legality or otherwise of fidelity contracts. There were twenty-two companies involved with fidelity contracts, almost all of them being, as the Commission's decision pointed out, 'important customers, being among the principal users of vitamins'. The Commission named the companies as the following:

Pharmaceuticals:
Beecham, Capsugel (Parke Davis), American Cyanamid Company, Merck (German), Sandoz, Upjohn, Wyeth.

Food:
Afico (Nestlé), Nitrovit (Imperial Food Ltd), Pauls and Whites Foods Ltd, Isaac Spencer, Unilever.

Animal Feed:
Animedica, Dawe's, Guyomarc'n, Organon (Akzo), Protector, Provimi (Central Soya), Radar, Ralston Purina, Ramikal Werk, Trouw.

These firms* with very few exceptions purchase the entire range of vitamins produced by Roche and obtain all or most of their requirements through such fidelity agreements ... The exclusivity established by Roche with its customers denies any access to these customers by other vitamin manufacturers. For quantities of any importance the rate of rebate given by Roche is such that it is made practically impossible or at the very least onerous for other producers to sell to the customers of Roche ...

The European Commission's case was based largely on internal documents I had given them, and on other papers they had uncovered during their own sorties into Roche companies in the E.E.C. Roche had argued that they could not have known that what they were doing was going to be considered illegal, as the definition of what constituted 'an abuse of a dominant position' was not clear, and as far as Roche were concerned they had only operated a normal business discounting system. The Commission disagreed: 'The Roche circulars referred to above provide evidence that the object desired and the effects expected by Roche were the substantial restriction of competition. Roche could not have been unaware that behaviour restricting competition to such an extent was incompatible with Article 86.' Roche were duly fined.

For the European Commission, and for the Competition department in particular, this had been something of a test case. Talking on Granada's *World in Action* programme in 1975 the department's Director-General, Willi Schlieder, had said, 'This case is extremely important to bring multinational companies under control. National governments are of course disposing of a certain power to control them but their power ends at their boundaries, therefore it's absolutely necessary to have an international agency like the Commission who is able to look in different countries into their affairs and to control them.'

* 7 American companies, 5 British, 2 Swiss, 1 German, 1 Dutch and 6 others.

The Commission wanted to prove that they could exercise some control over the behaviour of multinationals, and by fining Roche they were doing just that. And it wasn't just a question of empty principle. Seventy-five per cent of the sale of bulk vitamins goes into animal nutrition and the price of bulk vitamins in the E.E.C. can therefore have a direct bearing on the price of meat or poultry in the shops, which in turn directly affects the household budgets of ordinary E.E.C. citizens who have no idea that deals are being struck by the multinationals to keep prices high and by so doing to make their shopping more expensive. It was more for their sakes than for anything else that I had reported Roche and the other multinationals to the E.E.C. Commission.

And now I was facing prosecution. This was something of a test case too. It was a test case for the relationship between Switzerland and the E.E.C. If I was found not guilty, then the court in effect would be saying that the Swiss/E.E.C. Free Trade Agreement, and the principles contained in it, took precedence over Swiss domestic law and therefore I could not be guilty of spying against the State, because it had been in the State's interests for me to have given the information to the E.E.C., who was Switzerland's partner in the agreement. If, on the other hand, I was found guilty, it meant that Switzerland thought that what I had done had been against the interests of the State, and if they thought that, then they were putting their own domestic interest in preserving commercial secrecy (however illegal the secrets) above their obligations to the E.E.C. contained within the Free Trade Agreement. This was pointed out at Basle Criminal Court by my lawyer.

It made no difference. On July 1st, 1976 I was found guilty of persistent economic espionage (under Article 273 of the Swiss penal code) and persistently betraying trade secrets (under Article 162). Other countries limit charges of spying to military secrets alone. Even the Swiss found it hard to believe that I had been convicted just for reporting illegal trade practices to the E.E.C. Soon after my arrest the newspapers had reported that I had sold secret Roche formulae to foreign companies! It's a logical conclusion, given the charges, but the papers were wrong. All I had done was talk to the E.E.C., as I thought, quite legitimately. Commissioner Hofer testified at my trial that he had the impression when he first interrogated me that I had no idea I had done anything wrong. But the court were unimpressed by any arguments of ignorance. I was sentenced to twelve months' imprisonment, suspended for three years (on top of the three months I had already spent in prison on remand), banished from Switzerland for five years, ordered to pay costs, and to forfeit the sum of 25,000 Swiss francs bail. I was not there to hear the sentence. Despite protests by my lawyer to the court, and representations by the E.E.C. Commission to the Swiss government, my trial was held mainly *in camera*. I was not prepared to be present at a trial that was not being held in public. In my view it was a travesty of justice. There was no national security risk, no obscenity likely to damage public morals, just a big multinational which wanted to keep its business practices away from the glare of public opinion. But in Switzerland the interests of Roche coincided with the interests of the State. If Roche had a valid reason for wanting to keep its secrets secret, the State had a valid reason for keeping them secret, and the trial could be held *in camera*. A small part of it was held in open court, but most of it took place in closed session. A copy of the sentence was sent by my lawyer, Dr Bollag, to Willi Schlieder in Brussels.

I instructed Dr Bollag, who had phoned the result through to me at my house in Latina, to appeal against the conviction immediately. The first appeal would have to be heard in the Basle Appeals Court, and neither Dr Bollag nor I thought there was much chance of the conviction being overturned there. Our hopes were centred instead on the final stage in the appeals process, the Federal Supreme Court, which was a national rather than a cantonal court, and which we thought should have more awareness of the international implications of the first conviction (as well as being based in Lausanne and not in the city in which Roche had its headquarters).

In August 1976 Roche announced its intention of lodging an appeal against the European Commission's decision to fine them with the European Court of Justice in Luxembourg. Roche felt they had been politically victimized, and they also accused the European Commission of basing their case 'on documents provided by a former employee of Roche whose action is still the subject of legal proceedings instituted by the Swiss authorities . . . ' If Roche were going to argue at the European Court of

Justice that the E.E.C. had used documents procured by illegal means (which would invalidate Roche's conviction) then they were certainly going to watch my progress through the Appeals Court with great interest, in the hope that I remained convicted. It was not the size of the fine that bothered Roche, but the fact that the Commission had dared to fine them at all. Even Willi Schlieder admitted that the fine was 'relatively modest' in relation to Roche's annual turnover. It amounted to around £240,000, which was a fraction of one per cent of their total declared turnover. Under E.E.C. law it could have been as high as 10 per cent of the turnover.

Many members of the European Parliament, particularly amongst the Socialist Group, thought the fine should have been set higher. They were incensed that Roche had got away with a very light fine, while I had been imprisoned and my wife had been put under such pressure by the Swiss authorities that she had committed suicide. Now that I had been convicted by the Basle court, and it appeared that Switzerland was putting her own interests above her international obligations, the Socialist Group were calling for the European Commission to withdraw from the agreement with Switzerland, until such time as Switzerland saw fit to honour her part of it. On September 15th John Prescott, the British Socialist M.P., put down a question to the Commission in the European Parliament: 'What representation has the Commission made to the Swiss government about the conviction of Mr Adams for supplying it with evidence concerning the activities of the multinational Hoffmann-La Roche, and will it now recommend that the Association Agreement between Switzerland and the Community will be suspended until its obligations are clearly understood by both parties?' The European Commission, in the shape of the Vice-President, Sir Christopher Soames, responded cautiously. They would, of course, continue to give me every kind of assistance should I decide to appeal. (I had decided, and informed them of the fact, but apparently Sir Christopher did not know that.) My conviction in the Swiss courts did raise problems for the Commission. 'It could affect the Commission's ability to investigate the business practices in the Community of firms established in Switzerland. The Commission needed to apply the competition provisions of the E.E.C. Treaties and of the Free Trade Agreement between the Community and Switzerland.'

But the problems were not such that the Commission intended to take any drastic action to remedy them. Far from it. Sir Christopher continued, 'Let me assure the House that the Commission has no intention of recommending the suspension of the Free Trade agreement with Switzerland. This Agreement has now been in force for nearly four years. It has been to the greatest benefit of both the Community and of Switzerland, and apart from the problem which is the subject of this question, no difficulties have yet arisen in its application.'

The Socialist Group were not satisfied with this reply. They wanted the Commission to confirm that it was legally possible for the Commission to give notice of intent to withdraw from the Swiss/E.E.C. agreement. What's more they thought the Commission should give such notice. John Prescott returned to the attack, 'This house will note that a Community subject who has provided information to the Commission, which imposed a miserable fine on a multinational company, has been jailed, bailed, fined, further sentenced, hounded from Switzerland and has lost his wife by suicide; . . . that it is not a tolerable answer that was received from the Commissioner. Parliament knows it is possible, and I ask the Commissioner to confirm that it is possible, under the E.E.C./Swiss Agreement, to discuss the desirability of its suspension, as the Swiss government have not offered any repentance in this matter.'

Sir Christopher took refuge in a recital of all the Commission had done for me, and in the fact that my conviction was not yet final because I had not been through the Appeals procedure. Likewise, Roche's conviction was also the subject of an appeal, and there was little the Commission could do until all the legal processes had been completed, though the Commission would 'watch the situation'. It was possible to withdraw from the Agreement, but he repeated the Commission was not going to do so. And that was how it was left. An advice note produced a month later by the Parliamentary legal advisory body, the Directorate General for Research and Documentation, Legal Services, concluded that, 'The sentence of the Swiss court on Mr Stanley Adams . . . represents a clear instance of collision between Swiss domestic law and the rules of international law created by the Agreement between the European Economic Community and the Swiss Confederation.' My conviction, the lawyers thought, 'must therefore be seen as being incompatible with the proper functionings of the Agreement'.

Switzerland, when pressed, declared a willingness to 'see the letter and spirit of obligations arising under the Agreement respected', but as they refused to recognize that my arrest and conviction had anything at all to do with those obligations, maintaining that it was a quite separate issue of Swiss internal law, this willingness was no solution to the conflict between Switzerland and the E.E.C.

Meanwhile I waited for my appeal to be heard in Basle, and Roche waited for theirs to come before the European Court of Justice. They must have hoped that when our two cases were over they would be able to drop out of the headlines, at least temporarily, but they were wrong. A much greater catastrophe brought them back into public notice and, incidentally, in a small way, tied the two of us together again.

9 Seveso

On July 10th, 1976, in a small industrial town in the north of Italy, a chemical factory supposedly making ingredients for perfumes and flavourings exploded, venting a cloud of white fumes across the town. The factory was ICMESA, owned by the multinational Givaudan, which was itself wholly owned by Hoffmann-La Roche. The town was Seveso, and the white cloud contained one of the most poisonous substances known to man, dioxin. Dioxin is 70,000 times more powerful than cyanide and cyanide is lethal in minute doses.

The most detailed account of what happened at Seveso at the time of the explosion and afterwards is in a book called *Super-poison*, written by a team from the *Sunday Times*, Tom Margerison, Marjorie Wallace and Dalbert Hallenstein. It tells how plants died, birds fell from the sky or dropped dead off their perches, rabbits, kept to supplement the local diet, were found dead with blood seeping from 'the mouth, ears and rectum', dogs and cats 'staggered drunkenly before falling over and dying'. The people of Seveso suffered initially from 'reddening and burning of the skin, acute diarrhoea and vomiting, headaches that made them dizzy and pains in the kidney and liver'. Later came the chloracne, red weals on the skin like a virulent form of teenage acne, and impaired eyesight; therapeutic abortions for women who were pregnant, because dioxin was thought to cause deformities at birth; and later still, acute damage to liver and kidneys which many doctors suspected of causing deaths, although official death certificates registered other causes.

ICMESA had started production of T.C.P. (trichlorophenol, the substance which gave off dioxin when overheated) without notifying anyone, despite numerous accidents in other factories in different countries, which were well known in the industry. It was clear that ICMESA had not followed sensible safety precautions, nor had precautions been enforced by the Italian authorities.

The managing director of Givaudan, Guy Waldvogel, who answered directly to Adolf Jann, Roche's president, authorized the manager of ICMESA to offer the local authorities 100 million lire (about £42,000). The offer was refused. Waldvogel is quoted as saying, 'I don't know why. Some people said it was a bribe. The cheque was simply refused and returned. It was badly managed.'

The *Sunday Times* team summed up their findings in Seveso as follows:

The final immorality of ICMESA was that Hoffmann-La Roche had the benefit of a profitable product while the inno-cent citizens of Seveso unknowingly took the risk. They are now paying with their health for Roche's profits and for the arrogance of the engineers and managers who set up Depart-ment B. We do not yet know how bad the medical situation in Seveso really is: the ineptitude of the epidemiological pro-gramme may mean we shall never know . . . 'Capitalism means progress,' Dr Adolf Jann, president of Hoffmann-La Roche, is reported as saying in a television interview about Seveso, 'and progress can lead sometimes to some inconvenience.'

The disaster of Seveso was covered extensively in the Italian and in the foreign press, and once again Roche was in the limelight. Publicity about my case during the previous three years had obviously marked me out as a former employee of Roche, so several Italian journalists immediately turned to me as someone who could enable them to discover more about the workings of Roche and about how a Roche factory could have suddenly started using a hazardous chemical process without apparently declaring it to the Italian authorities. The initiative came from the journalists and never from me, but I had to make a crucial decision: to co-operate with the Italian journalists and risk further problems for myself, or simply to refuse to be interviewed. In everything I had done in the Roche/E.E.C. affair, I had genuinely tried to act on my principles without considering the conse-quences to myself. Again in this case I decided to apply the same rule and agreed to be interviewed by a journalist from *L'Europeo* of Milan, an independent and serious weekly magazine. *L'Europeo*'s new editor was Gianluigi Melega, a campaigning journalist who was fast boosting *L'Europeo*'s hitherto falling circulation with investigative stories about the Vatican and property deals. (*L'Europeo* was owned by the Rizzoli Publishing House, and Andrea Rizzoli was a Christian Democrat and close friend of Giulio Andreotti, Prime Minister of Italy.) In due course I was visited by a journalist named Giuliano Ferrieri.

Ferrieri wanted to know about my connection with Roche, what had happened to me, and what I thought about the present disaster in Seveso. He asked all the questions, and I answered whatever I could, and his editor, Melega, sanctioned publication of the complete article. The first part dealt with my own past history, the E.E.C. case against Roche, my imprisonment, Mariléne's suicide, and my conviction in the Swiss courts. The next part dealt with Seveso. I gave Ferrieri the facts as I understood them.

Roche took over the company Givaudan of Geneva in 1965 when Givaudan owned 51 per cent of ICMESA's shares. In 1969 Roche ordered Givaudan to buy the rest of the shares. I was asked why this might have happened and aired my suspicion that it was because of the drop in world production of T.C.P. which followed plant closures after accidents at B.A.S.F. Ludwigshaven in Germany, Philip-Dufar in Holland, and Coalite in England.

One of the first moves Roche made when they finally owned ICMESA completely was to install new plant for the manufacture of T.C.P. They did this without applying for any special permit from the Italian authorities, locally or nationally. Indeed, its production licence states 'Permit to produce pharmaceutical products and colourants, not in any way dangerous.' The factory and plant of ICMESA were designed by a Swiss engineer, Rossello, who later stated publicly that the plant was not built totally to his designs, of which he had kept copies. Roche/Givaudan/ICMESA had economized on safety precautions which Rossello had included.

Ferrieri wanted to know the possible destination of the T.C.P. I explained that ICMESA was producing 70 tons of T.C.P. a week, too much for the perfume trade. I mentioned that T.C.P. was a basic ingredient in the defoliant 245T (known as Agent Orange). It had been used for general agricultural purposes until there were health scares about its possible effects and it was taken

off the market in many countries. Indeed, in Italy it was withdrawn in 1970. I knew from my time in Roche that a lot of
business is done through brokers, so it is impossible for the
producer to know exactly where the product is going or will
eventually be used. The ICMESA management knew that all
their T.C.P. was shipped to a Givaudan factory in Clifton,
U.S.A., but from there it could have gone anywhere. I left
L'Europeo's readers to draw their own conclusions about its likely
destination.

Giuliano Ferrieri's final question to me concerned any possible
links that Roche might have had with Italian politicians which
could have explained the protection from bureaucratic intervention that ICMESA enjoyed while it manufactured T.C.P. All I
could say was that it was well known that Gianbattista Medri, the
manager of Roche's Italian subsidiary in Milan, Istituto delle
Vitamine SpA, was a strong Christian Democrat, and Medri was
the link between Roche and high-ranking politicians from that
same Italian political party. Medri was quoted in the book by the
Sunday Times journalists as having played a part in the negotiations over the E.E.C.'s case against Roche in the vitamin market.
He also admitted helping put Roche in touch with the relevant
political authorities in Italy over the Seveso crisis, which indicates
that if nothing else he had the channels of communications oiled
and ready for use. Previously I had been told by a senior official in
the E.E.C.'s Competition department that during the time when
they were preparing the case against Roche the E.E.C. had
received three letters from Italy, pleading Roche's cause. They
had come from Giulio Andreotti, then Minister of Economic
Affairs in Italy and a Member of the European Parliament. The
letters contained more detail than an Italian minister could have
known about a Swiss company. Whatever effect these letters had
on the E.E.C. decision, it is a well known fact that the fine against
Roche imposed by the E.E.C. was a very small one indeed – (0.01
per cent of turnover instead of 10 per cent). So it is human to think
that the letters from the Italian minister were helpful – if not in
avoiding the fine, at least in reducing it to a minimum.

I understood the three letters to be in the possession of the
European Commission, unless of course they had been destroyed
or perhaps returned to the minister. I had no reason to doubt their
existence or to think that the Commission official who told me

about them was lying. In all fairness I should also state that the
E.E.C. Commission has never confirmed their existence. In fact,
quite the reverse. In answer to a parliamentary question in 1977
which asked, 'Has the Commission received any representation
from other E.E.C. governments on behalf of Hoffmann-La
Roche in this matter?' the Commission replied, 'The answer to
the honourable member's question is: No, no representations
have been made to the Commission on behalf of Hoffmann-La
Roche.' On being pressed later the reply was again, 'The answer
to the question is No. No approaches have been made to the
Commission on behalf of Hoffmann-La Roche. To make this
quite clear and avoid misunderstanding . . . I would like to say
this: no approaches have been made to the Commission, in other
words no one has made any representations to the Commission,
in other words the Commission has been subject to no outside
intervention. I think that is clear . . . '

There is, it appears, a conflict amongst sources that will never
be resolved.

Before the interview was published in *L'Europeo*, Gianluigi
Melega, the magazine's editor, received a telephone call from the
magazine's owner, Andrea Rizzoli, who wanted to know if it was
true that *L'Europeo* was going to carry a story about Stanley
Adams and Andreotti's connection with Roche. Melega said it
was. Rizzoli asked him to kill the story. In a later interview with
B.B.C. Radio Four Melega explained what happened.

> I got a phone call from Mr Rizzoli who at that time was a close
> friend of Andreotti, in close connection with Andreotti, asking
> me not to print the story, that the magazine should not print the
> story. I said we were willing to take later any sort of interview
> from Mr Andreotti, and have his point of view, but we were not
> going to kill the story of Mr Adams. So we printed and I myself
> was fired from the chief editorship of the magazine three weeks
> later. And from what I have seen happening to myself, or
> happening to him (Adams) as well, it's obvious that when you
> stand up against giants, whether they are industrial or politi-
> cians, you may get bruised in the process. This does not mean
> that one should stop, but it means that you reflect on these
> matters.

Melega was later elected to the Italian Parliament as a Radical M.P., which he still is today. Before he was fired he published a letter from Andreotti denying the connection.

An article in an American newspaper on his firing pointed out that Rizzoli, as well as being a close friend of Andreotti, was heavily in debt to the Italian banks, to the tune of millions of dollars, 'and with but very few exceptions, the men who run Italian banks and hand out soft loans to needy publishers are all Christian Democrat appointees'. (After Andrea Rizzoli's death his son Angelo became Chairman of the company but it is now (1983) under Court management and Angelo Rizzoli is in prison awaiting trial on various charges of fraud.)

In the early spring of 1977, when the latent effects of dioxin were becoming more apparent in Seveso, with people complaining of 'swollen livers, headaches, blurred vision, sore eyes, tingling in the hands and feet, and a jumble of nervous complaints', investigations into how the accident happened and its implications were under way. I received a police summons in Latina to travel to Monza near Milan to appear before a magistrate whose jurisdiction covered Seveso.

At the time I had no idea why I was being called, and was worried enough to contact friends at *L'Europeo* who arranged for a lawyer to meet me at Milan railway station and go with me to the magistrate's office in Monza. The lawyer could not go into the magistrate's office with me, but we had a prearranged signal whereby I could let him know if anything was wrong and he would take the necessary action. It shows how jumpy I had become. I saw Andreotti's influence everywhere. I still had Melega's unfair and abrupt sacking in my mind. In fact I need not have worried. The magistrate only wanted to know everything I could tell him about Roche and its hierarchy, its philosophy and the possible connections between Seveso and Italian politicians. I did not hesitate to tell him everything I knew, including of course the Roche–Medri–Andreotti link. It was neither the first time nor the last that magistrates heard the name Giulio Andreotti mentioned in connection with scandals, and wanted to know more.

The story of Seveso deserves, and has, a book to itself. It is a prime example of the way in which Roche put the interests of itself and its shareholders (money and profits) above the interests of the people, and of the way in which politics and the tangle of political influence in Italy becomes a way of life in itself, a way which makes it impossible for people to move and make decisions freely in almost any sphere of activity.

The court hearing on the ICMESA dioxin tragedy was eventually held in Monza in September 1983, and on the 23rd the three judges gave the five Roche men prison sentences of five years each. The managers concerned, who have all appealed, are three Swiss, one Italian and one German.

I myself had become entangled in the Italian system, and quite unable to keep out of the web of Italian politics. Perhaps, with my background and philosophical views about fighting for what is right, I didn't want to keep out.

10 Starting Again

In April 1974, when I first moved to Latina, I had applied for a residence permit. Italian bureaucracy moves slowly, but my company lawyer advised me that my permit should come through within a few months. By Christmas of that year it had still not arrived. In the new year I was arrested and imprisoned in Switzerland and when I finally returned to Italy in late 1975 and made enquiries about my permit I was told that it was still 'under consideration'. An application for residence does not normally take eighteen months to consider, and I began to suspect that there might be some connection between the delay in granting my residence permit and the past history of my arrest and imprisonment in Switzerland. I asked the E.E.C. Commission for help. Mr Aurelio Pappalardo, an Italian official, had by then succeeded Aldo Carisi as Director of Inspection in DG4. He came to Rome, saw me (on Schlieder's orders) in summer 1976 and approached the Italian authorities. He too was told by the Ministry of the Interior that my request for residence was 'under consideration', but he was assured that the delay had nothing to do with my involvement in the Roche case. I waited a bit longer, but nothing happened. By now I was seriously worried. Although I had been a British citizen from birth, and had been honorary British Consul in Colombia for five years, I had lost my British citizenship when Malta became independent and I and my children now had Maltese passports. This meant that we did not hold the passports of any member country of the European Community and without a residence permit we had no right to live or work in Italy. I had absolutely no desire to find myself deported to Malta and forced to find a living there. I had left Malta as a young man immediately after the war and had never been back. After thirty years' absence I no longer spoke Maltese and my family were either dead or scattered round the world. Worse still, there was the possibility that I could be deported not to Malta but back to the country from which I had come, Switzerland, and from which I had been banished for five years. I had no idea what the legal implications of that might be. I approached the E.E.C. Commission for help in trying to regain my British citizenship. François-Xavier Ortoli, President of the Commission, asked the Rt Hon. George Thomson, the E.E.C. Commissioner in charge of Regional Development and a former Labour minister in the House of Commons, to write to the British Government on my behalf. On July 28th, 1976 he wrote to the Home Secretary, Roy Jenkins.

Dear Roy,
    I am writing to draw your attention to an application for U.K. citizenship by registration which is currently being made by Mr Stanley Adams. Mr Adams has been, as you may know, a central figure in the proceedings which the Commission has taken against the Swiss company, Hoffmann-La Roche, and he has suffered considerable hardship from the Swiss authorities as a result of passing to the Commission the information which enabled the Commission to pursue Hoffmann-La Roche for commercial malpractice . . .
    The facts of the Adams case are as follows . . .
    Mr Adams is currently living in Italy, with no assurance that he will receive an Italian residence permit and he is naturally anxious that he should at least recover his British citizenship. Mr Adams is of Maltese origin and until July 1969 held a British passport. At that time the Maltese government ruled that, on Malta's achieving independence, Maltese citizens who wished to keep British nationality should opt for it within a certain period. Mr Adams was living in Venezuela at the time, and, unaware of the necessity to take action in order to retain his British nationality, took no steps to do so, thus ending up with a Maltese passport.
    The Commission has throughout taken the view that Mr Adams had acted in the public interest within the Community and that he had suffered unduly harshly for what he had done. The Commission therefore helped to secure his release, paid his bail, and financed his defence. During the period I held responsibility for Competition matters, it was agreed to support

his appeal against sentence. He is now in effect exiled from his chosen place of work and his future employment prospects are, to say the least, uncertain. I should therefore be very grateful for anything you can do to ensure that there are no difficulties about his recovering his British citizenship.

Roy Jenkins did not reply. He was about to take up his post in the E.E.C. as the next President of the Commission, where I was to have further dealings with him which I felt to be unsatisfactory. It was left to his successor, Merlyn Rees, to answer. Two months later on September 20th, 1976 he wrote explaining that as a citizen of Malta (which incidentally had become independent in 1964) there was no way that I qualified for registration under British legislation.

> . . . I regret that there is no way in which, in his present circumstances, Mr Adams can be considered for registration as a citizen of the United Kingdom and Colonies. As you will see from the enclosed leaflet . . . Mr Adams has no entitlement and he is not qualified to apply for registration at my discretion on grounds of either residence or 'relevant employment' . . . If in the future he became qualified to apply for registration the information you have given in your letter would certainly be taken into account in considering any application he might make, but I cannot of course give any assurance at this stage that it would be successful.
>
> If Mr Adams wishes to come to this country he would need to establish a claim to do so under the immigration rules. These are published as House of Commons paper no. 79 entitled Statement of Immigration Rules for Control on Entry, Commonwealth citizens. Mr Adams may wish to peruse a copy or alternatively discuss any claim he may have to enter at the nearest British mission where he lives. He should, in any case, seek an entry clearance before coming here from any such Mission. On the information you have given the work permit scheme would seem to be the only method of entry open to him.
>
> I am sorry that I cannot send you a more welcome reply.

It was clear that I was not going to be treated as a special case, or given particular consideration on compassionate grounds. I was measured against the regulations and found wanting. Only if I found myself a job in Britain and applied for a work permit would I be allowed to enter the country and stay there, but my residence would be conditional on employment and that was something I wanted to avoid at all costs. When I had first realized that there was a chance I might not get my pig farm off the ground, I had written to several different companies, first in the pharmaceutical field, and later in other industries, looking for work. Some of these were companies who would have been only too happy to poach me from Roche when I was working there if they had been able to. All the replies I had were negative, and some companies did not even bother to reply. I could not find work as a desk clerk, never mind as a manager. To all intents and purposes I was on a blacklist, unspoken and unwritten, but none the less there. Big business did not want me. Knowing this made me more determined than ever to make a go of my own business. All my money was invested in it, and it was the only way I could be sure of earning a living. British citizenship would have given me the right to live in Italy as an E.E.C. citizen while I tried to build up the farm. It would also have given me the right to live in Britain if later I decided to sell the farm as a going concern and look for other business opportunities in the U.K. Without citizenship I was dependent on someone else's good will to give me a job and good will was temporarily in short supply.

But at least there was no shortage of it within the European Parliament, which still remained active in my defence. At the beginning of 1977 I was invited to Luxembourg, to attend a debate on my case which was scheduled for January 12th. In the press conference that was held to cover the issues on that session's agenda, I was asked to speak to the international press (including journalists from Switzerland, which gave me some pleasure). The Rt Hon. Tony Crosland, M.P., then Britain's Foreign Secretary, and President of the Council of Ministers for the European Community, spoke directly before me. When he had finished speaking, he wished me luck and urged me to 'fight on'. He was a man I greatly admired and I appreciated his encouragement. My press conference was chaired jointly by Dr Mario Zagari, M.P. from Italy, who was Vice-President of the European Parliament and an Italian ex-Minister of Justice, and by John Prescott, the British M.P. for Hull East who was then

Vice-Chairman of the Socialist Group. John Prescott put down a comprehensive list of questions in Parliament on behalf of the Socialist Group, who were looking after my interests (as indeed they still do today).

They wanted to know:

1) When did the Commission convene the Joint Committee under the 1972 Swiss/E.E.C. agreement to discuss the implications of this case, and what conclusions did it reach? (The Swiss were saying that they had not been officially approached on the matter.)

2) Has the Commission been informed as to the date of Hoffmann-La Roche's appeal to the European Court against their fine? Is there any delay, and will the Commission make a statement? (This was important to me. My lawyer was of the opinion that if the European Court of Justice found Roche guilty, then the Swiss higher courts would be forced to find me not guilty. It seemed a logical supposition at the time. I was hoping that the Roche case would be heard before my final appeal.)

3) Has the Swiss government given any assurance that no Community Citizen will face prosecution for industrial espionage if they provide information to the Commission similar to the action taken by Mr Adams about the illegal practices of such companies? (This was a key question. The Swiss had given no such assurance and, as far as the Socialist Group could see, had no intention of giving any such assurance while the interests of their multinationals were at stake.)

4) Has the Commission received any representation from other E.E.C. governments on behalf of Hoffmann-La Roche in this matter? (A reference to the Andreotti letters mentioned in Chapter 9.)

5) On what date did the Commission publicly move against Hoffmann-La Roche companies in the Community and was Mr Adams previously informed? If not, why not? (If they had warned me I would never have gone to Switzerland, and all my troubles could have been avoided.)

6) When was the Commission first made aware of Mr Adams' decision to appeal against his conviction by the Swiss courts, and is it compatible with the statement given by Commissioner Soames to the European Parliament in September? (Christopher Soames had given the impression at the last debate that

the Commission could do nothing until they knew whether I had decided to appeal or not, but I had informed them the previous July, two months before the debate, that I had instructed my lawyer to lodge an appeal.)

7) Has the Commissioner received any request from Mr Adams for assistance in acquiring citizenship of one of the Community countries? (This was in the hope of reviving chances of my getting British citizenship, or, failing that, finding another E.E.C. country who would offer me citizenship, even Luxembourg.)

Presenting his questions, John Prescott emphasized the importance the debate had for me as a person.

The point I really want us to exercise our minds on is that, while the different parties to this dispute are contesting it in the courts, the consequences are different for each party. The Commission are concerned with assistance to Mr Adams in his difficult situation. Roche were fined a very miserable sum, only a fraction of the maximum fine that could have been imposed for this activity, and which is of little consequence to them. For the Swiss authorities it is obviously a matter of some concern and one which, no doubt, they are watching closely. But no one faces the personal consequences that Mr Adams himself has faced.

You will recall that after interrogation by the Swiss authorities, when the man was arrested, his wife unfortunately within a number of hours of that interrogation committed suicide. He himself eventually got out of prison with the aid of the Commission and went to Italy. Now, he is in a situation where, as a Maltese citizen, living in Italy, he is attempting to rebuild his life. He has rendered this Community a considerable service – one that I think would rate the possibility of our considering him for Community citizenship. One of the questions, question number 7, is one largely geared to considering whether British citizenship could be granted to him, and particularly with his background. He was forty years a British citizen until the Maltese Independence Act, and also acted in an honorary capacity as Consul for Britain in a Latin American country. To that end I have a meeting both with the Home Secretary in Britain on January 24th and I hope for a meeting with President

Roy Jenkins about this matter. We are taking steps to help him in Italy in order to see if we can achieve for him what has been much delayed, a residence permit. Under those circumstances we could personally help Mr Adams considerably; and through the power of this Parliament in its publicity, and the Commission by its contacts, together we should be able to achieve these two things.

But there are a number of other questions of equal concern down on the paper . . . questions about whether there is delay in dealing with the matter by the European Court, whether in fact the Commission in its activities has been subject to certain pressures, matters that have been mentioned in press speculations which one finds difficult to substantiate, questions which clearly need voicing in this Parliament to the Commission, to ask whether there is any truth in these matters. Why was Mr Adams not informed of the action by the Commission against the company and allowed to visit Switzerland and therefore be arrested by the Swiss authorities? In question 4, for example, I ask the Commission, and I want it to be absolutely precise about this, whether it has been approached by any other country, giving an opinion that perhaps Roche was correct in this matter, or has there been any correspondence between the Commission and member governments about the case of Adams and Roche? If so, in what way and in what manner is it related to the issue? I hope we can have some reasonably precise replies about that.

. . . The position therefore at the moment is that if any other Community citizen was to provide information about this company or other companies in similar circumstances, and they happened to be situated in Switzerland, they could face prosecution on a charge of criminal espionage just by providing information to show that certain illegal practices under the Rome Treaty were taking place.

. . . The final point really is that this man, Mr Adams, served this Community very well. He did the Community a service. The least that we can do is to assist him. He is looking to this Parliament to protect him, to protect his interests and give him some form of justice. I hope that will be considered as an honourable part for all parliaments to play and that tonight we will make some small progress towards achieving the protection of his interests and taking a step that Parliament should take on behalf of the interests of Community citizens.

Nobody could accuse the Socialist Group in the European Parliament of not trying. They did their best to help me, but the European Commission, in the shape of Vice-President Wilhelm Haferkamp, dealt with most of the questions in what I felt to be a vague and inadequate manner. The E.E.C./Swiss Joint Committee had discussed the Hoffmann-La Roche case on June 5th, 1975. The Swiss delegation 'declared its willingness to examine this question in terms of the letter and spirit of the Agreement in accordance with the procedure and the obligations laid down in it.' There had been no delay in the timing of the Roche appeal to the European Court of Justice. The papers had been lodged at the correct time. On the question of similar cases to mine arising in the future: 'A procedure for the exchange of information between the Commission's departments and the Swiss Mission has been laid down. The Commission takes the view that this procedure should ensure that there will be no repetition of cases similar to the one we are discussing today.'

Haferkamp enlarged on this in later debate. 'This question is the subject of pending legal action. We can do nothing that interferes with the proceedings. Therefore, while avoiding any such interference, we have at the same time attempted to find pragmatic solutions to prevent a repetition of similar cases.'

No representations were made to the Commission on behalf of Hoffmann-La Roche, from any E.E.C. country. The Commission had first moved against Roche subsidiaries in October 1974. They hadn't informed me because, 'At that time the Commission's departments had long since lost contact with Mr Adams, who had not given his new address in Italy. Mr Adams had previously declared his willingness to confirm his information as a witness in court if necessary.'

You would have thought that an investigatory body like DG4 would be able to trace a new address without much difficulty, or alternatively that if I had agreed to be a court witness if necessary they would have attempted to keep tabs on where I was, but apparently they didn't. They didn't tell me not to go into Switzerland, because they didn't have my address. In fact I lived seventy miles from the E.E.C.'s Rome offices. (The E.E.C. has offices in the capital cities of each of the ten member countries.)

I had informed them, Haferkamp said, that I was going to lodge an appeal against the Basle Criminal Court's verdict in July 1976. The appeal was lodged in October 1976. I had approached the Commission to ask for help with citizenship. Commissioner Thomson had asked the British Government if it was possible and had been told that under existing legislation it was not.

And that was that. A lot of questions had been aired. Quite what had been achieved I wasn't so sure, but it was reassuring to know that at any rate many friends were fighting for me.

I returned from Luxembourg to Italy and continued the fight myself. My first concern was the elusive residence permit. The European socialists had asked Dr Mario Zagari to help. He did indeed intervene on my behalf with Francesco Cossiga, the Italian Minister for the Interior (who was a personal friend of his). Up until now the Ministry of the Interior had always refused to come clean and give the true reasons why my application for *Soggiorno* had been shelved. Indeed, when Mr Pappalardo came to Rome on behalf of the E.E.C. he was told that my application was being considered (not shelved). No indication was given of any connection between the Roche matter and my application.

Now Dr Zagari was told confidentially but clearly that until the court case was decided the Ministry of the Interior would not even consider my application (I supposed they referred to my pending appeal rather than the case pending against Roche in the European Court of Justice).

As things stood, the Italians did not want to give me residence, even though the sentence received in Switzerland was a suspended one and I did not have to serve any prison sentence. There was no chance that the Swiss could increase my sentence, but they could reduce it or cancel it. I presumed the Italians were not willing to grant me residence unless the sentence was cancelled, and I didn't think that was likely to happen, though it might be possible when my case reached the Federal Supreme Court in Lausanne. The Minister of the Interior answered only to the Prime Minister, Giulio Andreotti (the man who thought I wasn't fit to take up space in a newspaper). I didn't think Francesco Cossiga was taking decisions of his own accord . . . I looked for other means of applying pressure.

Eventually, in desperation, I phoned up some journalist friends of mine in Rome who were prominent political writers, and asked them for advice. They came round to my house in Latina and we sat and talked it over. Enrico Manca, Italian Socialist M.P. and one of the Party leaders, also came with them. They went away promising to see what they could do. A little later I received a call saying that they thought they had found the politician who could help me. His name was Oscar Mammi, M.P., a Republican Party leader, a man with a lot of political experience, and with a reputation for being a serious and honest politician, and he happened to be the Chairman of the Italian parliament's Home Affairs Committee. They introduced me to him and I fixed an appointment to go and see him in his office in Rome. I told him exactly what had happened, and he said he would send for my file and assess the situation for himself. As Chairman of the Home Affairs Committee, he had the right to call for it and nobody could refuse him. And that's what he did. A short while later, on June 8th, 1977, he wrote me a letter simply saying that he was pleased to say I would be getting my residence permit. I phoned his office to see if anybody could give me any more details and spoke to his assistant who told me that when Oscar Mammi had examined the file he had found nothing in it at all that could have prevented me being granted my residence permit. He had therefore ordered that I be given my permit immediately. When I asked why he thought it had been held back for so long, his assistant told me that he thought someone had been putting pressure on the Italian Home Affairs Minister to let the file lie dormant and do nothing. Of course, once Mammi had requested it, and it was out in the open, nothing could be done except to give me my residence permit. (Although they did make sure it was not a permanent one, but renewable yearly, which is unusual . . .) Oscar Mammi himself later confirmed in a television interview that there had been no valid reason in my file for withholding my residence permit for so long.

While I was trying to settle my residence, the European Commission, at my request, was putting pressure behind the scenes on the Italian government and finance institutes to renew the grants and loans they had promised before. Eventually the diplomatic pressures, visits, letters and telephone calls, bore fruit and again the Italian government was induced to review the position. In February 1977 the Cassa per il Mezzogiorno agreed to sign the grant contract and the Mediocredito Regionale del Lazio agreed to sign the contract for a twelve-year, low-interest loan, and I was nearly back where I had been in 1974 before all the trouble started. I now had my residence permit, my grant and my long-term finance. But I had lost over three years and had almost used up my capital on keeping myself and my children. I had had no income at all during this period. There was now an urgent need to move the scheme ahead as fast as possible if my children and I were not to starve in the future. We were not eligible for any kind of Italian state benefit. If we didn't have the money to buy food, we didn't eat. That was all there was to it.

Although I now had my grant and long-term loan restored I still had problems. I couldn't find a single commercial bank in Italy prepared to offer me the bridging loan I needed to cover myself against the slow arrival of Government funds. With the Government contracts as guarantees there would normally have been no problems at all, and certainly there were none in evidence before my arrest. Commercial banks of course were not subject to outside diplomatic pressures as Government institutes were and they remained firm in their resolve not to lend me any money. Most bank managers would have been Christian Democrat appointees, and it may be that they had an eye to the way the political wind was blowing, but for whatever reason, and they didn't have to give me one, there was no money forthcoming in Italy.

I started to look outside for finance, but no outside bank would accept Italian government documents as guarantees. They just didn't have any faith in the Italian government. I had to find some other way of guaranteeing the loan. The British firm, Meteor Pigs Ltd, from whom I planned to buy my stock, offered to help. Meteor Pigs was a co-operative of twelve independent pig farmers in Rushden, Northants and I aimed to buy 525 purebred gilts and boars from them, which had a value of over £120,000. It was an important order, and there would be fresh orders later for replacement of stock. They set about looking for British sources of finance for me, but without much success.

I was beginning to get desperate. It was impossible to start building without some form of pre-finance. The money just wouldn't arrive from the Government in time to pay the builders and keep the work going. It would grind to a halt within weeks for lack of funds and then the grant and loan would be cancelled because the building wasn't finished. I couldn't risk that happening, but I had no income and my savings were almost at zero.

On September 27th in Basle Appeal Court, again in my absence, and again in closed session, I lost my appeal against the conviction by the Basle Criminal Court. The diplomatic flurries at the Commission and in the European Parliament had left the court unmoved. The Basle Appeal Court did, however, remove the sentence of five years' banishment from Switzerland, arguing, quite logically, that I wasn't working in Switzerland any longer and if I did I would scarcely be likely to have the opportunity to offend again, so there was no need to protect Swiss interests by banishing me. I can't say I was unduly surprised at losing the appeal. It was what I had expected, but it was none the less depressing. I instructed my lawyer to lodge an appeal with the Federal Supreme Court in Lausanne. If my conviction were to be overturned it would be the judges in the Lausanne court that would do it. As judges in the highest Swiss court, they should be more aware of issues of constitutional and international law. At least, that's what I hoped.

Meanwhile I continued hunting for sources of finance so I could get the building of my farm under way. Meteor Pigs Ltd had no success in their hunt for finance either, but finally their General Manager, Mr Tony Pallet, introduced me to a 'financial consultant', Terence Noble, who he thought might be able to help. I contacted him. We spoke by phone, we exchanged letters, and finally I came to London to meet him. He met me at the airport in his Rover and took me to lunch at the 21 Club. Once the Manager of an American bank in the City (London), he still had many connections in America, particularly in California. There was a company called Venture Capital which he hoped would be able to find me the loan I needed on the guarantee of the Italian contracts. We agreed that he would make the necessary arrangements and he drove me back to the airport so I could get back to my children that night. All this of course cost money, which I could ill afford, but I had little option if I was going to get the business going.

On November 7th, 1977 Terry Noble wrote to Venture Capital, to the senior partner, Mr H. J. Heilbroner, outlining my requirements for a loan and giving details of my intensive pig-farming scheme. Various correspondence followed, I went back to London a couple of times, and finally it transpired that the American partners of Venture Capital were coming over to England to transact various items of business, mine among them. There were two main partners in Venture Capital, H. J. Heilbroner and his junior partner Harold Saperstein. They also had a European representative, Paul Calder, who lived permanently in Monaco but spent a lot of his time in London. On December 9th I returned to London with my Italian lawyer to meet them. I was met by Terry Noble at the airport and we had lunch again at the 21 Club, and then went on to the Dorchester where we were to meet the others.

Paul Calder was there and the two Americans. At least, I was told the two Americans were there, but they remained in their hotel rooms and didn't come down. I never saw them there. The deal was explained to me. There was a facility fee of 15,000 U.S. dollars (£8,000) payable in advance, and then on receipt of the money there would be a further percentage, two or three per cent, payable to Venture Capital for their part in the deal. Meteor Pigs were anxious that the deal should go ahead, because once I had my farm built I would be buying pigs from them and the contact meant the possibility of big export orders in the future. I would also be buying a feed mill from one of their associates, H. J. Digwood. In order to help me Meteor Pigs and H. J. Digwood offered to advance £4,000 each towards the facility fee. I would repay them within fourteen days (which was how quickly we had been led to believe the money would arrive), and give them a cheque now in Italian lire as a guarantee which they would cash at a given time. I signed the deal and so did the witnesses. I was then handed a shares portfolio from one of Venture Capital's American clients who was willing to guarantee the loan for me. All I had to do, I gathered, was present this portfolio to a Swiss bank, or one in Luxembourg, or Strasbourg, wherever I liked, and the contents would be sufficient to guarantee the loan that I needed. They then left. I phoned the manager of a reputable bank in Lugano and told him the portfolio was on its way and I wanted to borrow about 2 million Swiss francs (£500,000). I returned home to Latina, relieved that I had finally found the source of finance that I needed.

The relief lasted until the bank in Lugano phoned me and told me that the portfolio was worthless. The owner was not offering the bank the facility to hold the shares in their vaults as a guarantee to the loan, but merely offering them for inspection to show how much the owner was worth. If I defaulted on the loan the bank had no formal claim at all against the guarantor, which made the deal worthless. There was no way they could advance me money on those conditions. I presented the portfolio to several different banks, including one in Luxembourg recommended by Venture Capital. All the banks said the same thing. The portfolio meant nothing. Venture Capital said they would try and find a Mexican bank instead to advance the money, since it was alleged that the guarantor had considerable property and excellent connections in Mexico.

Several letters and telexes later it was clear to me that I was not going to get any finance and I had lost the £8,000 facility fee. Meteor Pigs Ltd and Mr Digwood would soon start pressing me for its return, although they had held off so far while it looked as if I might sort things out.

On February 8th, 1978 I received the following letter from Venture Capital consultants:

Dear Stanley,

We are still in the process of attempting to obtain a Mexican Bank guarantee on your behalf, but it appears tenuous.

As you know, Harold is very impressed with you and your capabilities; consequently double effort is being applied on your project. A good indication of his respect for you is the fact that we very much want you to represent us in Italy – as supported by our certificate of appointment forwarded to you.

Stanley, we have already domestically spent far in excess of our retainer thus far; however we are still continuing to explore every possibility. We must say, in all due candour, that if the Mexican Bank Guarantee falls through, our chances for success are minimal.

With best regards,

H. J. Heilbroner

I was not remotely interested in representing Venture Capital Consultants. I was a great deal more interested in getting my money back. When it became clear that the Mexican bank was not going to produce anything either I spoke with political friends in the House of Commons. The representatives of Venture Capital had left the country and I heard no more about it. The *Sunday Times*, where they used to advertise, refused further advertisements, and that was all that could be done.

I had been forced to move from conventional banking to the fringes of entrepreneur finance in my desperation, and I had lost £8,000 for my pains. I suppose it's a risk one runs in those circumstances but it was one I could ill afford and I was angry with myself for allowing desperation to overcome my usual cautious instincts.

11 The Debate in the European Parliament

In April and May of 1978 the Federal Supreme Court in Lausanne heard my appeal. The case was again heard *in camera*, despite protests, and again I didn't attend. The Supreme Court upheld the judgment of the two lower courts. Despite all that had been said outside Switzerland about the implications of the earlier verdicts, inside Switzerland I remained convicted of persistent economic espionage and persistent breaches of commercial secrecy. And this was the final verdict. No further appeal was possible (at least not in Switzerland).

My lawyer had tried to argue that,

Switzerland could not grant protection for commercial secrets in conflict with its obligations under international treaties; in Article 22 para. 2 of the Free Trade Agreement it had undertaken to take the appropriate measures to fulfil the obligations arising from this agreement and in Article 27 para. 3 a) to provide the Joint Committee with any useful information and to provide obligations under international treaties would have to be overcome by the former giving way to the latter.

The judgment stated: 'The appellant does not state to what extent Swiss national economic interest in the maintenance of commercial secrets is excluded by the international agreements existing between the E.E.C. and Switzerland and this is also not clear.'

It went on to say:

The appellant's objection is however of itself already invalid. The Free Trade Agreement is a pure Trade Agreement which is limited essentially to the regulation of industrial free trade ... Article 23 of the Free Trade Agreement does not establish any law on the conduct of private individuals, it merely establishes which practices are incompatible with the proper operation of the Free Trade Agreement, but does not forbid them, does not even describe them as illegal, and, in contrast to Articles 85 and 86 of the E.E.C. Treaty, does not declare them invalid or provide for sanctions . . .

National legal provisions therefore continue to apply, even if principles of competition of the Free Trade Agreement are infringed . . .

The protection of commercial secrets is therefore not in conflict with Switzerland's international obligations under the Free Trade Agreement. There is no conflict between internal law and international treaty.

The argument that I had done nothing against the interests of the State and therefore could not be charged as a spy under Article 273 of the Swiss penal code was dismissed.

Business secrets which a Swiss economic undertaking wishes to keep secret count as facts of economic life and maintenance of their secrecy, in the Swiss view, is a legitimate interest and they therefore are to be protected *vis-à-vis* other countries and thus they count as commercial secrets in the sense of Article 273; their disclosure violates not only private but indirectly also national economic, i.e. State, interests.

In other words, even when the facts of 'economic life' that Roche wanted to keep hidden were illegal and broke the provisions of an international agreement that Switzerland had signed, they were still protected under Swiss law. What's more, anyone who attacked Roche by revealing those secrets was deemed to be attacking the interests of the Swiss State. The two were linked together. What was good for Roche was good for Switzerland, and woe betide anyone who challenged that link or dared to report them to an outside body, even if that body was a partner in an international agreement.

According to the material findings of the Criminal Court and the lower instance the appellant knew that Switzerland was not a member of the E.E.C. and the E.E.C. Commission was a foreign, i.e. non-Swiss government office. This excludes any misconception as to the facts. It is irrelevant whether the E.E.C. Commission is the competent authority for judging the business practices used by Roche and denounced by the applicant.

My lawyer, Dr Bollag, told me of the court's verdict and in a telephone conversation advised me that this was the end of the road. I asked if there was anything else we could do, and he said no, the appeals process was complete and there was nothing further to be done. We had lost. In July Dr Bollag sent copies of this judgment, with full legal comments, to Willi Schlieder.

On November 13th of that year, after waiting in vain to hear further, I wrote to John Prescott, M.P., at the House of Commons.

Just to keep you informed that the Federal Supreme Court (Lausanne) have rejected our appeals on the 21st April and the 3rd May 1978, and that, according to my Basle lawyers, there is now nothing further we can do in Switzerland. This means that my sentence will remain valid, in spite of all that has been done and said in Brussels and at the European Parliament by my Socialist friends. My Basle lawyer (Dr Bollag) has sent copies of the judgments mentioned to Mr Schlieder's office some time ago. These documents are in German, but no doubt you can obtain official English translations in Brussels, from Mr Schlieder. `

I trust that you and your colleagues in the European Parliament can do something for me. Could we not take my case to the European Court of Justice? Or the Court in Strasbourg (Human Rights)? I understand that the Roche sentence will be out in mid-December '78 . . .

Schlieder, himself a lawyer, should have known, and presumably did know, that the only remedy left for me then was the European Commission of Human Rights in Strasbourg, and that there was a six-month time limit in which to submit my appeal. Yet neither he nor the E.E.C. Commission gave me guidance on this crucial point. By the time I wrote to John Prescott it was already too late. How was I to know?

If the European Court of Justice were to uphold the European Commission's decision against Roche, and find that Roche were guilty of breaking Article 86 of the Treaty of Rome, then my position would be much stronger. It would be hard for any international court to hold that one party could be guilty of an illegal act, and another party guilty for reporting that act. Illegal activities were not normally considered worthy of the protection of the law.

The Roche judgment was finally delivered not in December, but a couple of months later, on February 13th, 1979. The European Court of Justice endorsed the Commission's decision to fine Roche and found that Roche were indeed guilty of abusing a dominant position in the market by their use of fidelity contracts. In their original submission to the court Roche had argued that the E.E.C. had infringed the procedural rules of fair trial because: 'The decision to initiate a procedure was taken on the basis of information which came into the possession of the defendant (the E.E.C.) illegally.' (Just as it was important to me that Roche should be found guilty, so it was important to Roche that I should be found guilty, so they could argue that my acts were illegal and therefore make their conviction invalid.)

Roche asked for an annulment of the Commission's decision to fine them on the grounds that:

A certain number of documents . . . came into the Commission's hands irregularly, in particular because they were handed to the Commission by an employee of Roche who procured them unlawfully and is on that account guilty of an offence punishable by Swiss criminal law. The irregular procurement of the documents vitiates the procedure and the Commission has, moreover, violated international law by carrying out investigations in a third sovereign state.

The Commission vigorously denied ever having conducted any of its investigations on Swiss territory and the Roche lawyers later conceded and withdrew this submission so it was not examined by the court in Roche's defence. Reading the judgment of the European Court of Justice I began to understand why in my first interrogation it had been so important for Superintendent Hofer to establish whether I had approached the European Commission, or they had approached me. The Swiss wanted to know if they had a case against the Commission, which explained why the E.E.C. lawyers and the Inspectors had been so reluctant to meet with me on Swiss territory. It probably also explained the rumours at the time of my release from prison that the Swiss had issued warrants for the arrest of members of the E.E.C. Commission's Competition department if they entered Switzerland.

Much of the argument around the European Commission's decision to fine Roche centred on whether or not Roche had a dominant position in the market, whether they had a dominant position for each vitamin named by the Commission, and if they did whether they could be said to have abused that position by using fidelity rebates. The European Court of Justice found that Roche had a dominant position 'as far as concerns the markets in vitamins A, B2, B6, C, E and H. On the other hand it was wrong to find that there was such a position on the vitamin B3 market . . . The Commission was also right to regard the said contracts containing fidelity rebates as an abuse of a dominant position.'

Roche attempted to argue that the concept of abuse of a dominant position in the market was ill-defined and that they should not therefore be fined in what must be to some extent a test case to define the concept. They couldn't have been expected to know, they said, that they were running the risk of a fine when they drew up the contracts. The Court dealt summarily with this argument. A prudent commercial operator, the Court said, would know that any company holding a large share of the market had to be careful about the way they behaved. The law allowed for any company uncertain of whether its practices broke the competition laws or not to take advice from the European Commission. 'The applicant did not however consider that it should avail itself of this opportunity in order to obtain that legal certainty of which it claims it has been deprived.' The European Court of Justice concluded 'that the applicant intentionally pursued a commercial policy designed to bar access to the market of new competitors.'

Because the European Commission had made a mistake in its assessment of the B3 vitamin market, because it had only assessed the dominant position of Roche over three years rather than the five which it had taken into account when fixing the fine, and because Roche had withdrawn the contracts, the Court reduced

Roche's fine but dismissed their application to have the Commission's decision overturned.

Roche had appealed and lost but had the fine reduced. I had appealed and lost, but had my sentence reduced (losing the five-year period of banishment). We were both guilty in the eyes of the law, Roche of breaking competition law, I of reporting that Roche had broken competition law. The logic seemed a little faulty, but logic apparently didn't enter into it.

I had for some time been unhappy with my lawyer, although I could scarcely blame him for losing my cases, given the obstinacy of the Swiss government, or the Swiss judiciary. In May 1977, after my first conviction and before any appeals were heard, I had written to John Prescott asking if he knew of any Swiss socialist lawyers who might be prepared to work alongside Dr Bollag. In June 1977 I wrote to Willi Schlieder saying I wanted to change my lawyer. As the Commission was paying for my defence it seemed a courtesy to consult them. I named several lawyers, among them Dr Andreas Gerwig, M.P., from Basle. Schlieder's assistant, a man named Mensching, phoned me back and said they thought it would be unwise to change lawyers at that point, that Bollag was doing a good job, and I should stay with him. I accepted their opinion and did nothing. Now, in 1979, having lost all three cases, and with Dr Bollag saying there was no more to be done, it seemed the logical time to change lawyers if I was going to try and fight the case further, although I had no idea at the time how I could fight it. At the beginning of 1979 I discussed the matter with John Prescott and the Socialist Group again.

In February 1979, during a telephone call from the European Parliament in Luxembourg, John Prescott suggested to me a Socialist lawyer from Berne, by the name of Dr Erich Diefenbacher, who had fought cases against the Swiss State in the past. (This lawyer was not one of those named in my letter of June 1977.) Dr Erich Diefenbacher, who was standing right near John Prescott at that time, took over the telephone (as soon as I had agreed to appoint him as my new lawyer) and mentioned two things to me: firstly that I could have applied to the European Commission of Human Rights and secondly that in Swiss law there is a particular article, Article 113, which enshrines in Swiss domestic law the principle that international law supersedes domestic law. I had never heard of either of these facts before. The European Commission of Human Rights lays down that an application for a hearing must be submitted to them within six months of exhausting all possible domestic remedies in the country of origin. It was nine months since my final appeal had been heard in Lausanne. I was too late.

Erich Diefenbacher was not the only one to refer to Article 113 in Swiss law. Meanwhile, Swiss parliamentarians had been becoming active on my behalf. The Swiss Socialists got together with the European Socialist Group to discuss how they could co-ordinate their activities. On January 30th, 1979 Dr Jean-Noël Rey, a Swiss Socialist M.P. and Party Secretary, wrote to Jean-Pierre Simon, Deputy General-Secretary of the Socialist Group, suggesting the following action:

1) Intervention by your group (European Socialists) with the Commission as to the position of the Swiss government after the sentence of the Supreme Court of Switzerland re Adams, concerning the passing on or offering of economic information (on non-defence matters) by individuals and/or legal entities to organs or organisms of the E.E.C.

2) Parliamentary intervention of our group as to the interpretation of Art. 273 of the Swiss Penal Code (economic espionage) in view of obligations Switzerland has entered into towards the E.E.C. by concluding the Treaty of Association.

3) Parliamentary intervention of our group demanding why the Swiss Department of Justice in the Adams case in a special legal opinion has sustained the position taken by the lower courts (of Basle) as to the most restricted interpretation of Art. 273 of the Swiss Penal Code.

4) Parliamentary intervention of our group, why all levels of Swiss courts (as well as the Swiss Department of Justice) in the Adams case omitted the application of Art. 113 of the Swiss constitution which would have impeded any prosecution of Adams. (Art. 113 of the Swiss constitution renders – after the ratification of an international treaty – ineffective all previous national legislation being in contrast to the new international treaty i.e. in our case, the Treaty of Association to the E.E.C.) This concerns also the non-application of the long established rule of Public International Law, whereby International Law

sets aside contrasting National Law and National law sets aside contrasting Cantonal law.

5) Establishing efficient direct contacts between the two groups, for the first period preferably on a person to person basis, thus effecting a close co-operation in the matter concerned.

On February 13th, 1979, the day that the Roche judgment was declared, the European Parliament held another full-scale debate on my case. All the questions that had been postponed till my court cases were completed, and the Roche appeal to the European Court of Justice had been heard, were now coming home to roost. There could be no more postponement. This time I quote from the debate in some detail because it was the final summing up of the European Parliament's position and the Commission's position once the legal processes had finished.

President – The next item is the oral question with debate (Doc. 612/78) by Mr Prescott, on behalf of the Socialist Group, to the Commission.

Subject: Mr Adams and Hoffmann-La Roche.

The recent judgment of the Swiss Federal Appeals Court that Mr Adams in giving information to the Commission and the Community about the illegal Community trade practices of the Swiss multinational company Hoffmann-La Roche – commits an act of espionage prejudicial to the security of the Swiss State – raises doubts as to the validity of the E.E.C./Swiss 1972 Trade Agreement. Obligations under this agreement require each party to allow such information to be available and not subjected to criminal charges including espionage.

Will the Commission answer the following questions:

1) How many times has the 'Joint Committee' under the Trade Agreement been convened, when was the last meeting, who requested it and were the principles in the Adams case discussed?

2) Who appointed Mr Adams' lawyers, what were the costs involved and is the Commission convinced that all legal courses have been exhausted including an application to the European Court of Human Rights?

3) Is the Commission aware of the legal opinion that the

judgment of the Swiss courts is in conflict with Art. 113 of the Swiss constitution concerning obligations arising from international agreements and was this part of Adams' defence submission?

4) What assurances have the Commission received from the Swiss government that should any other citizen provide similar information about illegal acts they will not face charges of espionage?

5) Does the Commission accept that the Swiss government had the necessary power under Article 105 of the 1934 Act to have intervened in this case and prevented a criminal prosecution if it had so wished?

6) What period of notice is required from either contracting parties to the 1972 Trade Agreement between Switzerland and the E.E.C. to terminate it and in view of this Swiss Court's decision in the Adams case, does it consider this decision to make Swiss domestic law to be incompatible with the obligations in the Trade Agreement?

I call Mr Prescott:

Mr Prescott: – Mr President, the question from my group referred to as Adams v. Roche has been a matter of some controversy in the Community for the last six years. Basically the case is that Mr Adams, who was in the employment of Roche, gave information and documents to the Commission, which proved that this multinational company, based in Switzerland, was conducting illegal practices and abusing its dominant position in regard to illegal loyalty payment agreements within the Community.

Today the European Court, to which the company appealed against the fine imposed by the Commission, confirmed this judgment. It reduced the fine somewhat, but it confirmed the guilt of the actions of the company Roche. So we are having this debate with the clear interpretation of the European Court that the action of the Commission in fining this company for its illegal activities is upheld. Consequently, the giving of information by Mr Adams to the Commission was not in itself an illegal act from the point of view of the Community. That is why it is a matter of contention to my group, and indeed to this House, that Mr Adams was arrested some years ago: he was placed in gaol for three months and was eventually charged; his wife committed suicide while he was in gaol and the authorities refused to allow him to attend her funeral. What an indication of the vindictiveness of the Swiss authorities!

This is further evidenced by the nature of charges brought against Mr Adams. He was accused under Article 162 of giving secret information, thus committing a criminal act. But to compound the offence the Swiss authorities then proceeded against Mr Adams under Article 273 which said that the giving of such commercial information to the Commission was an act of espionage. Their various courts, in the appeal procedures over the years, have now confirmed the judgment, which is the issue of part of this case, that to give information about the illegal activities of a company operating in the Community will be considered an act of espionage and the man concerned considered a spy. So it is now clear from all the court decisions that whatever the agreement between the Community and Switzerland, which is relevant to this debate, anyone giving information about a company registered in Switzerland under these circumstances will be considered a spy by the Swiss authorities. There are only two other States, I believe, who have such laws. One is South Africa, and the other is South Korea – and I think that speaks volumes in itself. It is the view of my group that the Swiss authorities have been somewhat vindictive, to say the least. They could have allowed just the prosecution for a criminal offence under Article 162, which would still be controversial to those interested in the Community, but they prosecuted for an act of espionage. This information about the company's commercial practices was considered a threat to the security of Switzerland.

Perhaps I am a little cynical: the other advantage which doubling the charges gave to the Swiss authorities was that they were then allowed to hold a closed trial, so the charges that were brought by Switzerland in the name, almost, of Hoffmann-La Roche, were not subject to public examination in public court but to the secret kind of trials which are associated with activities considered to be a threat to the security of the State. It is the view of some of us that this action itself is in breach of the Human Rights Convention to which Switzerland is a party. Each person is entitled to a fair trial and a public hearing. Perhaps a public hearing would have revealed the vindictive attitude of the authorities in this particular case.

Now I appreciate that the Commission feels it cannot pass comment on the internal affairs of a non-Community country. One understands the argument, but the Commission has taken action, which I and Parliament applaud, in providing the legal defence for Mr Adams to the tune of over U.K. £30,000 or approximately 60,000 units of account. Clearly, to defend an alleged spy in Switzerland with Community money is an act of some internal interference, almost an act of judgment in itself, though one which I support, and so does my group.

John Prescott went on to pursue once again the question of Switzerland's relationship with the E.E.C. and the validity of the Swiss/E.E.C. agreement in the light of the court decision. (This appeared in debates for years with clockwork regularity, largely because the Swiss continued to do nothing to assure the Community of their good will).

So what we fear in the group is that Switzerland, which has a reputation for being on the side of good when nations are at war, with the wonderful work of the Red Cross, is putting itself into the position of being a flag of convenience of multinational companies. We feel this questions the very basis of the agreement between Switzerland and the Community and should be sincerely examined.

Mr Commissioner, I hope, in your reply you can give us information that this meeting will be convened to discuss the matter with the Swiss authorities because I give you fair warning that the Adams case is not finished. I would recommend to my group that we support him in his application for a petition for fair trial, because the constitutional laws were not fully applied in Switzerland, I am legally advised. And secondly, an application to the Human Rights Court will ensure that this matter continues. We hope that you can give us some encouragement today that the requirements of justice in the case of Mr Adams and the right of information in this Community about the actions of multinationals will be upheld in the near future.

Mr Wilhelm Haferkamp, Vice-President of the Commission, answered again for the Commission. The Joint Committee had

8 and 9 *Left*, Willi Schlieder, Director-General of the E.E.C. Competition department 1970–81; *right*, Albert Borschette, E.E.C. Commissioner for Competition 1967–76 (died 1976)

10, 11 and 12 *From left to right*, François-Xavier Ortoli, President of the European Commission 1973–6; Roy Jenkins, President of the European Commission 1977–80; Gaston Thorn, President of the European Commission since 1981

13 The Common Market Commission has its headquarters in Brussels. In this building sit the E.E.C. President and his fourteen Commissioners, all Directors-General and some 5,000 bureaucrats who between them manage the Common Market on behalf of the 250 million European voters.

14 This building in Strasbourg, France, is one of the three seats of the European Parliament. It houses 434 M.E.P.s elected from the ten member states and business is conducted in seven official languages.

met twelve times since the agreement began. The last time was December 1978. 'The fundamental issues in the Adams case were not discussed in the committee but they have been the subject of frequent conversations. These conversations are continuing.' (A subtle distinction which presumably meant either that the Swiss were not prepared to talk formally, or make any changes, or that neither the Commission nor the Swiss thought the matter of sufficient importance to be bothered with . . .) The Commission had paid for my defence, and I had chosen my own lawyers.

> The internal Swiss criminal proceedings came to an end with the verdicts of the Swiss Federal Supreme Court on April 21st and May 3rd, 1978. Mr Adams has not yet suggested to the Commission that he wishes an appeal to be made to the European Court of Human Rights. He has not expressed any reaction to the Commission following the two judgments of the Swiss Federal Court.

This was scarcely an accurate statement. I had been in constant contact on the telephone with Willi Schlieder's office. I had expressed dismay at the verdict, and at my lawyer's opinion that I could go no further. I did not refer to an appeal to the European Court of Human Rights, because I was told there was nothing more I could do. I was waiting on *their* advice. A letter sent to me much later by Dr Bollag when I asked him why he didn't refer me to the European Court of Human Rights stated:

> I received my instructions partly from you and partly from the E.E.C. Commission. During the whole procedure you were in direct contact with the Commission who kept you constantly informed of all the possible alternatives. It was after the final decision of the Federal Supreme Court on your case that the E.E.C. Commission started talks through diplomatic channels with the Swiss about the interpretation of the Free Trade Agreement between Switzerland and the E.E.C.

I still had no idea why the European Commission did not mention the possibility of an appeal to the European Court of Human Rights.

Third question: In the Commission's view it is not for the Commission to comment on judgments of Swiss courts, or on their compatibility with the Swiss Federal Constitution. In the criminal proceedings against Mr Adams, the defence made the point to the Swiss Federal Court that an action under Article 273 of the Swiss criminal code was in conflict with the obligations accepted by Switzerland in the Free Trade Agreement with the European Community. The Swiss Federal Court maintained on the contrary that there was no conflict between Article 273 and the obligations under the Free Trade Agreement.

Fourth question: The Swiss government has made no declarations of the kind referred to in the question. There are permanent contacts between the Commission's offices and the Swiss Mission in Brussels. The Commission assumes that this will ensure that there is no repetition of a case like this.

They appeared to have little basis for that assumption. The Swiss hadn't exactly shown good will so far. After all, they brought the prosecution in the first place.

Fifth question: It is not for the Commission to comment on the competence of the Swiss authorities. As is generally known, Article 273 of the Swiss criminal code deals with crimes against State Security. Article 105 of the Federal law on actions under Federal criminal law stipulates that the desirability of instituting proceedings must be assessed.

This was new to me as well. I hadn't realized that legally the Swiss could use their discretion as to whether to prosecute or not even if the charges were substantiated, and that they must therefore have made a deliberate policy decision to prosecute.

Sixth question: Either party may terminate the agreement by giving notice to the other. The agreement lapses twelve months after the date of such a notice. The Commission does not intend to propose termination of the agreement . . .

What that all amounted to, as far as I could see, was that the Commission had backed themselves into a corner on my case.

They weren't getting any co-operation or assurances out of the Swiss, who intended to leave things exactly as they were, and they had no intention of taking a stand and jeopardizing the Free Trade Agreement, whatever the European Parliament might say. In fact, I rather think that by this stage the Commission devoutly wished they had never heard of me. I was proving a severe inconvenience in the smooth running of multi-state affairs.

The next person to speak in the debate was a Dutch member, Mr Wilhelm de Gaay Fortmann, who was speaking on behalf of the Christian Democratic Group. He pointed out:

> For human and juridical reasons it seems important for the Commission . . . to make known to Parliament its opinion on the legal influence which it considers the trade agreement has on Swiss law and on practical occurrences. From this angle I was disappointed by the answer given by the Vice-President of the Commission who did what a lawyer should rarely do: he attached excessive importance to the sovereign juridical authority of the Swiss government. In my view the Commission must now deliver a formal opinion on the matter since the ruling of the Swiss Federal Supreme Court would enable parent companies established in Switzerland to prohibit their subsidiaries in the Community from giving information to the Commission if the provision of such information would conflict with Swiss national legislation. That fact in itself seems to me to make it necessary for the Commission to decide whether the ruling is compatible with the trade agreement between the E.E.C. and Switzerland.

Mr Raymond Forni, a Frenchman from the Socialist Group, spoke:

> Mr President, ladies and gentlemen, I fully agree with the statement made just now by Mr Prescott, on this Adams–Roche affair. We have rightly criticized the Commission's attitude in a number of areas. We have repeatedly expressed our regret in this Parliament at the fate of Mr Adams and we have also regretted the Commission's inertia in certain instances, particularly in respect of the advice which it might have given to Mr Adams on the placing of his case before the

responsible bodies under the European convention on the Rights of Man . . .

There would seem to have been a manifest infringement of certain elementary rights of a citizen, Mr Adams. How can we consider the decision taken and the sanctions imposed on him to be legal now that Roche has been sentenced by the Commission and Court of Justice of the European Communities to pay a fine because of abuse of dominant positions for which it had been criticized and which had been detected thanks to the information provided by Mr Adams . . . ?

My last point, which I make with no trace of irony, is to congratulate Mr Adams on his courageous action and encourage the Commission to see to it that justice is done to him so that other citizens will not be discouraged but will continue to provide information on the attitude and behaviour of multi-national companies within the European Community.

John Prescott summed up with a suggestion:

I want to indicate that I would consider tabling a motion to refer the matter to the Legal Affairs Committee in view of the fact that the Commissioner has made clear in his statement that they do not consider terminating the agreement. But if the Swiss are legally in breach of the agreement, then the E.E.C. Commission must discharge its obligations, since the agreement has already been broken by the other party. So, Mr President, I would like to give notice that I will put a motion down asking our Legal Affairs Committee to give us their interpretation of the breach of the agreement, and the Commissioner can appear before it and give them more information.

A short while later Parliament adopted the resolution tabled by Mr Prescott, Mr Forni, Lord Ardwick, Mr Patijn and Mr Johnston which instructed the 'Legal Affairs Committee to investigate the implications for the 1972 E.E.C./Swiss Trade Agreement and to report back to it' and instructed 'its President to forward this resolution to the Commission for its information'.

12 Italy – the End of the Road

If words were pound notes then my daughters and I would have been millionaires, instead of which we were penniless and near bankruptcy. When I failed to find any pre-finance for my pig industry I had looked round for other ways to start building. Eventually I found a builder, the owner of a construction company, who was willing to build only for costs and be paid the difference later when the grant and loan money came in. I found it impossible to believe that somehow I wouldn't get the project off the ground. I had never not succeeded before and I was optimistic enough to believe that even now if I looked hard enough I would find some way of solving the problems. Persistence had always paid off for me in the past. And it was criminal even to consider letting the opportunity go. A licence to build a large industry such as I had planned was like gold dust in that part of Italy, and I had Government grants and finance as well – all things that were not come by easily. Once the project was built I knew that I would have no problems at all making it profitable. Italy desperately needed meat, and I was going to be producing a large quantity of it. Once everything was on course then I needn't worry anybody else any more. I could be independent, earning my own living and owing nothing to anybody. A lot of effort had gone into the renewing of the grant and loan, and they were not something that could just be thrown away. Not that there was any chance of that. The land was virtually unsellable in its pre-building state and I couldn't have found a job anywhere else if I'd wanted to. I'd tried, and failed when things had looked difficult before. The only hope I had was in making a go of the pig industry. I had consulted key experts in Britain and America, and I knew it would work. But I was dogged by problems.

Some were just the problems of building in Italy, others may have been politically motivated. I was living in Middle Italy, the heart of Giulio Andreotti's Christian Democrat power base. In the area where I lived everyone who was anyone was a Christian Democrat appointee, and I was out of favour. But it was difficult to say which problems were a result of natural Italian inefficiency, and which were politically motivated, the two were so intertwined.

I had only been building for a couple of months when the local authority engineer came along to inspect the site and stopped the construction work. He said we were not building according to plan. My architect had altered the original plans, but the new plans had been correctly signed by me and filed with the local authority. At least, they'd been correctly filed by us, but apparently incorrectly filed by the local authority who denied all knowledge of them. It took four months and many hours of expensive legal time before the authority finally acknowledged that the mistake was theirs. They had got the plans after all, they'd just mislaid them . . . and their engineer had been working off the old plans. We were allowed to start building again.

An overall work schedule for the year's building was submitted to the Government grant and finance agencies. In addition, at the beginning of each month, the construction company would draw up plans of the work it intended the builders to cover that month and I would approve these and pass them on to Rome. Neither the Cassa per il Mezzogiorno (grant agency), nor the Mediocredito Regionale del Lazio (finance agency) paid in advance. They both paid in arrears, on presentation of the invoices for work done (and usually four to six months late). At the end of each month the local authority engineer came out to inspect the work and see if the target had been achieved. A couple of months after we had been allowed to restart building, we fell a little behind schedule. I don't remember why. I was on the site by eight a.m. every day, as soon as I'd seen the children off to school, to supervise and see how things were going. It was beautiful too in the sun of the early morning.

I used to enjoy just standing there and breathing the fresh air, watching my plans beginning to take shape, and seeing in my mind the breeding rooms, the maternity wards, the fattening huts and the feed mill site. But I couldn't play God. If the workmen didn't turn up, there wasn't much I could do, or if the supplies were delayed, or if it rained, or if there was a strike somewhere, or if the builder was simply over-optimistic in his estimate of what could be done in a month.

Delays happen in building everywhere, and in Italy they're an occupational hazard. Where there is Government finance it is normal to invoice as usual for the work planned and catch up on any shortfall when you can.

In my case however things were different. I was accused of fraud and all building was halted. I had not done what I said I would do (or what the construction company said we would do) so technically it was considered fraud. I hadn't made any false declarations, or invoiced for work that had not been done, or received money that wasn't owing to me, but work was still stopped. The argument was that if the engineer had not come, and if I had not said anything, then I might have been paid the full amount to cover what I said I was going to do. But the engineer had come. He always did, and I had no intention of defrauding anyone, least of all for such a comparatively small sum. Technically the authorities were within the law, but it was one in a million times it was applied, in that way. If it was applied routinely nothing would ever get built in Italy, or anywhere else that worked on the same principle. When the owner of the construction company who was working with me saw what had happened he pulled out. As far as he was concerned, he told me, it was obvious that I was a marked man, and even if we managed to get permission to start building again he was sure the authorities would find another way of stopping me. He had already lost quite a bit of money, and he didn't want to risk any more.

I can't say I blamed him. I felt a bit that way myself. But I didn't have a choice, so I continued trying – first to get permission to start building again, and secondly to find someone else to build with me, but without success. It was 1979. I had no income and had been living on borrowed money for nearly two years. If my land had been difficult to sell before it was totally impossible now, covered as it was with concrete foundations for a large industrial pig farm. It looked increasingly as if I wasn't going to get my business built. Without the business there was little hope of paying anybody back, and my creditors were beginning to get restless. Meteor Pigs Ltd and H. J. Digwood in England were pressing for the return of the £8,000 facility fee that had been lost to the Americans. So far they had refrained from presenting my cheque, but were now threatening to do so at the end of March. If they did, there was no money in my account to meet it, and it would automatically become a legal matter and I would be declared bankrupt. If I couldn't earn money, and I couldn't borrow it, then my children and I would starve. We were not entitled to any kind of Italian state benefit. All medical and dental treatment had to be paid for. If I didn't work, we wouldn't eat. I was worried too about the possibility of being deported from Italy. My residence permit was renewable yearly, and dependent on my having a valid reason for being there, and a viable means of support. If the pig farm no longer existed, then I had no legitimate reason to be in Italy, and my permit might not be renewed. And if we were deported, where would we go and how would we live?

I was tired of endless problems. I was depressed and I was frightened. I don't think anything is more terrifying than the thought of not being able to feed one's own children. They were the innocent victims in all this, and I was haunted by the thought of what might happen to them. So far I'd done my best to shelter them. I'd moved them from the fee-paying school they'd been at to state schools. (Without a residence permit we had not been entitled to State education before.) Nathalie had just reached secondary age, so the transfer seemed natural, and Sandy and Stephanie were willing to move to a bigger school with a wider mix of people, which was the reason I gave for the transfer. It was absurd to be proud, but I didn't want them to worry about my lack of money. They were too young to be expected to carry all my problems as well, though they were very independent for their years. Growing up without a mother had made them more self-reliant than other girls of their age.

I loved them very much and felt my responsibilities as father and mother in one. Every morning I drove them to school and picked them up again at half past four, with strict instructions not to wander out of the school gates until I arrived. (Stephanie was only six.) In the evening I cooked supper for all of us and listened to their accounts of the day's events. Driving them to school was going to be a problem soon. The Jaguar, a symbol of my more prosperous days, had been taken away as security for debts before I could sell it. Its value was well over that of the debts it had been taken to cover. The car I had replaced it with was shortly to follow in the same sorry direction, sequestrated to cover debts. When it did, my daughters were going to have a long walk to school. But this was a minor problem compared to all the others. In one sense I was very fortunate. My three girls never added to my problems. They were a great comfort to me and the one reason why I never gave up, though I often felt like it.

On February 20th, 1979 I changed my lawyer. I wrote to Dr Diefenbacher.

Dear Dr Diefenbacher,
This is to confirm my cable of today addressed to you and reading as follows: By letter today have terminated relations with Bollag, Basle. Please be good enough to take up my mandate and try in way of revision to get an annulment of the previous sentences of the Basle Criminal Court and Court of Appeals, as well as the sentence of the Federal Supreme Court of Switzerland. This cable and written confirmation thereof will serve as your power of attorney and entitles you to take all measures which you will deem useful in settling my case against the Swiss Confederation. Copy of this cable is also sent to Mr John Prescott, the House of Commons, London.

Using the cable as his authority Diefenbacher tried to get hold of my files from the courts, so he could begin the task of seeing whether there was any way of re-opening my case. He hoped it would be possible using Article 113 of the Swiss Constitution, which states that international law takes precedence over national law, but more importantly he was intending at that time to argue that under Article 6 of the European Convention of Human Rights, to which Switzerland was a signatory, I had not had a fair trial because it had not been held in public, and that Roche's conviction in the European Court of Justice, which had happened after my final appeal was heard, meant that the evidence used could not have been obtained illegally, otherwise the European Court could not legally have used it to convict Roche. If that were the case, it made a nonsense of my conviction. The Swiss courts were reluctant to hand over my files to a new and well known Socialist lawyer. An application to Lausanne for the judgments of the three cases and an account of the basic pleas entered for the Lausanne case met with the statement that the client would already have the judgments, and the Federal Court in Lausanne kept no records of pleas, they would be with the Cantonal Court in Basle. Diefenbacher wrote to Basle. Normal procedure would have meant that as soon as the courts had confirmation of his authority, which was given by the cable I sent, they should have released the whole file to him, including the accounts of those parts of the trial which had been held *in camera* . . . They did not. Telephone conversations were fruitless, so eventually Diefenbacher went to the court in person, accompanied by a witness, to ask for the files. He was told that my cable was no proof whatever that he was my lawyer, and asked to produce a written power of attorney, and a justification of his wish to inspect my files. This was followed by a letter asking for the same things before the file could be released. The demands were of course legitimate but highly unusual in the normal way that the Swiss legal profession operated. A written letter of authority was usually considered sufficient proof of a lawyer's appointment. The requests were being made by the judge in charge of the case, Felix Staehelin. I had a written power of attorney drawn up in Italy, witnessed by a notary public and sent to Dr Diefenbacher, who finally managed to get hold of the files.

Once he had the files and had time to study them I began to learn a lot of new things. I had never been to any of my trials, and I didn't read German so even the published judgments were impossible for me to follow, and a lot of the material was unpublished and unreleased because the trials had been held *in camera*. I only knew therefore what Dr Bollag told me.

I knew that Dr Felix Staehelin had taken over as presiding judge in my case in 1977, before my first appeal was heard, because Dr Bollag had written to tell me. What I didn't know, and what Dr Bollag did not tell me, was that apparently Staehelin had been a well known corporation lawyer for the Basle chemical industries. He was a retired Colonel of the Military Justice Division of the Swiss army, and was not a regular judge but a judicial suppliant. Why he had been given my case I don't know. Perhaps it was just the luck of the draw, or perhaps someone thought his knowledge of the chemical industry might be helpful . . .

I learnt too that Roche and the Public Prosecutor's office had been in close contact throughout the case (which did not surprise me). The extent of the contact surprised Dr Diefenbacher though. In 1980 he was interviewed by Granada Television for their *World in Action* programme and replied to the question about whether it was unusual for a big corporation to be so closely involved with a prosecution: 'The corporation claiming to be damaged by any act, of course, must give evidence and facts and so on, but I believe, according to my experience . . . in the legal administration of the Canton of the City of Basle . . . the extent to which the Public Prosecutor's Office has been acting practically on the orders of Hoffmann-La Roche is most extraordinary.'

Later I was to find out more about how I had actually been identified as the informant, but for the time being I knew only that my suspicions about Roche's involvement in my case were justified.

In Latina, in 1979, four years after my arrest in Switzerland I was still suffering from the repercussions of my prosecution. I had asked the European Commission, through Willi Schlieder's office, to intervene with the Mediocredito Regionale del Lazio and the Cassa per il Mezzogiorno to see if it was possible to prevent them cancelling my loan and grant, which they were likely to do as building had stopped, but I feared they would have little success. I was at my wits' end to know what to do.

On March 9th, 1979 I wrote to John Prescott, a cry of despair: 'We have no income of any kind. If I do not succeed in building up the pig industry which I came here to build, then I may as well join my poor wife and leave the children in the hands of the E.E.C. Commission.' I detailed a number of ways in which it might be possible for the Commission or Parliamentarians to help me. 'Well, those are the possibilities. I know that if the right people intervene then we will succeed and my sufferings will be over in due course. On the other hand I also know that if we do not succeed in getting the wheels turning again, my company (that is myself) will soon find itself bankrupt and forced to close down shop and leave Italy. There is not much time . . . ' (I had persuaded Meteor Pigs not to present my cheque to the bank, which gave me a little breathing space, but the situation was still desperate.)

In June of that year Dr Diefenbacher suggested that I should consider the possibility of taking a job if one could be found for me if the pig project failed. I replied:

I must immediately inform you that I would be absolutely willing and ready to accept a position with some government or some international organization, should we fail to arrange things so that my farm continues forward as planned.

It is hardly necessary for me to remind you that I have now been without an income for over five years, that I have done my very best to bring up my three children without the help of any organization, that I have therefore placed myself in a terrible situation of debt and that never has the E.E.C. or any other body stopped for a moment to think of how the Adams family manages to live . . .

No job was forthcoming.

In June 1979 the first direct elections for the European Parliament were held. John Prescott decided not to stand but to remain in the House of Commons, and handed my files over to the newly elected Socialist M.E.P. for Sheffield, Richard Caborn. (Another British M.E.P. with whom I was to have contact years later was elected at the same time. He was Dr Christopher Prout, Conservative M.E.P. for Salop and Stafford, and a barrister specializing in international law.) Richard Caborn phoned me to make contact and I wrote to him bringing him up to date with the latest situation. I was still very worried about the question of my nationality and my daughters' nationality. Nothing had happened since the parliamentary debate in 1977 when it was suggested I be given citizenship of one of the E.E.C. countries, and my attempt to get British citizenship had been turned down. I did not under any circumstances want to find that we were expelled from Italy and forced to return to Malta to live, a country I no longer felt I belonged to. I asked Richard Caborn to see what the possibility was of my being granted nationality of another E.E.C. country. I didn't ask him to try Britain again. Now that the Conservatives were back in power I thought that probably I had less chance than before. I reminded Caborn that time was running out for me, and anything that the European Parliament or the European Commission could do for me would have to be done soon or it would be too late. 'Each day, each week and month I have to find ways to live. The sooner that we get something settled in my case the better. As Erich Diefenbacher knows, at this very moment (due to lack of funds) I stand a good chance of being put on the street without a home and furniture, and naturally without work/income. What do I do then with the three children?'

By this stage, as I told Richard Caborn, I owed several months' back rent and the landlord was threatening to evict me, the bailiffs had been in to the house to list all my possessions against debts owing and at any time could decide to foreclose. I had no possessions left to sell. All I had was listed and marked by the bailiffs and could not be disposed of. I couldn't even move to cheaper lodgings because the very act of moving would bring all my creditors about my head with immediate demands for payment. In some ways I was glad. It would have been hard to move. One of the rooms in the house had been Mariléne's room and still had a lot of her things in it. The children thought of it as Mummy's room, and it was important to them. I didn't want them to lose that last connection until I had no option.

The Italian Socialists, particularly Dr Giorgio Ruffolo, M.E.P., did try and intervene on my behalf, but they got nowhere. After a particularly desperate letter in September 1979 Dr Erich Diefenbacher wrote back to me:

Dear Mr Adams,
This is in reply to your phone disc message 22 September and your letter 19 September which reached me only on 25 September 1979. I am sorry to tell you that I find it very needless for you to reproach me for the fact that, if at all, things are going very, very slowly. All I can tell you is that I am trying very hard to make ends meet all over . . . Dear Mr Adams, it sounds stale, and I know it, but for the moment I have no other advice; patience and courage . . .

On September 29th I wrote again to Richard Caborn. I had just heard that the Mediocredito Regionale del Lazio definitely planned to cancel my loan and there was little hope that the Cassa per il Mezzogiorno would not then follow suit and cancel the grant. Diefenbacher had not yet been assured of payment by the European Commission and he had no funds to start any action on my behalf, either to re-open the case in Switzerland, or to pursue the possibilities of taking action against Roche for damages. The Socialist Group had promised to make funds available but so far nothing had happened.

> I must again make it clear that for the last five years I have been living on borrowed money. I am at this moment on the verge of being put out of this house and losing my furniture and belongings. That at this moment I have funds to last us certainly not longer than another three months, and that after December 1979 if nothing by then has been solved my three children and myself will be without means to live, however meagre . . .
>
> European Parliamentarians of the Socialist Group should bear in mind that it is not enough to state 'we will help Adams and his children', and then take months to solve the simplest matter in my case. They must realize that while they are trying to solve things for us, we must also have means to live with. I have never asked the E.E.C. or anybody else for any payment of any kind and I certainly do not ask for anything of the kind now. But surely I must be given the means (work, or farm, or damages) so that I can continue forward bringing the children up . . .
>
> Do the Socialist Group members know that up to now in Italy I have had to pay for the schooling of my three children? Do they know I have no medical and dental and hospital assistance of any kind here for myself and the three children? Do they know that I have no pension plan of any kind for the future? All these things, added to the fact that I have no income and have had no income for the last five years, make things evidently even harder for all of us.

It's hard to be patient when you can see disaster looming and are totally helpless to prevent it. Working through officialdom, or through the law courts, takes time, and I no longer had time.

I wrote to Erich Diefenbacher and Richard Caborn on October 19th:

> The enclosed copy of a letter dated 16.10.79 from Dr Enzo Mei is self-explanatory, and confirms that Mediocredito has definitely cancelled the finance contract, and furthermore that Dr Nerio Nesi, President of the Banca Nazionale del Lavoro,

and Enzo Mei himself are not able to help in this matter. This leaves us in a very difficult situation, and even a rather dangerous one. Please bear in mind that once the pig-farm project is no longer active the Italian government may (and probably will) ask me to leave Italy. As I made clear on a previous occasion, I hold an annual residence permit exclusively on the basis of the building of the pig farm. To remain in Italy I must prove that I am about to have some kind of work in Italy, i.e. the pig farm, some other business or a job. Otherwise I have no right to be here without means to support myself and my family.

I believe I made things clear in my letter to both of you of September 29th, 1979, also letters of September 19th and September 30th, 1979 addressed to Dr Diefenbacher. The telex from the Socialist Group of 7.9.79 sent to Dr Nesi is of no avail now.

Dr Diefenbacher rightly asks me (in his letter of 27.9.79) to have 'patience and courage'. But for how long? What do I do at the end of this year when we have no means to feed ourselves? Where do we go if the Italian government asks us to leave Italy?

Since the plenary session in Strasbourg took place in July 1979 I have heard so many things. But I have not seen one single step forward in my case. Where is the delegation which is supposed to meet with me? When is Dr Diefenbacher going to be placed in a position to be able to commence proceedings against Roche? I have made telephone calls and sent telegrams to both of you but without receiving any replies. I beg you to bear in mind always the sad situation I and my children find ourselves in at this moment and to do something soon to improve things for us.

In early November the Socialist Group paid for me to fly to Strasbourg to talk to them and to members of the Legal Affairs Committee who were preparing their report for the European Parliament on the implications of my case for Swiss/E.E.C. relationships. My lawyer Dr Diefenbacher was also present.

We also discussed possible legal moves for the future. The plan was to seek a way of getting compensation for me from the E.E.C., quietly, and damages from Roche, preferably out of court with the E.E.C.'s help, and an annulment of my Swiss sentence. We were talking in terms of an overall minimum of two million Swiss francs (over £500,000) as being a reasonable amount to ask, taking into consideration the tragic death of my wife (for which no money could compensate), my loss of capital and of income, and the fact that I had three children to bring up and educate. If the behind-the-scenes negotiations didn't produce anything, then it was agreed that Erich Diefenbacher would take steps in Switzerland to re-open my case, and if the Swiss refused to re-open it, then that would give us the necessary lever to enable us to take the case on to another court outside Switzerland. The fear was that going to the Human Rights Commission would take too long to solve my problems by securing damages for me, though we thought it was an avenue we could explore.

Following the visit, on November 15th I wrote again to Richard Caborn, sending a copy to Ernest Glinne, Chairman of the European Socialist Group since the June elections.

> While all this is going on, we must continue living, and as I made it clear, we now have enough to last us another month or so. If Ruffolo does not succeed in convincing some bank here to grant me a loan very soon, then some other way must be found. For whichever way we deal with the matter, and whichever way we get success . . . it will no doubt take months, if not years before I see any funds coming to us.

On November 21st, 1979 I wrote again to Richard Caborn and Ernest Glinne. 'Since my letter of November 15th sent to both of you I have other bad news . . . Yesterday I received a Court Communication in Latina dated 14.11.79. This accuses me of fraud against a Government institute.'

The fraud concerned the fact that I had promised to complete the building of my pig farm by a certain date, and I had not fulfilled that promise. The action was brought both by the grant agency and the loan agency, who had each paid out one instalment of finance to me – money which had gone into the building of the farm. A judge had been appointed to hear the case and I expected soon to be summoned to a preliminary hearing. I finished my letter to Caborn and Glinne with the following words. 'Closing this letter by repeating that in one month's time my family and I will not have funds to live on, to pay rent, to pay debts etc etc. Ruffolo has not contacted me so far. Furthermore, kindly remember that the Court Communication just received is a serious matter, which may get me into serious trouble (even prison) if we do not have it withdrawn urgently.' On December 19th, 1979, in total despair, I sent the following cable to Ernest Glinne.

DESPERATION FORCES ME TO CABLE YOU STOP NOBODY HAS SO FAR MANAGED TO HELP US MATERIALLY AND AS YOU HAVE ALREADY BEEN INFORMED END THIS YEAR MEANS LITERALLY FINDING OURSELVES ON THE STREET WITHOUT HOME FURNITURE AND FOOD STOP RESULTS OF RUFFOLOS EFFORTS WITH NESI AND OTHERS ARE COMPLETELY UN-KNOWN TO ME STOP IF EEC OR SOME BENEFACTOR OR BANK DOES NOT HELP US FINANCIALLY IMMEDIATELY THE THREE CHILDREN AND MYSELF WILL SIMPLY DISSOLVE INTO NOTHINGNESS WITHIN COUPLE OF WEEKS STOP EEC COM-MISSIONERS SHOULD BEAR THIS IN MIND AND SEARCH THEIR CONSCIENCES STOP IT WILL BE FUTILE TO SECURE DAMAGES FROM MULTINATIONAL IF MEANWHILE THIS FAMILY STARVES TO DEATH ABANDONED BY ALL CON-CERNED STOP KIND REGARDS AND THANKS. STANLEY ADAMS.

On December 20th I was arrested.

13 Prison in Latina

It was the Thursday before Christmas. My children were just getting dressed and I was awake but still in bed. The young girl who used to help us in the house (we no longer had anyone living in) had just arrived and let herself in with her key when there was a loud knock on the front door. I was startled. Nobody ever called at this hour. It was only just gone seven o'clock. Anna answered the door and came upstairs to tell me there were two men outside who wanted to speak to me. 'Send them away,' I said, through the bedroom door, 'I'm not dressed. I haven't shaved and I'm about to have a bath. Ask them to come back in half an hour.' A minute later she returned. The men insisted they had to see me now even if I wasn't dressed. I didn't have the faintest idea who they were or what they wanted, but I wrapped a dressing-gown round me and reluctantly descended to find out what the matter was.

They were policemen in plain clothes who asked me to go with them to the *questura* (the Carabinieri headquarters). I protested, of course. I wanted to know what it was all about, couldn't it wait till a more civilized hour, I wasn't dressed yet, I hadn't shaved, I had to get the children off to school . . . But they were adamant. I must come with them now. They could give me ten minutes to get dressed, and that was all. They agreed to wait outside in their car so as not to alarm the children and I dressed quickly, asked Anna to tell my daughters there was no school today and keep them at home for the time being until I returned, and left with the men for the *questura*.

Neither Anna nor my children knew where I was going, or who the visitors were. Once inside the *questura* one of the men pulled out a piece of paper and showed it to me. 'I didn't want to tell you before,' he said, 'because I know you have young children and I didn't want to cause any kind of scene that might distress them, but this is a warrant for your arrest.'

I couldn't believe it. I looked at the warrant. It had been signed by the prosecutor assigned to my case, Dr Alfonso Di Paolis. I had expected to be summoned for questioning, or asked to provide papers, or called for a court hearing, but not to be arrested out of the blue just before Christmas. It was unheard of. The charge was a purely technical one. No one had actually lost any money. Construction had been stopped, it was true, but the first instalment paid to me, which had gone into the building, was guaranteed by the mortgage the two finance agencies held on my land; and this was worth far more than they had paid out. Furthermore, at the request of these agencies I had taken out a Lloyd's insurance policy in their favour, to cover such eventualities. In any case, the conditions of the loan were that no repayment was expected for the first two years. I had anticipated a threat to foreclose on the land, but to be arrested like this, no.

The magistrate, Dr Di Paolis, was known to have views on the far right of the political spectrum. He was a member of the M.S.I., 'Movimento Sociale Italiano' (the new Italian Fascist party) and later became President of the local businessmen's club (Circolo Cittadino) that catered mostly for those with similar views, not uncommon in Italy. I had known that he was not likely to be sympathetic to me as a person, given my background which was well known in the area, but I hadn't expected this. I asked if I could telephone my lawyer. Being Italy and not Switzerland the police said yes. I phoned my lawyer at his home, where he was just getting out of bed, and told him what had happened. Dr Edoardo Vinciguerra was not a criminal lawyer, but a commercial lawyer who had been acting for my company since 1974 when I first moved to Latina. He was a good lawyer and president of the local Bar Association. Vinciguerra assured me he would go straight down to his office and see if he could fix a meeting with Di Paolis and get him to change his mind about sending me to prison. He then spoke to the police officers, asking them to keep me at the police station as long as possible to give him time to talk to the magistrate first. Latina prison was a little way out of town and I needed to get back to my children as fast as possible. It would be quicker if they could avoid taking me to prison in the first place.

The police obligingly said they would do what they could. I was finger-printed and had my photograph taken for the records. It reminded me of a similar exercise five years ago in Lugano, and I devoutly hoped that this time I really would be out in hours. At nine o'clock my lawyer phoned to say he couldn't get to see the magistrate till eleven o'clock. The police couldn't wait that long. They had to take me to the prison now. I asked what I was supposed to do with my children. I had three young daughters at home, and soon they would be on their own. What was to happen to them? The officers were sympathetic. They phoned Di Paolis' office to find out. Dr Di Paolis told them to have the children picked up and taken to the female police unit which looked after the children of alcoholics, drug addicts, prisoners, anyone who was unable for legal reasons to care for their own children. The officers told me they would send a policewoman round straight away. That was the last thing I wanted. I protested strongly. They shrugged their shoulders. I was going to be taken to prison and there was nothing else they could do. I phoned my company lawyer again and another friend, also a lawyer, Dr Paola Piazza; I asked them both if they would phone Di Paolis and say they would take care of the children between them. They wouldn't have to, I reassured them, I would find other friends to do that, but it was essential that they phone Di Paolis immediately and offer to take responsibility for the children before they were taken away. As lawyers they had access, and would be listened to. I couldn't bear the thought of my little girls spending Christmas bewildered and frightened amongst strangers, not knowing why they were there or, worse still perhaps, knowing why they were there and not understanding why their father had suddenly been taken away to prison.

It was half past nine when I arrived at Latina prison. The normal routine of admission began. My tie, belt, ring, wallet, watch and shoelaces were all taken from me and I was given a number and taken to an isolation cell. I couldn't shake off the sensation of history repeating itself, but I refused to despair.

On my return from Switzerland in 1975, after Mariléne's death, my neighbours had been very kind to me and often invited me round for drinks or a meal in the evening. It was on one of these evenings, in February 1977 at a bridge party in a neighbour's house, that I had met Paola Piazza, a single woman of thirty-five. We had become firm friends, and our friendship had flourished. My children had rapidly become friends both with

Paola and her grandparents, Vincenzo and Vittoria Cagliano, with whom she lived. Paola and the old couple were very kind to my daughters. As Paola was a lawyer I knew that she would do all she could to make sure I was interrogated as quickly as possible by the magistrate so I could be released on bail. It was Paola who took over the care of Nathalie, Sandy and Stephanie, telling them that I had been urgently called away to the European Parliament in Strasbourg, and would be back soon. The children were used to these trips, and accepted the story. (It was only two months since I had been away last.) Paola knew her way round the Latina law courts and made contact with the criminal lawyer now representing me, a man named Dr Giorgio Zeppieri, who had been appointed for me by my company lawyer, Dr Vinciguerra, as soon as he realized I had been arrested on a criminal charge. Between them Paola and Giorgio Zeppieri succeeded in persuading the magistrate to come and interrogate me urgently.

Dr Di Paolis arrived at the prison the next day. The Italians have a more civilized attitude towards these things than the Swiss and I was allowed to have my lawyer present during questioning. I'd never met Zeppieri before, but he guided me as best he could without knowing much about the case and put in an immediate application for bail, which was granted. It was made clear that I had very little money, so I was asked to surrender only my passport to make sure I didn't leave Italy. By Friday night I was home again. I had collected the children, thanked my friends and settled down to recover from the shock and prepare for the coming festivities. I was very relieved. I had thought I would get out quickly, but I had been afraid that I might not make it in time for Christmas.

The next day, Saturday, I went down to Zeppieri's chambers at his request to fill him in on the background to the case. We went through everything in great detail. Finally he decided that there were one or two points that needed clarifying or elaborating on and he decided we should go back to the magistrate, just to straighten the record, as soon as possible. I didn't really see why it was necessary, but he said it would help my defence later, so I accepted his advice. We set a time for Monday.

That weekend the house was full of preparations for Christmas. I had bought a large Christmas tree and set it up in the living-room. Nathalie and Sandy and Stephanie all helped me decorate it. There was tinsel everywhere. I hung some of the presents I had bought the children on the tree. We weren't exactly having an extravagant Christmas, but with the little money we had I managed to get a selection of small gifts, enough to excite the children. Paola was coming for Christmas and there were presents for her too. There was much scurrying and whispering as the children hid their presents or wrapped them secretively in corners away from the others. School had finished and the build-up to Christmas had begun.

On Monday morning, Christmas Eve, I went to court with my lawyer to see the magistrate, promising my children I would be back soon to take them into town for last-minute Christmas shopping. Paola came with me. I didn't expect to be long, an hour at most.

Zeppieri and I were ushered in to see Di Paolis straight away. He started questioning us, with his assistant, a policeman, taking down notes. After about three-quarters of an hour we had finished and he asked me to wait outside in the corridor while he talked to my lawyer. I paced up and down, hoping I'd be able to get home soon because there was a lot to do yet before I was ready for Christmas. The children would be waiting for me and I had to get the lunch ready before we could go out. Fifteen minutes later a plainclothes police officer came up and told me to go with him. I asked where, but he just repeated his request, escorted me to his car, and drove me down to the police station. There they informed me that Di Paolis had decided to withdraw bail and commit me to prison again. I was dumbfounded. It didn't seem possible. I had been safely out on bail. There had been no request from the court for me to go and see them, I'd done it without being asked on the advice of my lawyer, and now here I was being driven back to prison. It was like a re-run of an old film. Only this time it was Christmas Eve and as we drove through the town the shops were bright with lights and thronged with last-minute Christmas shoppers. In desperation I waited for a reprieve, for the car to stop and turn back, for the old-style hero to arrive and rescue me, for the policeman to turn round and say 'I'm sorry sir, we've made a mistake.' But it didn't happen. I was locked inside Latina prison once more and taken to the isolation cell. As the door closed behind me I was frantic. Tomorrow was Christmas Day. The children were expecting me home to take them shopping. I was the only person who knew exactly which presents were for whom, and there were several small gifts I hadn't yet had time to wrap up which were still hidden in my bedroom. Why, I thought desperately, do things always happen to me at this time of year? I tried to get a message through to Paola to tell her where things were, so she and the children could have some kind of Christmas together and I wondered what story she would use this time. The European Parliament would scarcely be meeting over Christmas and my daughters were bright enough to realize that. Anyway I'd left that morning saying I'd be back in an hour or so. I hoped she would be inventive enough to find something convincing. Whatever it was, the children would still be hurt that I had suddenly left them alone at Christmas, but I thought that was better than knowing where I was.

This time I did give myself up to despair. The cat-and-mouse game which I had played for years, in which I was always the mouse trying to keep one step ahead, without knowing the rules, had become too much for me. In Latina prison I broke down and wept, for days and days. I was grateful to the male prison nurse who looked after me so solicitously. I think he realized I was having some kind of nervous breakdown, and he took care to keep me heavily sedated, with injections at night and tablets during the day. He was concerned for my physical and mental health and did what he could for me. I lost weight rapidly and became quite ill. On January 7th, alerted by Paola, Erich Diefenbacher wrote to the Socialist Group. 'On January 5th I spoke again with Miss Piazza, Mr Adams' friend, after learning that Adams still has not been released from detention. Miss Piazza informed me that Adams is passing through a very difficult period of extreme exhaustion and depression and that there is immediate danger of suicide. His three little children do not know that their father again is jailed.'

On January 10th I wrote to Erich Diefenbacher. 'I write to you from Latina prison. This letter will go out of here secretly, uncensored, carried and mailed by friends . . . My dear Erich, I am at my end. I must make certain things very clear. My children do not know where I am – for obvious reasons, we do not want to repeat what happened five years ago, and this could be my last letter to anybody.'

Erich replied on January 24th with a copy of a letter he had

written to Ernest Glinne in Brussels, sending copies to other
members of the Socialist Group.

> As I explained to all of you repeatedly and also during the
> hearings in Strasbourg on 5–8 November 1979 it was absolutely
> vital to substitute the credit given to Adams by Mediocredito
> with credit from another bank long before his action concern-
> ing Roche. At the same time a job should have been found for
> Adams somewhere outside Italy and someone trustworthy
> should have been charged with the sale of Adams' pig farm. I
> cannot bear the responsibility of just keeping on repeating the
> same things and seeing that our Party is not acting as it should
> on behalf of a man who professes to be a Democratic Socialist
> and has acted accordingly. His claims for damages have only
> come after his means of living have been destroyed by the
> co-ordinated action against him without any other than oral (in
> Parliament) interference in his favour.
>
> There is no use for a new meeting in order to discuss what
> should be done. The only thing would be to substitute the
> credit of Mediocredito by another bank, the technical details
> are known. Furthermore someone from the Group should
> be appointed to go to Latina, in order to settle the debts of
> Adams, get him and his three small children out of Italy and
> find him a job. After this has been done, serious discussion as to
> the further proceedings on political and legal level should be
> undertaken . . .

On January 27th I sent a telegram to Richard Caborn, STILL
CONFINED STOP ALREADY SENT CABLE TO GLINNES HOME
INFORMING THAT UNLESS VERY URGENT ACTIONS TAKEN MY
SITUATION ENDS TRAGICALLY STOP BEG YOU SPEAK ERNEST
NOW STOP YOU MAY PHONE NEWS TO MY FRIEND STANLEY
MARTIN WHO WILL TRANSMIT – ADAMS
On January 31st I wrote to Richard Caborn, telling him I was
still inside and warning him that it was no good relying on the
Italian Socialists either to get me out of prison or to help relieve
my threatened bankruptcy because they simply weren't powerful
enough to do it, even if they wanted to. (And I wasn't always sure
that they did.) Caborn was trying to raise some immediate funds
to help me within the Socialist Group, for which I was grateful,

but it still didn't solve the problem of what I did after my debts were paid (if I ever got out of prison).

On February 10th I wrote again.

Dear Mr Caborn,

I am still in prison, I have now been here 50 days exactly. Once more the E.E.C. proves to me its slowness to help to get me out of trouble, which follows me as a result of what I have done for the Community in 1973.

I take this opportunity to thank you personally for all you have done and are still doing for me, and I know (do not doubt it) that when I have solved my various problems it will be mainly thanks to yourself and to Mr Ernest Glinne . . . My health is very poor and if I stay here much longer I will not come out on my own feet . . .

Looking back on my time in Latina prison now, I find it hard to say how suicidal I really was. I certainly felt suicidal. I was very exhausted and finding it impossible to see any way out of my problems. I was like a rat in a maze. Whichever alleyway I chose to run down I was sure the door would shut at the end, leaving me trapped once more. If it had not been for my daughters, perhaps I would have finished my life then. But I couldn't leave them alone to face the world with neither mother nor father. They knew by now what had happened to Mariléne, and I couldn't do that to them again. I was helped too by the warmth of human life around me. That sounds a strange thing to say about prison, and it is true that being locked up is a terrible thing, but in Latina prison there was a kind of camaraderie among the prisoners that was very supportive. In the Swiss prisons I'd been kept totally isolated, locked in solitary confinement, but in Latina I was moved after two weeks to a cell with other prisoners. The cell slept four, but at first there were only two of us, myself and a big guy called Toni. Later we were joined by a young house-breaker from Naples, Ciro, and just before I got out a fourth prisoner came in, but I didn't have time to get to know him so well. Mostly it was just myself, Toni and Ciro. Toni was a car thief, not a very good one, who was regularly returned to prison soon after he had completed one sentence to start another. But he knew the system and he knew his way around, which was invaluable. He appointed himself as my bodyguard when I first arrived and looked after me, letting it be known that if anyone bothered me they would have Toni to deal with. As he was six foot two and very broad this was an effective protection.

The food wasn't good, but that didn't matter so much. In Latina prison, life was lived in the Latin manner. Each cell was allowed to have a small cooking stove – a gas ring like a hurricane lamp with a specially sealed canister of gas so the stove couldn't be used to set fire to cell or bedding. Prisoners were allowed to bring in as many saucepans as they wanted, and if they didn't like the meal of the day then they cooked their own. Toni had the run of the place and used to coax the menus out of the kitchen so we knew in advance when to expect something edible and when to make our own arrangements. Provisions were easily come by. They could either be brought in by visitors (and visits were allowed once a week) or they could be bought if you had the money. Every evening, about seven o'clock (cell lock-up was six o'clock), a guard would come round for the orders. Through the little grid in the cell door you would hand him any letters you wanted sending, unsealed, and a note of anything you wanted to buy with your name and your prison number on it so they could deduct the money from the amount you had deposited. Then the next morning, a guard would go out and post the letter and do the shopping for the prison. Anything that you had ordered you could collect from the commissary in the morning, during what was called the 'hour of freedom'. You could even order fresh meat if you wanted. Our cell was festooned with groceries. We had coffee, tea, bread, potatoes, onions, garlic, pasta, spaghetti, fruit, salt, pepper, assorted tins . . . everything we might need, including an Italian coffee-making machine. Eating in the cell became like a picnic, and we planned our meals with great care.

The 'hours of freedom' were a time in the morning and the afternoon when you could either go into the great courtyard to take the fresh air, or socialize with other prisoners or both. All the cell doors were open during this time. It was forbidden to close them. It was in one of these hours that I made the acquaintance of two cells full of Greeks. They were a complete ship's crew whose boat had been impounded when they were found smuggling cigarettes in the Bay of Naples. They didn't understand or speak any Italian and had no idea how they were going to get out of prison again, as their Naples lawyer ignored them, apart from writing periodic letters demanding more money. The captain, Peter, who was about thirty-six, was married to an English girl from Liverpool and spoke some English. He had a baby son called Paul, he told me, and showed me his family photographs proudly on several occasions. I had a copy of the Italian penal code with me in prison, and I started to try and work out a way of getting the Greeks released. (Two of the youngest Greek crew members were in the cell immediately opposite mine on the first floor. They were lads of about nineteen and they were totally unable to cope with being in prison. On several occasions in the early morning I watched them through the peephole in my door as they were carried unconscious to the first-aid rooms after suicide attempts.) I wrote a nasty letter to their lawyer (which gave me great pleasure, given my own feelings about lawyers at that time), telling him to get off his backside and come and visit his clients instead of demanding more money. I don't think he ever visited, but he did stop demanding money. Then gradually, writing for them in Italian, and getting them to sign, I worked towards getting them bail. Eventually we got an assurance from the court that they would be released on bail on payment of a certain sum of money and probably deported back to Greece.

All this used to happen during the 'hour of freedom'. In the morning I'd see them out in the exercise yard and tell the captain not to bother going out this afternoon but to come and have coffee with me in my cell because I'd just received some letters or documents for them. Once we got the promise of bail we had to find the means of raising the money. I realized they must have been smuggling for someone, so I persuaded them to tell me his name so I could make contact and ask him to put up the bail money. Obviously this couldn't be done openly through letters which would be read by the prison authorities, so the contact was made verbally through some of my visitors who would then report back to me (after making various telephone calls) what had happened. The smuggling chief agreed to put up bail, but said the amount was too much, so I then started haggling with the Public Prosecutor's office until it came down to a manageable sum. In the end bail was set at around £2,000 for the whole crew and the chief smuggler agreed to pay. I arranged the payment of the money into court and the Greeks were released. They were freed before I was. Needless to say they were overjoyed and embraced me with tears in their eyes and kissed my cheeks when they left. They wrote to me for many months after I got out of prison and I still have a standing invitation to go and holiday in Greece with the captain and his English wife. I haven't been yet, but perhaps one day I will. They think they owe me something, but in a way I owe them something too. They gave me warmth and sense of purpose that helped me through the time I spent in prison. Toni and Ciro did the same. Toni couldn't read or write so I would examine the penal code and write letters for him, claiming his rights, and he would sign with a cross. Ciro could write, but didn't know how best to help himself, so I would advise him on his problems, telling him where to write and how to do it. If there was anything constructive I could do, I liked doing it. If I had been kept in solitary confinement (as was the case in Switzerland) and had not had the care and friendship of Paola and the prisoners I don't think I would have survived my time in Latina prison.

Paola came to see me every visiting day, bringing anything I might need to make life easier for me in prison, and news of my children. Because she was a lawyer she managed to get an extra visiting pass, so that although visits were only allowed once a week, Paola managed for all the time that I was in Latina prison to visit me twice a week. She never missed out, and her visits were a great comfort to me.

It was all very different from the time I spent in Basle prison five years previously. It made me realize just how inhumane that had been and also to suspect that even there I had been treated differently from other prisoners because of the offence I had been charged with. In Latina I was treated exactly the same as other prisoners. There was no difference at all.

On one of her visits Paola told me that all the central heating oil in my villa had been used up, and no supplier would deliver any more, because my credit was so bad. Until then my three daughters had been having their evening meal with Paola's grandparents, who had generously opened their home to them, and had been going home late in the evening with Paola to sleep in their own beds. Paola stayed in the house with them. But in January, even in Latina which is normally quite warm, it was too cold for the children to stay in an unheated four-storey house. I sent a telegram to neighbours of mine, Stanley and Miriam

Martin, asking for help. They were an English couple, with children a little older than mine, and our two families were great friends. Stanley worked at the NATO Communications School in Latina as an Instructor. They now offered to take my children in, and for the next few weeks looked after them with their own family.

Towards the end of January, when it looked as if I was not going to be able to get bail quickly, I reluctantly told Paola to send for the children's grandmother to pick them up and take them to stay with her. (Mariléne's sister Yvonne had died from kidney disease in October 1979.) Even though I couldn't see them where I was, I hated the thought of them being taken so far away from me, but I didn't feel I could impose on the good will of my friends any longer. On January 30th their grandmother came and fetched them, and they went back with her to Luino, eight hundred kilometres away on the Italian–Swiss border. All this time I had been writing to my daughters and receiving letters in return. Of course, they didn't write to me in the prison. I had given them the name of someone they could write to, as a staging post, with the excuse that I was moving around a lot and this person would know my address and be able to forward their letters to me. In order to write to them myself I asked Paola to buy me plain postcards, of dogs, or flowers, or horses, with no indication of place, not even a 'made in Italy' mark. Then I'd send the cards (one apiece, never to the three together) to friends outside Italy and ask them to forward them to the children, so they would have a foreign postmark. It was an elaborate system, but it worked. Sometimes the children would ask when they wrote why I never sent them views any more, or pictures of places where I was, only animals and flowers. I couldn't answer them. I tried so hard to keep from them any knowledge of where I was, and until now I was sure I had succeeded. But reading through old files some years later I came across a letter from Ernest Glinne to Erich Diefenbacher that showed my eldest daughter, Nathalie, who was then only eleven, had sent a telegram on her own initiative to Ernest Glinne in the December I was arrested, telling him that her daddy had been taken to prison and asking for help. She knew all the time, and she never told me then or afterwards that she knew. She let me go on thinking she didn't know, and playing my games, because she thought that was what I wanted her to think . . .

On Tuesday, February 12th, 1980, fifty-four days after I had first been arrested, I was finally released on bail. My lawyer, Zeppieri, had eventually got round to finding the farm's mortgage papers in my house (with Paola's help) which I had kept telling him were the key to my release. He had shown the papers to the magistrate, Alfonso Di Paolis, who until that moment had thought that I had been paid the two sums of 400 million lire each from the grant and the finance agency. He had not realized that I had only received one instalment, and had certainly not understood that that instalment was more than covered by the mortgage taken out by them on the farm. Even knowing that, he was reluctant to give me bail and refused to grant it. On Paola's suggestion my lawyer then asked the court to appoint a committee of three judges to decide the matter. The court agreed and the judges overruled Di Paolis's decision and granted me bail. I was not asked to pay any bail money, but simply to hand in my passport to the court, as surety that I wouldn't leave the country.

Paola was waiting faithfully for me at the prison gates, to drive me home. The house was cold and empty. The children were with their grandmother, hundreds of kilometres away, and I had no money either to pay for their fares back home, or to visit them, or to have them living with me. I left them where they were. I quite literally could no longer afford to feed them, and I was terrified of what might happen to me next.

14 The Donnez Report

Whilst I was in prison three petitions had been filed against me for bankruptcy. If they were agreed by the court, then I would be made bankrupt and all my assets and possessions sold off to meet my debts, leaving me with only the clothes I stood up in, with no home, no furniture, and nothing to live on. So far, friends in the Latina courts had managed to keep the petitions at the bottom of the pile of cases waiting to be heard, so they had not yet come before a judge, but there was a limit to how long this kind of shuffling could go on, and I knew that soon the cases would have to be allowed to proceed. My personal debts amounted to about £17,000. I owed money for legal costs, for rent, for telephone bills, for electricity, and for heating oil. The bankruptcy petitions had been presented by lawyers anxious to get their money back, and the more trouble I was in, the more money was needed for lawyers. It was a vicious circle. Even if I paid off the lawyers who were claiming against me now for the time they had spent sorting out the problems to do with the setting up of my pig industry, I would still have to find money to pay my present lawyers for their work in getting me out of prison. On top of that, if I wanted to stop my furniture being sold over my head, I had to find £4,000. If I wanted to reclaim my car, which had been sequestrated for debts, I'd have to find another £2,000. I had also borrowed large sums of money to feed and clothe my children and myself. Some of my creditors, who were also good friends, were not pressing legally for the return of their money, but I knew I would have to repay them soon. They needed the money and had waited so long for its return that even their tolerance was running out. The irony is that on paper I was solvent. My land was valued at £75,000 (if I'd been able to sell it, plus buildings, to someone who wanted to continue building a pig industry there, it was worth a lot more). The charge against it was only £41,000. If I had been able to sell it I could have repaid both the Mediocredito and the Cassa per il Mezzogiorno the first instalments they had paid me, with interest, and had enough money left to pay my own debts and gather myself and my children together to leave Italy and start again somewhere fresh. My time in Latina prison had convinced me that the sooner I got out of Italy the better. But I couldn't sell the land because the Mediocredito Regionale del Lazio and the Cassa per il Mezzogiorno held a mortgage on it, and I couldn't redeem the mortgage without selling the land unless I found a buyer willing to accept the mortgage as well, which was unlikely. So the grant and finance agencies would eventually foreclose and sell the land for a fraction of its real value, just to get their money back, and I would be taken to court over the other debts, declared bankrupt, and probably sent back to prison again.

According to certain sources, however, I had no need to worry because I had large amounts of money salted away in real estate in Italy and in the Isle of Wight. I don't know where this rumour came from but it started in Brussels and began to circulate while I was still in prison, and was current both within the European Commission and in Switzerland. According to the rumour I had been sent to prison because I had taken large sums of Italian government money and used them to speculate on the property market. Erich Diefenbacher was privately warned to be careful about pleading my cause because there was some suspicion that I was not as honest as he thought I was. On February 21st, 1980 he wrote to Ernest Glinne in Brussels.

... I furthermore must request that I be informed on all negative actions of Adams, part of which has been conveyed by third parties. I cannot base my decision, in the difficult legal, political and financial position I find myself in, on mere hearsay. Will you therefore be good enough to see that I get all necessary evidence be it from a political point of view or negative. In order to form a final judgment to be put before you I have to be furnished with facts and evidence ...

The rumour was widespread and caused me a lot of problems. I only heard of it later, and did my best to dispel it, but it kept resurfacing with remarkable persistence.

15 and 16 *Left*, Ernest Glinne, M.E.P. from Belgium, Chairman of the Socialist Group in the European Parliament since 1979; *right*, John Prescott, Labour M.P. for Hull East, leader of the British Labour Delegation to the European Parliament until 1979

17 and 18 *Left*, Richard Caborn, M.E.P. (Labour) since 1979 and M.P. for Sheffield Central since June 1983; *right*, Christopher Prout, M.E.P. (Conservative) since 1979 and member of the Legal Affairs Committee of the European Parliament

19 Press Conference held on January 28th, 1981 at the International Press Centre, London, organized by the Stanley Adams Appeal Committee and jointly chaired by (left) Michael Ivens, Director of Aims of Industry, and (right) Eric Moonman, ex-Labour M.P. and currently Director of the Centre for Contemporary Studies

20 Adams at home in his London flat, March 1981

My problems were further compounded by the fact that I discovered through friends that the Ministry of the Interior had ordered my deportation from Italy as a 'non desirable' alien following my arrest and imprisonment. The order had been issued on February 25th 1980, but as I was facing criminal proceedings it had to go before the Latina magistrate first. At any stage therefore, if the judge were to give his approval, I could be picked up and deported at twenty-four hours' notice or less. I was reduced to living in a permanent state of siege. I kept the door locked and the shutters down and only answered the door to friends according to pre-arranged signals. I didn't dare answer the door at random in case I found the bailiffs or the police standing on the doorstep. Any unexpected knock sent my pulse rate soaring and my heart thudding in my ears. The Socialists in the European Parliament had been given details of my most pressing debts and were doing what they could to help. They were pressurizing the European Commission to find enough money to prevent my being made bankrupt (with the risk that I would then be sent back to prison) and had themselves raised around £500 for me, at Richard Caborn's instigation, to help me cover immediate living expenses. (Italy being Italy it took sixteen days to reach me from the time it was telexed from Brussels to the time it reached a bank in Rome. We knew it had been sent, but no one could find any trace of its arrival!) On February 29th I wrote to Ernest Glinne, confirming that the money had arrived that morning and outlining my situation.

I take this opportunity to confirm also that the three petitions which exist against me in the Latina court (and which are being kept at the bottom of the pile by our friends) will be allowed to proceed in the normal way and go to a judge for study and decisions in a matter of fifteen days from now. Our friends can no longer keep these petitions hidden for us. I repeat that I can only avoid further trouble (and probably arrest) by paying the sums due before mentioned petitions are handed to a judge, which will probably take place on Monday March 17th, 1980.

It is important that I am kept fully informed by telephone of the steps being taken at your end as I may have to disappear from Latina before March 17th, 1980 if we do not manage to settle the mentioned debts beforehand. As you know, I am without my passport at the present time so I can only move within Italian territory. However, if I am not found at my address when called by any judge to Latina court I will avoid arrest and I would also hinder the judge from being able to take any decision on the petitions pending . . .

On March 3rd I wrote again.

If the debts are not paid before the petitions in question go before a judge there will be a new penal case against me, in addition to the one (for which I was arrested and spent 53 days in prison) brought by the Cassa per il Mezzogiorno. Whether I remain in Latina or not the penal case will be opened (unless we pay) and I will be arrested on sight in whatever part of Italy I may be found. Since I have no passport I cannot leave Italy . . .

The date of my possible court hearing was confirmed as March 19th. Meanwhile the Socialist Group continued making representations to the European Commission and on March 14th, 1980 I sent a telegram to Willi Schlieder's office:

HAVE BEEN INSTRUCTED BY SOCIALIST GROUP EUROPEAN PARLIAMENT TO INFORM YOU OFFICIALLY THAT TO GET OUT OF THE PRESENT EXTREMELY DIFFICULT SITUATION I REQUIRE IMMEDIATELY LIRE FIFTY MILLION (£20,000). AT LEAST LIRE ELEVEN MILLION ARE ESSENTIAL BEFORE 19.3.80. THIS REQUEST HAS INDEED BEEN MADE TO YOU ON SEVERAL OCCASIONS RECENTLY BY MESSRS GLINNE AND CABORN WHO HAVE PROVIDED YOU DETAILED FIGURES COVERING SUM MENTIONED. I REQUEST IMMEDIATE ACTION BY EEC COMMISSION AND AM SENDING COPIES OF THIS TELEX TO PRESIDENT SOCIALIST GROUP EUROPEAN PARLIAMENT AND MR CABORN AND MR JENKINS. KIND REGARDS. STANLEY ADAMS.

Roy Jenkins was the President of the European Commission then, and for much of the key time of my relationship with the Commission. The 50 million lire I was asking for was only a stopgap measure. The Socialist Group was exploring the possibility of claiming substantial compensation for me, but that would take time and I needed money immediately if I was to avoid being sent back to prison. The money I asked for would have covered my most immediate and threatening debts, and given me enough money to have my children home to live with me for a short while. After that I would have been back where I started.

Four days later, on March 18th, the Director-General of the Commission's legal service, C. D. Ehlermann, replied with the following telegram denying all knowledge of any approach having been made to the Commission.

IN REPLY TO YOUR TELEX OF 14 MARCH I WOULD LIKE TO POINT OUT THAT MR SCHLIEDER HAS NEVER RECEIVED ANY REQUEST FROM YOURSELF OR ANY THIRD PARTY FOR PAYMENTS OTHER THAN FOR THE COST OF YOUR DEFENCE. YOUR LAST MESSAGE REQUESTING THE COMMISSION TO ASSIST YOU IN OBTAINING CREDITS FROM ITALIAN FINANCIAL INSTITUTIONS WAS RECEIVED IN MARCH 1979. IT WAS ONLY IN FEBRUARY 1980 THAT TWO MEMBERS OF THE EUROPEAN PARLIAMENT ENQUIRED ABOUT THE POSSIBILITY OF DIRECT FINANCIAL AID OR COMPENSATION FROM THE COMMISSION. CONTRARY TO THE STATEMENT IN YOUR TELEX THE SERVICES OF THE COMMISSION HAVE NEVER RECEIVED ANY DETAILED INFORMATION OR FIGURES TO JUSTIFY YOUR REQUEST. IN ORDER TO ENABLE THE COMMISSION TO EXAMINE YOUR REQUEST WE REQUIRE PRECISE INFORMATION REGARDING THE NATURE OF YOUR FINANCIAL OBLIGATIONS. I.E. HOW MUCH YOU OWE TO WHOM AND WHY. YOURS SINCERELY C. D. EHLERMANN

Fortunately I had by now managed to postpone my court hearing by another week. I replied on March 20th giving the details the Commission requested, and reiterated that they had already been given them once, by Richard Caborn, the British M.E.P. who had been in touch with Willi Schlieder's office at the end of February. My hopes for a permanent solution to my problems were now firmly pinned to the recommendations made by the European Parliament's Legal Affairs Committee.

The Legal Affairs Committee was composed almost entirely of lawyers. The chairman, Mauro Ferri, was a Professor of Law and an Italian Socialist. The three vice-chairmen were

Rudolf Luster, a Christian Democrat from Germany, Amedée Turner, a Conservative from Britain and Robert Chambeiron, a Communist from France. There were twenty-one other members: two Communists, three Conservatives, five Socialists, six Christian Democrats, three Liberals, one Radical and one Progressive Democrat, from Italy, France, Holland, Germany, Luxembourg, Belgium and Britain (including Christopher Prout). It contained a complete cross-section of nationality and political beliefs, and it existed to advise the Parliament on matters of international law. In February 1979 the Committee had been instructed by the Parliament to draw up a complete report on my case and the legal implications, both for myself and for the Swiss/E.E.C. Free Trade Agreement (see page 120). By the end of January 1980 they had produced a draft report, which I had seen, and on March 19th, 1980 that report was officially adopted by twenty-two votes with three abstentions. Despite the breadth of political opinion on the committee, nobody voted against it. The *rapporteur* appointed to head the report was Georges Donnez, a French liberal, and the report became known as the 'Donnez report'.

One of its recommendations was that the European Commission should consider the possibility of making a payment to me out of the Community's budget, to make good the financial loss I had suffered over the years (and the Commission was well aware of this recommendation). It was this suggestion that I hoped might put an end to my problems financially. But the report was not just a device to solve my personal difficulties. It was far more important and far-reaching than that. It had been set up by the Members of the European Parliament categorically so that such a case could not happen again, since the Swiss government had given no such assurances, and at the same time the European Commission had refused to take any action against the Swiss, such as withdrawing, or even threatening to withdraw, from the Swiss/E.E.C. Free Trade agreement. The Commission had applied almost no pressure to the Swiss at all, not even raising the issue formally for several years after my arrest. For some time they had sheltered behind the fact that the whole issue was *sub judice*, as both myself and Roche had appeals waiting to be heard. But once those appeals had been heard, on the day that the final judgment had been given on Roche by the European Court of

Justice, the European Parliament acted. As soon as the Commission refused once more to withdraw from the Agreement, Parliament referred the whole matter to their Legal Affairs Committee, to decide if Switzerland were in breach of that agreement and if so, what action should be taken.

The Donnez report had two principal aims. One was to see justice done to me personally, and the other was to make sure the principles of international law were upheld. The report summarized the history of my arrest, conviction and appeals, and the parallel history of the case taken against Roche by the European Commission, and Roche's appeal to the European Court of Justice, in which it was confirmed that Roche had broken E.E.C. Competition law. The absurd illogicality of Roche being found guilty of committing an illegal act, and my being found guilty of spying for reporting that illegal act, had disturbed the European Parliament, and it now disturbed its Legal Affairs Committee. The Donnez report drew attention to the fact that under the Swiss/E.E.C. Free Trade Agreement (Articles 22 and 23) the Swiss were *obliged* to give the E.E.C. information about any practices that seemed to break the Agreement (as Roche's practices did). For a report by lawyers, the Donnez report was positively outspoken.

It is legitimate to ask whether the Swiss Confederation has in fact applied these provisions. The Swiss courts, at least, seem to attach precious little importance to them, since the judgment given against Mr Adams considers that the practices of Hoffmann-La Roche should remain secret and regards the fact that the practices were brought to the attention of the Commission of the European Communities as an attack on national sovereignty . . .

The Court of Summary Jurisdiction and the Court of Appeal of Basle, as also the Swiss Supreme Court of Appeal, all felt constrained to look at the allegations against Mr Adams in the light of the provisions of the Swiss National penal code without taking any account of the existence of international provisions which might present the matters under consideration in a rather different perspective. The judgment in the Adams case raises grave doubts, particularly in view of the fact that the international treaties concluded by the Swiss Confederation are an integral part of Swiss law. They require no ratification and take precedence over prior laws.

The fact is that the judge merely applied the provisions of the Penal Code in force in Switzerland. It is incumbent upon the Swiss Confederation to modify its laws so as to avoid a situation where an act which it is required under international law to uphold (duty of information) continues to be punished as an offence against the higher interests of the State under municipal law, where that act is committed by an individual . . .

In conclusion the Legal Affairs Committee considers that the Swiss Confederation erred in its assessment of the allegations against Mr Stanley Adams, having regard to its agreement with the European Community. The Swiss Confedation has been found guilty of shortcomings under the following heads.

a) legislative: insofar as Swiss criminal law has not been brought into line with the new situation created by the agreement of July 22nd, 1972;

b) judicial: in the sense that the judgment in the Adams case did not take due account of all the rights and duties flowing from an international treaty, whose provisions are an integral part of Swiss municipal law;

c) administrative: since the Swiss government did not feel obliged to take the option of not bringing criminal proceedings provided for under Article 105 of the law of June 15th, 1934, despite the fact that Hoffmann-La Roche's practices were contrary to the aims pursued by the Swiss Confederation following the conclusion of the agreement of July 22nd, 1972.

Having thus disposed of the Swiss Confederation, the Donnez report moved on to the next section entitled 'Action to be taken by the Community in relation to Mr Adams'.

It is clear that the European Community has a particular responsibility to Mr Adams, whose statements enabled practices contrary to the E.E.C./Switzerland trade agreement and the E.E.C. Treaty to be stopped and punished. Mr Adams has suffered considerable misfortune in his personal and family life as well as substantial financial loss . . .

Therefore the Community must act to help Mr Adams.

First of all the Commission of the European Communities

should ask the competent bodies of the Swiss Confederation to take amnesty measures in favour of Mr Adams to erase all the consequences of his trial.

Furthermore, as Mr Prescott told Parliament, 'an application to the Human Rights Court will ensure that this matter continues.' If such an application is made, then clearly the Commission should provide Mr Adams with every assistance.

As far as Mr Adams' financial loss is concerned, the Commission of European Communities should consider the possibility of making a payment to him from the Community's budget to make good that loss. The Commission could also ask the Italian government (it will be recalled that Mr Adams has taken up residence in Italy) to do what it can for Mr Adams.

The final section of the report was entitled, 'Action to be taken by the Community in relation to the E.E.C./Swiss Confederation Trade Agreement'.

Quite apart from the individual case of Mr Adams, the Community must take steps to resolve what seems to be the most striking contradiction in the whole affair, namely, the fact that a state which has signed an agreement with the Community continues to apply its internal laws punishing anyone who exposes conduct contrary to the agreement. The application of Articles 273 and 162 of the Swiss Penal Code to the situation envisaged by the E.E.C./Swiss Confederation agreement represents in practice a form of protection to natural or legal persons acting contrary to the provisions of the agreement.

The Commission of the European Communities should therefore approach the Swiss authorities to seek firm assurances that there will not be a repetition of cases of this kind in the future, and the Commission should provide evidence of such assurances to the European Parliament.

It will be recalled in this connection that during the sitting of Tuesday 13th February 1979 a question by Mr Prescott, 'What assurances have the Commission received from the Swiss government that should any other citizen provide similar information about illegal acts they will not face charges of espionage?' received the following answer from Vice-President Haferkamp, the foreign affairs spokesman. 'The Swiss government has made no declaration of the kind referred to in the question. There are permanent contacts between the Commission's offices and the Swiss Mission in Brussels. *The Commission assumes that this will ensure that there is no repetition of a case like this.'*

The Commission must therefore inform us whether its assumptions have proved to be justified by communicating evidence of the assurances referred to above.

Should the Commission not be able to supply such evidence, it must find a different solution to achieve the same result. By way of example, the Legal Affairs Committee would suggest the possibility of having an explanatory note added to the text of the agreement which would specify that Articles 273 and 162 of the Swiss Penal Code do not apply to acts intended to facilitate the enforcement of the agreement.

The Donnez report, like all European Parliament Committee reports, was made up of an explanatory statement, which I have quoted from above, and a motion for resolution to be passed by the European Parliament and acted upon. The motion for a resolution was as follows.

On the Adams case and on the trade agreement between the E.E.C. and the Swiss Confederation.
The European Parliament
– having regard to the 1972 trade agreement between the E.E.C. and the Swiss Confederation.
– having regard to the final decision of September 27th, 1977 of the Basle Court of Appeal sentencing Mr Stanley Adams to one year's imprisonment (suspended) and the forfeiture of a surety of 25,000 Swiss francs.
– having regard to the decision of the Commission of the European Communities of June 9th, 1976 and the judgment of the Court of Justice of the European Communities of February 13th, 1979 on the activities of Hoffmann-La Roche.
– having been informed that Mr Adams, who has taken up residence in the territory of the Republic of Italy, is now in considerable financial difficulty.
– having regard to the resolution adopted by the European Parliament on February 14th, 1979.

– having regard to the report of the Legal Affairs Committee.

1) Invites the Commission of the European Communities to ask the competent bodies of the Swiss Confederation that amnesty measures be taken in relation to Mr Adams with respect to the consequences of his being found guilty of criminal offences.

2) Asks the Commission of the European Communities

– to make an extraordinary payment to Mr Adams in order to make good the psychological and physical consequences of the action he took to put a stop to the illegal practices of Hoffmann-La Roche.

– to approach the Government of the Republic of Italy with the request that it do all it can to assist Mr Adams should the need arise,

3) Invites the Commission of the European Communities to furnish the Legal Affairs Committee with firm assurances that in future any person revealing activities contrary to the E.E.C./Switzerland Trade Agreement shall not be prosecuted in the Swiss courts, in particular under Articles 273 and 162 of the Swiss Penal Code.

4) Instructs its Legal Affairs Committee to present a further report should it consider the assurances referred to in paragraph 3 insufficient.

5) Instructs its President to forward this resolution and the report of its Committee to the Commission and the Council of the European Communities.

The Donnez report, its recommendations, and the motion for a resolution to go before the European Parliament, were all I could have wished for. It not only pointed a way to a practical solution of my difficulties but by stating clearly that I should never have been convicted of spying or breaking trade secrets, and was not guilty of any crime, it dispelled any lingering doubts that people may have had about my character and integrity. What's more, the first clause of the motion for a resolution opened the way to my seeking justice in Switzerland itself, and having my conviction wiped out. I was convinced that this time, if Parliament were prepared to pass the Donnez report, I would really see an end to all my troubles. This time, thanks to the political efforts of all my friends, I believed there would be a way out of the maze.

The only question left was one of timing, and that was crucial. The report had to be debated as soon as possible if I were not to find that just as there was hope of a solution I was made bankrupt and imprisoned again, perhaps days before help arrived that could have prevented it. Once back in prison it would take more than money to get me out again. As each month passed, delaying tactics on the bankruptcy hearings became more and more difficult, and my debts and the interest on my debts were mounting all the time. Meteor Pigs Ltd, the British firm I had been dealing with between 1975 and 1979, had started pressing me again for the money they had lent me to pay the American finance consultants (which had vanished with them), and the Italian lawyers working on my present case needed paying and I'd had to borrow money to pay them the first instalment on their bills. Rent and telephone and electricity bills continued to mount, and I was now living only on the small help from my close friends who could not really afford to support me. My children were still with their grandmother and their schooling had been hopelessly disrupted. An official from the European Commission had apparently been to Rome and Latina and done some talking behind the scenes, but strangely enough he had not contacted me and I was not sure what the reason for his visit was. On April 5th, 1980 I wrote to Richard Caborn.

I have been out of prison since February 12th, 1980, and have not yet received any help from the E.E.C. There has been a lot of talk, a lot of telephone calls especially during March '80 from Schlieder's office. There have been a lot of promises from young German Mr Mensching (Schlieder's assistant) around 17th March, '80. I remember that at that time Mensching informed me that he did not think the E.E.C. would manage to telex me some funds by March 19th, '80 but he assured me that they were doing everything so that I receive at least part of the funds before long.

Then there was the telex from C. D. Ehlermann, Director-General Legal Services, dated March 17th and received by me on the 18th. I answered that telex on March 20th giving full data, but got no funds in any case. Why did things stop from that date on? It is my impression that the E.E.C. Commission (and Mr Ehlermann in particular) are convinced that since their man came to Latina and Rome, everything is settled for Adams. They seem to imagine that just because some postponements have been given by the Latina judges I have nothing else to worry about . . .

The Commissioners and Officials of the E.E.C. have never bothered to ask me how I manage to live. They have never bothered to ask how my three motherless children eat, dress, go to school and generally keep fit and happy. They have never moved a finger to help me financially so that at least I may get back the three children to live here with me in Latina, instead of leaving them 850 kilometres away near Lugano . . . just because I cannot support them.

I have written this dozens of times, but I must repeat it once more: at the present time I stand a good chance of being put out of the house for non-payment of rent for the last four months, soon to become five months. Should that happen, lawyers . . . will sell all my furniture and belongings as the Latina court have long ago approved sequestration . . .

If my letters sounded desperate, it was because I was desperate. I seemed to be on the verge of a solution, only to find that it was going to be taken away from me by court action days before the money actually arrived to prevent me going to prison. The strain of living in daily fear of the bailiff's knock on the door, and in fear of finding myself standing in the street, destitute with nowhere to go, was becoming too much for me.

The Socialist Group did their best to help. They put a request for urgent procedure to the European Parliament during the sitting of April 15th in an attempt to get the Donnez report heard that month. The request was rejected. Finally a date was set on the Parliamentary Agenda for the session of May 19th–23rd, 1980. My lawyers managed yet again to get a postponement of the bankruptcy hearings until Monday June 2nd. But it was made very clear that this was the final postponement, and the full amount must be paid by that date, not just a deposit of a third of the amount. It also looked at the time as if I was going to be summoned to a Rome court to be tried on the same charge that I had been arrested for in Latina. My lawyer again managed to postpone that hearing, but nobody knew for how long. At least there was no longer any danger of my being deported. On April

1st the Latina court had ruled against it (all this without my officially knowing of the existence of the deportation warrant at all). But this was a small consolation. The only reason the magistrate had not agreed to my deportation was that he wanted me tried on the charges outstanding, and he wanted the bankruptcy hearings to take place before I left Italy.

I hoped to be able to go to the debate on the Donnez report, but despite an official letter of invitation from the European Parliament the magistrate, Dr Di Paolis, would not allow my passport to be released to me so I could travel.

On Friday May 23rd, 1980, on the last day of the European Parliament's sitting, late at night, the Donnez report was still waiting to be debated when the President of the European Parliament decided to refer the rest of that session's business to the following session, a month later. But first he called on Ernest Glinne, Chairman of the Socialist Group. Glinne spoke,

This morning at 9 a.m., when the sitting opened, I stressed the importance we attach to Item 95. A few minutes would suffice. We limited our own speaking time to two minutes and we withdrew four of the five amendments we had tabled. What we have here – and I measure my words – is a matter which, to some, may be one of life or death. We strongly feel that Parliament cannot adjourn without having considered Item 95.
President: Mr Glinne, I propose that all items still on the agenda be deferred with the exception of the item to which you have referred.

Are there any objections?

That is agreed.
President: The next item is the report by Mr Donnez, on behalf of the Legal Affairs Committee, on the Adams case and the Trade Agreement between the E.E.C. and the Swiss Confederation. I call Mr Donnez (French Liberal).
Mr Donnez: Mr President, I would thank you for having acceded to Mr Glinne's request. As a token of my own good will I shall be extremely brief.

This is a matter with which Parliament is familiar, I would even say too familiar, and I would venture to hope that we shall be discussing it for the last time.

To some extent – I shall not repeat the facts of the case in order to keep our debate short – Mr Adams is today the victim of a major conflict between Swiss criminal law, under which he has been sentenced for the disclosures he made to the Commission, and a judgment by the Court of Justice of the Communities condemning Hoffmann-La Roche for the highly peculiar manner in which it construed freedom of competition. This judgment against a leading pharmaceutical company was possible because of the statements made by Mr Adams. We learned from those statements how curiously a treaty between the European Communities and Switzerland has been interpreted. The details of the case point clearly to the relatively poor implementation of the treaty, to say the least, on the Swiss side. The Legal Affairs Committee therefore took the view that a way should be sought of compensating Mr Adams for the moral prejudice and damages he had suffered and that we should call on the Commission to take whatever steps are necessary with the Swiss authorities to avoid the repetition of such mishaps and their referral to this Parliament. You have read the motion for a resolution before you. I would venture to hope that Parliament will approve it in its entirety.

President: I call Mr Johan van Minnen (Dutch Socialist).

Mr van Minnen: On behalf of the Socialist Group, I thank Mr Donnez for his report, which shows how the multinationals crushed a man who gave information about their illegal practices. It also shows that the Commission is not being as forthright in the defence of this courageous man as one would have expected, and it reflects the public outrage that has helped us get support for Mr Adams.

We must stress one very important point: people who are prepared to give information against very powerful organizations like Hoffmann-La Roche must be protected by national and international law. This is a major test case in the European Community, showing whether it is prepared to defend the people who help it to enforce its own agreements . . . I call on Parliament to be true to its principles. I hope we support it unanimously.

President: I call Mr Christopher Prout to speak on behalf of the European Democratic Group.

Mr Prout: My group supports in its entirety the Donnez report. We also support the amendment tabled by Mr Richard Caborn.

We are especially concerned about the future of the Trade Agreement between the European Community and Switzerland which was signed in December 1972. We urge the Commission to obtain a firm undertaking from the Swiss authorities that there will never be a repetition of the Adams case. By prosecuting Adams for disclosing the infringements of Hoffmann-La Roche, the Swiss government appear to be in breach of their treaty obligations. Moreover, by upholding this conviction, the Federal Supreme Court of Switzerland appears to have misdirected itself in law.

I would simply add that I do not think that the Adams case should be the occasion for a witch hunt against multinational companies. I think that is a side issue. I think the two issues are the Swiss government and the Swiss courts.

Christopher Prout was a British Conservative and a member of the Legal Affairs Committee. He had been very supportive of me during all this time, and has continued to be so.

Mr Antonio Giolitti, an Italian Socialist Commissioner, replied on behalf of the E.E.C. Commission. He detailed all that the Commission had done to help me, paying my defence costs, making representations to the British authorities over citizenship for me, intervening in Italy to help me get a residence permit and to get my grant and loan facilities renewed. He went on to say,

As far as the Commission knows, there is no causal connection between what happened in Switzerland and Mr Adams' present difficulties in Italy. This being so, the Commission does not consider it advisable at present to make any further specific representations to the Italian authorities . . .

The Commission has never lost sight of the fact that because he has supplied information which made it possible to stop the illegal practices of a multinational corporation, Mr Adams had been held in preventive detention in Switzerland and received a suspended sentence of one year's imprisonment.

While it has no legal responsibility *vis à vis* Mr Adams, the Commission is prepared to offer him assistance, in the form of a gift and as an exceptional and strictly humanitarian measure, as soon as Parliament has expressed its desire to this effect in voting on this resolution . . .

He outlined again the Commission's position on the Community's relationship with Switzerland, summing it up in startling words. 'In this sensitive case it is in nobody's interest to dramatize matters at the risk of jeopardizing the otherwise excellent relations existing between the Community and Switzerland.'

(I thought the drama had been provided by Switzerland in the first place when they imprisoned me, and I thought that subsequently the relations existing between the Community and Switzerland were far from excellent, as did Parliament, but the Commission was obviously more concerned with not rocking the diplomatic boat. I found it strange that these words were spoken by a Socialist such as Antonio Giolitti.)

Mr Giolitti went on to say, 'Finally, as regards paragraph 1 of the motion for a resolution in which the Commission is invited to request the competent bodies in the Swiss Confederation to grant Mr Adams amnesty in respect of the consequences of his being found guilty of criminal offences, the Commission does not see how it can carry out Parliament's request . . . '

The Commission didn't see how they could carry out Parliament's request because under the Swiss constitution an amnesty is a collective measure not generally applicable to individual cases, and it would have to be voted through the Swiss parliament. This had already been pointed out to the Legal Affairs Committee, and the Socialist Group had tabled an amendment:

> Invites the Commission to ask the competent bodies of the Swiss Confederation to instruct the General Prosecutor of the Swiss Confederation to demand, by way of a review procedure, the re-examination and re-opening of the case based upon Article 113 of the Swiss Federal Constitution and Article 6 of the European Convention of Human Rights. In subordinate order, invites the Commission to ask the competent bodies of the Swiss Confederation that amnesty measures be taken in relation to Mr Adams with respect to the consequences of the fact that he has been found guilty of criminal offences.

This was designed to remove the constitutional difficulties and set the way clear for Erich Diefenbacher to re-open my case in Switzerland. It meant that one man (the General Prosecutor), acting on the instructions of the Swiss government, could move to re-open my case without requiring the authority of the Swiss Parliament (which had a right-wing majority and probably wouldn't have given it). It also meant that the Commission would not be asking for anything that was constitutionally impossible. But the amendment did not appear to remove the Commission's difficulties. The Commissioner simply changed his argument. 'Finally as regards the amendment . . . I have to say that the Commission cannot accept it because it is a fixed principle of Community institutions, and hence also of the Commission, not to interfere with the powers of the juridical authorities of third countries.'

The European Parliament was unmoved by the Commission's fear of 'jeopardizing the otherwise excellent relationship between the Community and Switzerland', or the hesitation about approaching Italy on my behalf, or their denial of legal responsibility for my situation. From the far right to the far left, the whole of the European Parliament voted in favour of the resolution. It is the only time in the thirty-year history of the European Parliament that there has been a unanimous vote across all the parties.

For those who had worked so hard for me over the years it was a great achievement. It was a vindication of their belief that the European Parliament could protect the interests of the individual and could make sure that justice was done. I was at home in Latina, on my bed the following afternoon, a Saturday, when the phone rang. It was Van Minnen, the Dutch Socialist, who said he wanted to be the first to tell me that the resolution had been passed unanimously and that the vote had made history in the European Parliament. Everyone was very excited. We had expected the resolution to be carried, but to be carried unanimously was a different matter. Parliament could not have stated its wishes more clearly. As far as the European Parliament was concerned, my conviction should be wiped out and I should be financially compensated for all that had happened, so that I could begin to live a new life, free from financial worries and with a clean reputation. All I was required to do now was to sit back and wait for it to happen.

The elected European Parliament had spoken.

15 The E.E.C.'s 'Last Assistance' and the Appeal Committee

I waited, I had high hopes of a just settlement. Whenever the possibilities had been discussed, either in conversations between my lawyer and myself, or with members of the Legal Affairs Committee, or any member of the European Parliament, we had always talked in terms of a legal compensation from E.E.C. that would have been estimated in a similar way to damages in a court of law, taking into account loss of earnings, reduced prospects, the failure of the farm and so on, as well as compensation for psychological damage and the tragedies my family had suffered. The sum discussed was never less than £500,000, and if I received an amount of that order I knew I would be able to cover all my debts, including the farm debts, pay off everyone I owed money to, and leave Italy with enough money left over to set myself and my daughters up somewhere else (preferably in Britain). If I was able to pay everyone in full, including the grant and loan agency, then I hoped that the criminal charges against me would be dropped and my passport returned to me, so I would be able to leave the country quite legally, with no charges outstanding.

In the period leading up to the Donnez report I had been interviewed for a B.B.C. Radio Four programme, *Real Evidence*, and for a *World in Action* programme made by Granada Television. Both programmes had given wide publicity in Britain to my story, and I had been very moved by the response of the people who heard or watched the programmes. They wrote, either to me or the programme, offering their help, their support, and their encouragement. There were anonymous notes, in ill-formed block capitals, 'PLEASE SEE THAT THIS £5.00 GOES TO THE MALTEZ MAN WHO LIVES IN ITALY AND WAS THE SUBJECT OF YOUR EXCELLENT PROGRAMME ON THE 12 MAY 1980.' Pound notes, two pound notes, three five-pound notes, tucked into envelopes with little messages. 'ENCLOSED A MITE TO HELP RICHARD (sic) ADAMS, AS HE WANTED TO HELP OTHERS . . . ' from people who wanted to help even if they didn't really know who I was and had never met me. 'I enclose £2, a mere drop but a mite for Stanley Adams and his family . . . ' 'Although the enclosed £1.00 is very small I should be most grateful if somehow it could be conveyed to him in the hope that it will bring him luck . . . ' 'I should like to contribute my pensioners mite. Whilst one cannot hope to solve his problems, it might just encourage him sufficiently to stop him following in his wife's footsteps . . . ' 'Dear Mr Adams, I heard of your unfortunate experiences on Mr Cook's programme. May I say how sorry I was to hear of your loss. It seems a terrible thing has happened, and what can an ordinary person do to help? . . . ' 'I would like to thank you for the stand you took and say that I hope your troubles will soon be over.'

Dear Mr Adams,
    I listened in distress last night to the programme broadcast by B.B.C. radio about the many sufferings you have experienced since you first passed on information to the E.E.C. Commission about the illegal trading practices of Hoffmann-La Roche in Basle. I worked in Switzerland for 18 years, and for ten of them I worked for another chemical company, so I have a special sympathy for your plight. I often compared working for them to life under a totalitarian dictatorship. The 'party line' was laid down by management and anyone who queried it was liable to be severely reprimanded, to say the least . . . That Hoffmann-La Roche were so vindictive towards you and that the Swiss police backed them up in no way surprised me. In Switzerland big business can do no wrong. But the results have been most tragic for you and it is particularly to be deplored that the E.E.C. Commission has not made greater efforts to help you.
    My wife and I extend to you our greatest sympathy and we hope fervently that your fortune will soon change for the better. I am enclosing a cheque for £50 as a small contribution towards solving your financial problems, though I realize that your needs are very much greater than this. Should you have the

opportunity of coming to Britain we shall be very happy to see you and provide you with accommodation . . .

I am appalled to hear today the story of Stanley Adams, on Radio 4. What on earth is the E.E.C. doing? It seems to me they spend all their time talking about butter, wine, potatoes etc.

Why has it been so long getting some help to this poor man and his family?

I was beginning to wonder what the E.E.C. was doing too. The European Parliament had passed the Donnez report on the night of May 23rd, and by Monday June 2nd I had to have paid in full the three debts for which I had been taken to court if I was to avoid being arrested and sent to prison again. It had been made very clear to me that the money must be paid before June 2nd (when the last postponement of the bankruptcy hearings had been granted). That meant it had to be paid in on Friday, May 30th, which was the last working day before the 2nd. All this was well known to the Commission. They had been instrumental in getting the final postponement of the hearings, and I had been on the phone to them before and after the Donnez report was passed to make sure they understood the implications of the position. Obviously I did not expect a complete settlement to be worked out in such a short time, but I wanted the E.E.C. Commission to advance me sufficient money to keep me out of prison while the details of a settlement were worked out with my lawyer. Monday 26th, Tuesday 27th, Wednesday 28th went by with no sign of any money arriving, despite my increasingly agitated phone calls. I had only Thursday and Friday left to pay in. I was terrified at the thought that I might be taken back to prison again, and I knew that if I missed the payment deadline I would be arrested within a couple of days (if I wasn't taken straight to prison from the courtroom on Monday). There was just no way that I could face all that again. Last time I had been seriously ill and I was terribly afraid that if it happened again I simply wouldn't survive, mentally or physically, and then what would happen to my three little girls? I was prepared to do almost anything rather than go back through those prison gates.

The European Commission understood how I felt.

On the morning of Thursday May 29th, the day before my final payment deadline, Mensching from Willi Schlieder's office phoned me. He said that the Commission had decided to give me 50 million lire (£20,000) on condition that I would sign a document saying that I agreed the Commission had no further responsibility for me, and that I would get no more money from them, now or in the future. If I would sign that piece of paper then I could have the money by the next day. (The implication being, that if I refused to sign it, I would not get any money in time to prevent my being sent to prison.) I was appalled. The Commission knew as well as I did that that was not the kind of sum of money that the European Parliament had had in mind when they had voted the Donnez report through. The money they were offering was enough only to clear the debts which threatened to send me to prison but it by no means covered all my current debts which by now were well over £100,000 (including the company debts on the farm), nor was it enough to provide me with any means of changing my situation in Italy or of starting afresh anywhere else. At best it only postponed imprisonment until the next set of debtors decided to sue for their money.

I told Mensching I would phone back in an hour. I wanted to tell them to go to hell, but I didn't dare. I tried to phone my lawyer, Erich Diefenbacher, only to be told that he was away from his office and would be out of contact till Monday, June 2nd, which was too late for me. By then I might be back in prison. I tried then to speak to Ernest Glinne, Chairman of the Socialist Group, in his Brussels office, but he was in conference. Finally I spoke to Jean-Pierre Simon, the Deputy General-Secretary of the Group, who I knew quite well. I explained the situation to him. If I said no, I wouldn't sign, I would be arrested in a couple of days. If I said yes, the European Commission would make me sign something that might make it impossible for me to pursue any further claim. Simon said he'd consult with Glinne and he'd come back to me quickly. About half an hour later he phoned me back and said he'd talked with Glinne and some of the others. Their advice was to accept the money and keep myself out of prison. The Socialist Group would take it up with the Commission later and sort it out for me. So I accepted their advice and phoned Schlieder's office to say that I would accept the money. We agreed, after some discussion, that the Rome office of the E.E.C. Commission would be instructed to give me a cheque for the amount that afternoon, if I would go into Rome to collect it. After lunch I made my way into Rome, arriving at the E.E.C. office around three o'clock. Although the final agreement had been made with Brussels at eleven that morning, the cheque was not yet ready for me. The officials were waiting for the letter and receipt I had to sign to come on the document sender from Brussels before they would hand over the cheque. There was no way they were going to let me take that cheque without agreeing to the accompanying conditions. Eventually the documents arrived, and I signed the receipt:

29. May 1980. Rome.

The undersigned, Stanley Adams of Via Romagna 18, Latina, declares to have received from Mr Caferri, an official at the Rome E.E.C. offices, the non-transferable cheque no. 070024493 of the Commercial Bank of Italy for Lire 50 million, being paid by the Commission of the European Communities in accordance with indications contained in the Commission's letter of today No. SG (80) D/6577 signed by the Secretary General.

The letter to me read as follows:

Brussels SG(80) D/6577

29. May 1980

Dear Sir,

I have to inform you that the Commission has decided to award you the sum of Lit.50 000 000 by way of special assistance.

The Commission has not forgotten that you were held in custody and given a suspended sentence of one year's imprisonment in Switzerland because you had supplied the Commission with information which enabled the illegal practices of a multinational concern to be brought to an end. The Commission has therefore awarded you this sum as an ex gratia payment and on strictly humanitarian grounds, although it has no responsibility towards you in any respect.

The Commission has also instructed me to inform you that this payment is the last assistance which you will receive from the Commission.

Yours faithfully,

E. Nöel,
Secretary General,
Commission of the European Community

I took the cheque. I was relieved because I had the money to keep me out of prison, and I was distressed because the Commission had used my fear of imprisonment to make me accept unacceptable conditions. I couldn't believe that they could have behaved in such a calculating and inhumane manner. After all that the European Parliament had done for me, and all that the Donnez report had said, the Commission were still determined to do things their own way, and their way was not what the European Parliament had wanted, nor, I liked to think, what the people of Europe wanted, since it was they who had elected the Members of the European Parliament to their seats to represent their interests, in the first direct election ever in 1979. The European Parliament had made it quite clear in the Donnez report that they wanted to 'make good the psychological and physical consequences of the action' I took, and to 'make good' my financial loss, not to deny all responsibility for what had happened and simply give me a handout from the 'goodness of their hearts . . . ' I had now been without income for seven years and the money offered by the Commission covered only a fraction of my present debts.

The next morning when I tried to cash the cheque at a bank in Latina I ran into further difficulties because the cheque was from a Rome bank which had no branch in Latina and the Latina bank could not give me all the money immediately. Eventually I accepted simply the amount needed urgently to keep me out of prison and collected the rest many days later. It was Friday, the last day of the working week, and as I paid the money into court, I breathed a huge sigh of relief. I nearly hadn't made it, and the consequences of defaulting, even by a few days, had been made very clear to me.

Once the debts had been settled, I sat down immediately to write a letter of protest about the way in which the European Commission had behaved, enclosing a copy of the letter and receipt sent me by the Commission. I sent my letter to the leaders of each political group in the European Parliament, to all the members of the Legal Affairs Committee, and to the individual M.E.P.s from all parties who had been supporting me inside and outside the European Parliament. I also sent a copy to my lawyer, Erich Diefenbacher, in Berne.

To all concerned

The enclosed photocopies are self-explanatory.

The Commission knew that on May 30th, 1980 at the latest I had to pay certain debts, as had been illustrated by my lawyer, Dr Erich Diefenbacher, and by Messrs Glinne and Caborn of the European Parliament.

After the debate in the European Parliament, Strasbourg on May 23rd, 1980, when the Donnez document was fully approved, the E.E.C. Commission did nothing. Until on May 29th, '80 (the last working day before I had to pay the mentioned debts) a junior official of the Commission telephoned me at my house in Latina and informed me that the E.E.C. Commission would grant me only Lire 50 millions on condition that I would accept the text of the enclosed letter and would sign the enclosed receipt. I consulted with Mr Jean-Pierre Simon of the Socialist Group (who in turn consulted with Mr Glinne) and on their advice I accepted the Lire 50 millions. Even though this sum is only a fraction of the amount of debts I have to pay. The E.E.C. Commission Official (Mr Mensching of Schlieder's office) phoned me around lunchtime on May 29th, '80 and instructed me to travel to Rome E.E.C. Commission Offices and collect the cheque, and sign the receipt mentioned.

I could not refuse. This morning (May 30th, '80) I already changed the cheque and paid some debts to keep out of prison. I certainly expect much more support from the E.E.C. Commission and believe that I should get at least around DM one million (£300,000) as a total from the E.E.C. Commission . . .'

Erich Diefenbacher's office had managed to track him down after I had phoned them on Thursday, and he had immediately sent a telex to the Commission, which they had ignored. He now protested vigorously as well.

May 30th, 1980
Subject : Mr Stanley Adams, Latina
Mr President and Gentlemen,
Reference is made to my telex 371 of May 29th, 1980 and your letter of the same date communicated orally to Mr Adams by your emissary in Rome.

I must emphatically protest against this unfair and unusual procedure. Unusual because it is known to at least two members of the Commission and furthermore to a number of high-ranking officials that I have been representing Mr Adams for more than 1½ years in this particular case (E.E.C./Hoffmann-La Roche/Swiss Confederation).

It is a fundamental principle of legal practice in all of Europe that authorities, knowing of the fact that an attorney is being retained, deal without any exception only with this lawyer and not directly with his client. For reasons unknown to me – which I ask you respectfully to explain to me at your earliest convenience – this rule has not been followed by the Commission and its officials when transmitting the 'payment for humanitarian reasons only' to Mr Adams on May 29th, 1980. Mr Adams, I am speaking on his behalf based on my general power of attorney, is *not* accepting the payment of Lit. 50 million 'as final settlement' of damages suffered as direct consequence of the actions of the E.E.C. Commission and/or its representatives (evidence for this may be produced at any time). I therefore ask you to reply at your earliest convenience to this telex/letter and the one of May 29th, 1980, the text of which is for reasons of security repeated at the end of this telex/letter.

I send a copy of this to the Socialist Group of the European Parliament, to Mr Mauro Ferri, Chairman, and Mr George Donnez, Rapporteur of the Legal Affairs Committee on the Adams case.

The telex that Diefenbacher had sent the Commission reminded them formally that he was representing me and that all negotiations in my interest were being carried out by him. He had asked them to transfer immediately the amount of money needed to avoid my arrest and told them he would be in contact with them on his return to Switzerland.

Diefenbacher was furious at what had happened. He had been going through the court records of my case in detail and had unearthed evidence which linked the Commission directly to my misfortunes. He had not yet told the Commission, nor had he told me, presumably as he was waiting to see whether a just settlement could be reached amicably and without embarrassing the people involved. When the Commission refused to accept any responsibility for what had happened he changed his mind. His statement referring to damages 'suffered as direct consequence of the actions of the E.E.C. Commission and/or its representatives' was the opening shot in what was to prove a long battle.

Three weeks later Richard Caborn and Ernest Glinne met with Roy Jenkins, President of the E.E.C. Commission, to discuss the Commission's actions following the Donnez report. They raised a number of questions including the state of negotiations with Switzerland, the level of my compensation, and the payment of Erich Diefenbacher's fees. It had always been understood that Diefenbacher would be paid by the Commission, as my previous lawyer Georges Bollag had been paid, and the Donnez report asked the Commission to give me every assistance if I should choose to go to the Human Rights Commission, for which I would need a lawyer. The Donnez report had also asked the E.E.C. Commission to ask the Swiss to re-open my case, and Erich Diefenbacher had already done some of the groundwork for that. There was no way I could get to the Human Rights Commission without first having my case re-opened in Switzerland, otherwise I would have run foul of the six-month rule again. One of the amendments initially put forward by the Socialist Group to the Donnez report had been 'to make an extraordinary payment to cover the legal fees of Mr Adams' representation since . . . February 1979' (when I had withdrawn my mandate from Georges Bollag and given it to Erich Diefenbacher). The amendment was withdrawn in order to speed up the debate of the report only because assurances were given that it had always been intended that Diefenbacher's fees would be paid by the Commission. He was simply taking over where Dr Bollag had left off. So far Diefenbacher had not received any money at all for the time he had spent on my case since early 1979 and he was understandably getting restless.

On June 24th, Dr Diefenbacher wrote to Roy Jenkins, asking for a meeting to discuss the question of the final settlement of Mr Stanley Adams' compensation and requesting that Mr C. D. Ehlermann, Director-General of the Legal Services of the E.E.C., be present at the negotiations. At the same time he enclosed a copy of his power of attorney, detailed the work he had

had to do for me so far, and enclosed a bill for his services, with the comment:

> Right from the beginning of my mandate it has been under-stood by all Parliamentarians supporting Mr Adams' case that my fees and expenses must be paid by the E.E.C. It was only based on this assertion made to me by Messrs John Prescott, Ernest Glinne, Georges Donnez, Christopher Prout and many others that I could dedicate the necessary working time to Mr Adams' case. My findings have been confirmed in all respects by the Legal Affairs Committee in the Draft Resolution of 31 March 1980 (Doc. 1–44/80) which with the well known amendment has been passed by the European Parliament unanimously on 23rd May 1980. An amendment proposed by the Socialist Group concerning the payment of my legal fees has been withdrawn upon the assertion by Mr Mauro Ferri, Chairman of the Legal Affairs Committee, and Mr Georges Donnez, Rapporteur of this Committee that it goes without saying that my fees will be paid by the E.E.C.

By July 9th, Roy Jenkins had still not replied. Diefenbacher wrote to Ernest Glinne and Richard Caborn, 'Referring to my letters of June 24th, 1980 to Roy Jenkins, I have to inform you that again I am without any reply from the Commission . . .'

What's more the Isle of Wight rumour had surfaced again. I didn't really need money. I was just a con-man who had de-frauded the Italian State of development money and used it to speculate on the property market, and owned considerable amounts of real estate in Italy and the Isle of Wight. Diefen-bacher's letter assured Caborn and Glinne, 'Adams denies under oath to have been engaged in any sort of real estate operations in Italy and abroad. Please let me have details concerning this fact . . . '

On July 18th, eighty days after Diefenbacher and myself had complained about the Commission's behaviour following the Donnez report, neither Roy Jenkins nor any Commission official had deigned to reply to us. I wrote to Ernest Glinne:

> I have this morning sent you a telegram to inform you that Dr Erich Diefenbacher, my attorney at Berne, had informed me

that he has not received any replies to his letters of May 30th and June 24th addressed to Mr Roy Jenkins, President of the E.E.C. Commission at Brussels. Dr Diefenbacher is rightly upset, considering that the Judicial Committee and Parliament passed the Donnez report some months ago. Furthermore, Dr Diefenbacher wrote his last letters to Jenkins dated June 24th, on your own advice, after you and Richard Caborn had meetings with Roy Jenkins in Brussels, and my attorney was given to understand that when Jenkins received the mentioned letters he (Jenkins) would act somehow. The whole matter concerns discussing the final sums of damages payable by the E.E.C. Commission to me and my children. Indeed, in his letters, Dr Diefenbacher asked Roy Jenkins that Mr Ehlermann, Director-General Legal Services of the E.E.C., be present at such discussions.

I do not know what can be done. All I know is that I am under the impression that everything is ending in nothingness, after all the work of the Group and the Legal Affairs Committee and many friendly M.E.P.s to get some justice for me. It is beginning to appear to me, that all the work of the European Parliament in this particular matter means very little or nothing at all, if the E.E.C. Commission does not wish to act as requested by Parliament. In addition to the fact I have not got what I expect from the Commission, my attorney has not been paid, so he is not able to take certain actions in my name, for lack of funds . . .

I need not repeat that the small sum given me by the E.E.C. Commission on May 29th, 1980 has long since been used to pay some debts. Indeed I still have many debts to pay. I am back again in the position of not having even enough money for food, and having to start borrowing once more.

In the same letter I discussed the possibility of starting a number of court cases. When I had met with Diefenbacher and the Socialist Group in Strasbourg, in November 1979 (the month before I was arrested by the Italian police), we had drawn up a plan of campaign. The first move had been to try and persuade the E.E.C. to provide compensation quietly. Then we were going to consider the possibilities of going to the Swiss courts to re-open my case and ask for rehabilitation, and after that we were going to consider the possibility of starting a civil case against Roche and the Swiss government jointly for damages. Now that the E.E.C. had failed to provide the proper compensation, I also wanted to sue the E.E.C. Commission for moral and material damages. And I wanted to set all the cases in motion immediately. The only problem was that there was no money to initiate court actions with. If the Commission were not paying Diefenbacher, then he couldn't even open the Swiss case, never mind examine the possibility of sueing Roche. We had never expected to have to sue the E.E.C. Commission, so the problem of the Commission paying Diefenbacher to sue themselves had never been contemplated! Funds for that would ,obviously have to come from elsewhere.

Not that we had given up all hope of getting a satisfactory answer from the E.E.C. Commission. On July 23rd Diefenbacher wrote again to Roy Jenkins. 'Reference is made to my letter to you of 24 June 1980 which has not received any reply. Will you be kind enough to let me have your answer within the next few days . . . ' Richard Caborn added his weight to a request for an answer. Writing on July 23rd as well, he said:

Dear Roy,
At the meeting with Ernest Glinne and myself, on June 17th 1980, you indicated that you would send me a report of the proceedings of the Mixed Committee of the E.E.C. and the Swiss Confederation which met to discuss action on the Donnez report (the Adams case). I have to inform you that I have yet to receive this report.

I would be grateful if you would also notify me of the nature of your reply to Erich Diefenbacher's (Adams attorney) letter, 24th June 1980 requesting payment of his legal fees.

On July 29th, exactly two months after their initial letter to me, the Commission replied. The letter was not written by Roy Jenkins, but by Claus-Dieter Ehlermann, the German Director-General of the Commission's Legal Services, and was addressed to Erich Diefenbacher.

The Commission has instructed me to reply to your letters to President Jenkins of 24 June and 23 July 1980.
I refer to the letter to Mr Adams from the Secretary General

of the Commission of 29th May 1980. As this letter clearly states the Commission awarded to Mr Adams the sum referred to in the same letter as an ex gratia payment and on strictly humanitarian grounds, although the Commission has no responsibility towards Mr Adams in any respect; it also stated that such payment was the last financial assistance which Mr Adams will receive from the Commission.

As regards your claim for payment of fees and expenses, the Commission, as you know, has never as far as it is concerned, adopted an attitude giving rise to the supposition that it would pay such fees. It therefore cannot possibly undertake to pay them.

It would be an understatement to say that my lawyer was angry. He phoned me as soon as the letter arrived (early August 1980) and it was then that he told me there was no way that the Commission could disclaim responsibility for what had happened, as it was one of their own officials who had told Roche in the first place that I was the informant. The man who had named me, Erich Diefenbacher said, was the Director-General of the Competition department, Willi Schlieder himself.

To me that was the ultimate horror. The information I had given on Hoffmann-La Roche had been given to DG4, the Competition department. Schlieder was in charge of the department and answerable only to the Commissioner, Albert Borschette. It was Schlieder I had met and talked to on my first visit to Brussels, it was Schlieder who I had turned to for help when I was arrested in Switzerland, and Schlieder to whom my anonymous cell mate had written with details of my imprisonment. When I encountered problems in Italy it was Schlieder, and his department, that I turned to for help, and it was Schlieder, according to the court files, who had named me as the E.E.C. informant to the Roche lawyer and Swiss M.P. Dr Claudius Alder.

I had always wondered why Roche suspected me in particular. There were at least twenty other people with access to the same information, and I had given them no cause for suspicion when I worked there. Until now I had thought it was mainly guesswork, combined with a natural inclination to blame someone who had left, rather than someone still there. I now realized it was more than that. I don't know exactly when it was that Willi Schlieder first named me to Claudius Alder. It might have been at the meeting held with Alder after the Roche companies in the E.E.C. countries had been raided in 1974 or it might have been later. Whenever it was, it compounded a mistake that DG4 had already made, a mistake I now learnt that had first focused suspicion on me. Official documents (which came into my possession later) proved beyond any doubt that the DG4 inspectors from the Competition department's headquarters had shown the actual papers I had given the Commission to representatives from Roche and had allowed them to photocopy those papers. Like most office papers these had internal markings on them, hand-written notes and jotted comments, which gave away their source. Until Roche saw these, they could have had no suspicion that I was the informant. For a department supposedly trained in the techniques and principles of investigation, and with the avowed aim of protecting their sources of information at all costs, this was an extraordinary mistake to have made. The greenest of journalists knows better than to break the rule that you never show to anyone copies of original documents received with markings on them in case they incriminate your source. This first mistake was now reinforced by Willi Schlieder actually naming me as the informant. The police file holds two references to this (one specific), and the published Swiss court judgment refers to the fact as well. On page 216 in volume 2 of the *Record of the Criminal Proceedings against Stanley Adams*, paragraph 4 and 5 of the memo of investigating officer Werner Wick of February 14th, 1975 reads:

Telephone conversation with Mr Portmann of Dr Bollag's law office. He demanded to see Mr Adams on account of an appeal against continuate imprisonment; at the same time he declared that he would be interested to know the actual state of investigation. Then Portmann appeared at 14.30 hours. He was informed that Dr Alder had made the remark when speaking to the undersigned that Mr Adams' attorney should be told that a high-ranking E.E.C. official, member of the Competition department, had named Adams as bearer of the documents and as informant. Possibly Mr Adams' attorney on account of this could cause Adams to make a confession.

Since the undersigned, in different informal conversations,

had attempted to cause Adams to confess unfortunately without success – this communication has been passed on to Mr Portmann. At the same time he received the opportunity to speak alone with Adams. Mr Portmann informed the undersigned that today at 15.30 hours, he will have a conference with Dr Alder.

On page 70 of volume 1 of the *Record of the Criminal Proceedings against Stanley Adams*, the memo of investigating officer Wick of March 24th, 1975 reads:

Phone call from Dr Alder. He would like to inform that Mr Schlieder from the E.E.C. Competition department had informed him on 1 February 1975 by telephone, amongst other things, that Stanley Adams had been the informant.

The statement on page 9 in the Basle court judgment of July 1st, 1976 (which Dr Bollag had forwarded to Schlieder at the time) reads:

The fact that Adams has been the informer results also from the telephone-communication of Dr Schlieder from the E.E.C. Competition department to Dr Alder, attorney of plaintiff (file page 240).

Why Willi Schlieder should have given Roche's lawyer my name remains a mystery. Perhaps it was simply carelessness, but I would have thought that the Director-General of an investigative body would know better. Even if you assume the enquirer already knows the identity of an informer you never confirm it. It is true that I had left Roche by the time it happened, but I had never authorized the E.E.C. Commission to use my name in any way unless they needed to produce me as a court witness. If they didn't need to do that, then I wished to remain totally anonymous, and I made that quite clear from the start. The fact that Schlieder had named me as his informant was obviously quite important in the interrogation leading up to my trial and in the trial itself, and there is no doubt that I was arrested in the first place, and my wife interrogated, because of mistakes made by the European Commission in their handling of the investigation, whether by showing

Roche the papers I had given them, or by naming me then or subsequently does not really matter. The truth is that I had trusted them, and they betrayed that trust.

I have always been – and still am – a great believer in the idea of a European Community. The Rome Treaty which set it up may have been written more with the interests of big business in mind, than the interests of the millions of voters in the European Community, but for all its faults, and there were faults, it seemed to me that the powers vested in the Community, and carried out by the Commission, did create a real chance of protecting the interests of the individual against the threat of multinational practices if the political will was there to do it. Until the E.E.C. had been formed such practices could only be partially controlled by the individual countries because their authority stopped at their borders. It was for this reason that I had chosen the E.E.C. Commission as the appropriate authority to deal with Roche and the other multinationals I had reported to them. Seven years later I was realizing that the E.E.C. had no interest whatsoever in the individual and was quite prepared to sacrifice anyone who got in the way or inconvenienced their bureaucratic progress. I had served my function by giving them the information they needed. (In fact, I gave them more information than they needed.) I had then been discarded. My name had been given to the lawyer of a company powerful enough to crush me, and when the company had taken action, under the auspices of the Swiss government, the E.E.C. Commission had stood by and watched and had later refused me any real compensation for what had happened, despite their responsibility for it, and despite their being in-structed by a unanimous European Parliament to make good any financial and psychological damage I might have suffered.

I was beginning to think that the European Parliament, for all its efforts on my behalf, was a meaningless institution without the power to force the Commission to do anything. There had been a great song and dance about the new era of European democracy when the European Parliament was elected directly by the people for the first time, in 1979, but what use was a democratic election of M.E.P.s if they had no say in how the Community was run?

Richard Caborn and Erich Diefenbacher both tried once more to get satisfaction from the E.E.C. Commission with regard to myself and to the payment of Erich's fees. Caborn wrote again to Roy Jenkins on August 8th.

Thank you for acknowledging receipt of my letter (23rd July 1980). However, I have since been informed by Erich Diefenbacher that no assistance is to be forthcoming for the service he rendered to Mr Stanley Adams. This was one of the main points Mr Glinne and I raised with you at our meeting in Strasbourg on 19th June 1980.

I would therefore request, without any commitment on either side, a meeting with yourself, Mr Glinne, and Erich Diefenbacher, so that a more detailed explanation can be given to what I believe, along with many other organizations and ordinary people in Europe, to be a very important case.

I hope this suggestion meets with your approval.

Diefenbacher wrote to Mr Ehlermann on August 18th.

Confirming receipt of your letter 29th July 1980 I regret to have to inform you that the attitude of the E.E.C. Commission is not acceptable. I have come into possession of evidence proving in a singular way the direct responsibility of the E.E.C. Commission for Mr Adams' most lamentable fate.

As far as my own fee is concerned I refer to the assurance I had from Mr Mauro Ferri, Chairman, and Mr Georges Donnez, Rapporteur of the Legal Affairs Committee, as well as other well-informed M.E.P.s.

I therefore have to insist on the conference asked for in my letters 24 June and 23 July 1980 to President Jenkins.

My own situation by now was extremely precarious. By giving me enough money to pay some debts, but not all of them, the E.E.C. had placed me in an impossible situation. I had paid the pressing debts only to find that as soon as word got round that some creditors had been paid, everybody else began demanding their money too. Some of my friends who had loaned me money and had not been paid were deeply hurt. Because they had not pressed me for their money back, they had been ignored, while the more ruthless creditors had been paid first. And there was nothing I could do about it, I had no more money left to pay them with. A number of other creditors then began the whole process again, filing bankruptcy petitions with the court in the hope of getting some of their money back. If the European Commission had made any representations to Italy following the Donnez report (and judging by their reaction to the request during the debate on the Donnez report, I doubted they had), it had made no difference to my life.

I was still facing a charge of fraud, bankruptcy was looming, and the grant and finance agencies had put in a claim for the full amount owing them which was the first move in their threat to foreclose and sell off my land. My children were still living with their grandparents because I could not afford to feed them. In addition I had recently discovered that Stephanie, my youngest daughter, had very little sight in her right eye. She should have been receiving treatment for it, and going regularly to hospital, but treatment cost money and I did not have it. I was haunted by the thought that it was my fault that we hadn't noticed and corrected the problem sooner. Medical bills were always a terror to me and I hadn't been able to afford regular checkups for the children. (Stephanie had been under three when Mariléne died.)

On August 26th I wrote a letter to Erich Diefenbacher and a number of friendly M.E.P.s:

Abandoned as I feel at the present time, I have decided to write you this letter. My feelings and morale generally at this moment are so low, that I may practically promise that the present writing could be the last. So many words have been said; so many others have been written; but in practical terms I stand today where I stood in early 1975 (just out of Swiss prison) if not worse. I do not even have enough to eat and enough funds to help bring up my three daughters decently . . .

In the Donnez report prepared by the Legal Affairs Committee of the European Parliament and then voted unanimously by the European Parliament in May '80, there are several points, which were aimed at providing me and my children with immediate practical help. Three months have now passed since the document was voted by elected men of a Parliament which represents the major part of the European continent. Yet, E.E.C. officials, paid as they are by the taxpayers of the nine member countries, and therefore there in their offices daily supposed to serve the interests of the people of the nine countries concerned, have in many ways prevented justice being carried out in my respect . . .

It is futile to repeat that I am penniless. Perhaps it would move your hearts more if I inform you that my youngest daughter (Stephanie, now aged eight) has lost completely the sight in her right eye. This is due to lack of care and attention of all kinds, which in turn is due to lack of employment/income and funds in hand on my part . . .

On September 3rd Roy Jenkins, by now making his presence felt as a leader of the forthcoming Social Democratic Party in Britain, replied to Richard Caborn, refusing a second meeting, again saying that there was no prospect of the Commission being ready to assist Dr Diefenbacher, and repeating that 'the Commission, without any obligation on its part and on strictly humanitarian grounds, granted Mr Adams an exceptional ex gratia payment and made it clear that this was its last intervention on his behalf.'

On September 24th, Dr Ehlermann replied to Erich Diefenbacher in similar vein: ' . . . I regret to have to inform you that the Commission does not think that any useful purpose could be served by any meeting of the kind that you suggest.'

The Commission had definitely decided that I would get no money and that my lawyer would not be paid for the work he had done so far, never mind anything he might do in the future. They were no longer prepared even to discuss the subject. As far as they were concerned the file was closed. Adams no longer existed.

Glinne and Caborn had asked Roy Jenkins at their meeting in June what action had been taken in the Joint Committee and through other diplomatic channels, since the Donnez report had been adopted and the motion for resolution voted for. This motion had been specifically amended to meet the needs of my re-starting a court case in Switzerland. It had called on the Commission to 'ask the competent bodies of the Swiss Confederation to instruct the General Prosecutor of the Swiss Confederation to demand, by way of a review procedure, the re-examination and re-opening of the case based upon Article 113 of the Swiss Federal Constitution and Article 6 of the European Convention on Human Rights . . . '

It had also suggested that the Swiss might be invited to consider the possibility of an amnesty for me. The short reply to their query about what had been done was 'nothing'. Roy Jenkins in his reply reiterated the statement the Commission had made during the debate, that the Commission and Swiss authorities were prepared to discuss in the Joint Committee any problems arising over the interpretation of Article 23, and said they were now in the process of doing so.

By refusing to take the Swiss to task and insisting on 'friendly' discussions, the Commission were not prepared to carry out Parliament's wishes. Parliament would have to be consoled with the fact that the Swiss did know about it, even if they had not been, and would not be, officially informed about the decision of the European Parliament.

The European Parliament again returned to the fray. On September 19th, 1980 they passed an emergency motion for resolution, tabled by Ernest Glinne (Belgium), Richard Caborn (U.K.), and Johan van Minnen (Holland) on behalf of the Socialist Group.

The resolution read:

The European Parliament
– having regard to the report by Mr Donnez as amended and adopted by Parliament at its May 1980 session,
1) Invites the Commission to ask the competent bodies of the Swiss Confederation to instruct the General Prosecutor of the Swiss Confederation to demand the re-examination and re-opening of the case based upon Article 113 of the Swiss Federal Constitution and Article 6 of the European Convention on Human Rights:
2) Instructs its President to forward this resolution to the Commission.

Justification (for urgent procedure)
The failure of the E.E.C. Commission to take any action on a unanimous decision by Parliament.

This resolution, like its predecessor, was ignored by the E.E.C. Commission.

But if the E.E.C. Commission had little sympathy with my position, that was not the case with the ordinary people of the

European Community. The programmes transmitted in March and May of that year had generated a lot of interest and concern for me, and from that came some very practical help. In September 1980, in Great Britain, a 'Stanley Adams Appeal Committee' was founded, and an appeal launched to try and raise sufficient money to enable me to leave Italy and come to Britain with my family. It had started with the B.B.C. Radio Four programme, *Real Evidence*. Among the many people who heard the programme and responded to it had been the wife of Mr John O. Lyle, president of the Tate and Lyle Group (the sugar conglomerate). She had insisted that her husband do something about my case. (He had been shaving at the time and had not heard the programme, but he managed to get a transcript from the B.B.C. and find out what it was about.) John Lyle was also Chairman of Aims of Industry, a British free enterprise organization, and he asked the director of Aims, Mr Michael Ivens, to look into the matter. In April 1980, Michael Ivens wrote to me via Ritchie Cogan, then producer of the Radio Four programme at the B.B.C.

Dear Mr Adams,
I was very shocked indeed to learn from the B.B.C. programme of the way you have been treated.

This organization was set up 38 years ago to put the case for free enterprise. But we believe that free enterprise must be responsible as well as enterprising.

I am afraid we cannot help with money – because that is not what we are set up to do – but I will certainly do all I can personally to help in the political and communications field . . .

I replied on April 26th, 1980, thanking him for the letter that Ritchie Cogan had forwarded. I explained that my most pressing problem at the time was money, but that the Donnez report was coming up for debate at the end of May and I would be very grateful for any help in persuading Members of the European Parliament to vote in support of the resolution and report. I told him that Richard Caborn was in charge of the motion, and that I was also trying to obtain a British passport, and John Prescott, the Labour M.P. for Hull East, was looking after that for me in the House of Commons, but anything Michael Ivens felt he could do to help would be very useful. When it later transpired that the political moves had foundered on the obstinacy of the European Commission, Michael Ivens and others got together to form the Appeal Committee as an alternative solution to my financial problems. The members of the committee were drawn from all political parties. One of the most remarkable factors about my case has been the way in which I have consistently been supported by people with radically different philosophies of life, people who would previously have thought it impossible they should even share a platform on any issue. The Appeal Committee followed this pattern. It was made up of Michael Ivens, director of Aims; John Lyle, president of Tate and Lyle; Sir John Foster, K.B.E., Q.C., chairman of 'Justice' (a law reform society) and a former Conservative M.P.; Eric Moonman, a former Labour M.P. and director of the Centre for Contemporary Studies; Peter Paterson, author and journalist; John Torode, leader writer for the *Guardian*; Edward Holloway, director of the Economic Research Council; the Rt Hon. Peter Archer, Q.C., M.P., a former Solicitor General under the Labour government; the distinguished academic, Professor A. R. Ilersic; and solicitor Ivor Walker, a Labour lawyer. Sir Charles Fletcher-Cooke, Q.C., M.P., former Conservative Home Office minister and currently Chairman of the Legal Affairs Committee of the House of Commons, took over from Sir John Foster, who sadly died in January 1982. At a later date, Arthur Davidson, Q.C., M.P., Opposition front bench spokesman on legal affairs, and Jennifer Horne, a barrister, also joined the Committee. All the secretarial work was done by Mrs Wendy Willson in her own spare time, without any compensation.

The appeal began with a campaign in the British press. Articles and letters pleading my case appeared in *The Times*, the *Financial Times*, the *Daily Telegraph*, the *Guardian*, the *Sunday Telegraph*, the *New Standard* and in different local and provincial newspapers. A specimen letter in the *Guardian* (September 1980) read:

In 1976 the E.E.C. fined Hoffmann-La Roche more than DM 1 million for breaches of the E.E.C. laws on free competition. The information on Hoffmann-La Roche's malpractices in the vitamins market was provided confidentially by Stanley Adams who worked for that company.

His identity was leaked to the company by someone at E.E.C. headquarters and he was arrested in Switzerland and charged with violating Switzerland's industrial secrecy laws. He spent three months in prison before being given a year's imprisonment suspended for three years. As a result, Mr Adams' wife committed suicide and he went to Italy to be with his daughters Nathalie now aged 12, Alexandra 10, and Stephanie 8. His life was in ruins.

After several years of pressure, the E.E.C. finally paid him a derisory £20,000 which only cleared about one tenth of his costs and debts. He and his family are in Italy, are short of food, and one of his daughters has gone virtually blind in one eye. He wants to make a home in Britain. He held a British passport until Malta became independent in 1964 and was a British consul overseas.

We are anxious to raise money to relieve Stanley Adams in his present dire situation, and to rectify the injustice he has suffered.

Anyone wanting to help should send a cheque to the Stanley Adams Appeal, c/o Birkbeck Montagu's and Co., 7 Bridge Street, London, EC 4A 4AT.

Yours faithfully,
Peter Archer, (Sir) John Foster, Edward Holloway, Prof. A. R. Ilersic, Michael Ivens, John Lyle, Eric Moonman, Peter Paterson, John Torode, Ivor Walker.

The setting up of the Appeal Committee gave me hope that I might after all be able to get out of Italy. I had already been making plans to leave, illegally if necessary, but without funds or the promise of support in Britain when I arrived there, I could do nothing. With the money given me by the E.E.C. Commission I had only been able to settle the most pressing of my debts; other pending debts were now coming to the fore and would soon make it imperative for me to leave the country to avoid arrest, if I didn't have the money to pay them. The court held my passport, but it had expired at the end of May, and no one had noticed. Once it had expired, I had written to the authorities in Malta, giving details of the passport and expiry date, and asking for a new passport, saying, quite correctly, that I couldn't manage to lay my hands on my old one at present. Since all the passport details were correct, and the old one had obviously expired and was now invalid, I had been sent a new passport. This I kept carefully hidden in my home, and told nobody that I possessed it. There was no way, however, that I could leave Italy without my children. If I jumped bail to leave, then I would be arrested if I ever returned to the country. I couldn't contemplate a situation in which I was unable to visit the country where my children lived. What if anything happened to one of them while I was trying to set up a home for them to come to, and I was unable to get to them? What if, once I had left the country, something intervened to prevent them following me when I was ready and I could not go back to fetch them out? It was just too dangerous. Equally, it seemed to me, I could not simply arrive in a new country with three children and nowhere to stay and no money to support us. For one thing, the immigration authorities would probably not allow us in, and for another, the children had been moved around enough already without having to face a bout of absolute homelessness. So I was stuck.

This dilemma was resolved by a phone call in early September 1980. It was from someone I had been in contact with since the making of Granada Television's *World in Action* programme. One of the crew members had asked me which particular aspect of all my problems bothered me the most, and I had replied that my main worry was not so much for myself, as for the children. I was worried about their stability, their education, and the danger that if something happened to me again, they would find themselves on their own without any support. She said she would see if she could do anything to help, and we kept in touch. In mid September she phoned me to say that through personal contacts she had managed to arrange boarding-school places for my daughters in a school called Kingsmead, a co-educational school in Hoylake near Liverpool, who were prepared to give special consideration to my children because of my history. If I thought it was a good idea, and was prepared to let my children go, then the fees would be taken care of by the school and an educational trust. The initial offer was for two terms in order to give me a chance to sort myself out, knowing that the children were safe in England and well cared for. After that the situation would be reviewed. If the children were to go, they had to go soon because the school term had already started and it was important they didn't miss too much.

It was not an easy decision, and not one that I could make on the phone there and then. I said I would talk with my daughters and phone back in a day or two. I didn't know what was the right thing to do. I had never been separated from my daughters for a long period, apart from the time recently that they had spent with their grandparents. When they were little Mariléne and I had discussed boarding schools together and decided firmly against them. Mariléne had been sent away to a succession of different schools and had not been very happy there. She didn't want her children to go through the same experience. One of the reasons we had decided to move to Italy and set up a business there was so we could have our daughters at home with us going to local schools and not see them suffer the disruptive education they would have had if I'd stayed with Roche and travelled abroad, moving from country to country at the end of each three-year contract. But the situation was a little different now. Mariléne was dead, the school in England sounded a lot more homely and warmer than some of the convents Mariléne herself had been to, and if the children were in England and had somewhere to stay, then it gave me a better chance of escaping from Italy myself and following them to Britain. The children had only recently returned to me from their grandparents, because I didn't want them to miss any more school and the new term was about to start. It had been wonderful seeing them again, and I wished desperately that I could keep them with me, but I wasn't sure it was the best thing to do. I discussed the whole matter with them, and told them what had been suggested, and what it would mean. If they went to England, I said, then I would follow them. But the final decision I left to them. They were growing up now and were mature for their age. Nathalie was twelve, Sandy ten, and Stephanie was eight. 'Talk it over amongst yourselves,' I said, 'and let me know what you decide. If you decide you want to go, then you shall go, but if you decide you are happy and prefer to stay where you are, and you don't want to move, or leave Italy, then I won't make you. You can stay here and go to school where you go now.' They listened carefully, asked a lot of questions, and then disappeared upstairs to talk amongst themselves. Eventually they came down from their rooms and said they had decided. They wanted to go to England, if I could promise them that I would follow. I promised.

The Appeal Committee sent me enough money to buy their tickets to Britain and to get what we needed to help them face the cold of a British winter. Michael Ivens also sent money from the Appeal Fund direct to the school so they could be equipped properly with warm clothes when they arrived. I bought just enough to wrap them up for the journey. It was a hectic time, packing and shopping and just being together for a last few days.

On September 19th, the day the European Parliament debated my case yet again, I took my children to Rome airport and put them on a British Airways plane to Manchester, where they were being met by friends who would take them to the school and see them safely settled in. They looked so vulnerable standing there before they boarded, with their airline name-tags hanging neatly from their necks so they shouldn't get lost, and their few precious possessions clutched in their hands, I could hardly bear it. They were half excited and half frightened. Nathalie had a little school English, and had been trying to learn as much as she could, but Sandy and Stephanie spoke no English at all. To go to a strange country to live among strangers who speak a language you don't understand is a frightening experience for most people, never mind for three little girls who would have neither father nor mother to help them. They were very brave, and very trusting. I prayed fervently as I left the airport that their trust wouldn't be betrayed, either by me or by the people who were going to look after them.

16 Escape to Britain

One day in July 1980 I had been at home in Latina when the phone rang. A man's voice on the other end said, 'My name is Marc Nelissen. You don't know me, but I have read about you and would like to help.' He told me later that he had read two articles in Belgian newspapers, one of which, in *Tribune Libre*, had been written by Ernest Glinne and had described my situation immediately after the Donnez report and resolution had been voted on, and one of which had been published in a Flemish-language magazine called *Knack*. Marc Nelissen now wanted to know the best way that he and his brother Luc could help me. Marc was an accountant and Luc an industrialist. I told him that my greatest need was for money, and he asked me a lot of details about how I lived, what I lived on, what my main problems were. I explained that I did not even have a car to take my three daughters to school each day, as my vehicles had been sequestrated some months ago. We talked for a long time and eventually he rang off, saying he would come back to me shortly. Later he phoned to say that he and his brother Luc had discussed the matter and decided to give me a second-hand car. I accepted gratefully. The next time the Nelissen brothers phoned it was to say that they had found a car and were getting it serviced and fit for the road, and when it was ready they would drive it to me, which they did. They left their home near Antwerp on a Friday and arrived at my house in Latina late on the Saturday night. I entertained them for a couple of days and then they took the train to Rome airport where they bought tickets for a flight back to Belgium. It was an incredible thing for two people to do. They had never met me. They had only heard what I had done and what had happened to me. They didn't know if they would like me or not, and yet they were prepared to give me their time, their money and their energy. I was touched and grateful.

Between receiving the car in July and that day in September when my children left to go to school in England, I felt that things had changed. Driving home that afternoon I was determined that somehow I would keep my promise and follow my children to England. The very fact that I was driving gave me hope. I had a car again and the car was another sign to me that ordinary people were prepared to help even if the political institutions of Europe were unable or unwilling to do so.

Now I could pursue my plans to leave Italy. I had a new passport safely hidden among the books in my library. I knew that I would never be able to fly out because the airports were too closely monitored, and that my best hope lay in either crossing on foot over the mountains or driving across at a busy checkpoint. Of the two I preferred the latter, if only because in this way I would be able to take a considerable amount of luggage with me to England.

I still hoped that it would be possible to leave legally, with all my debts paid and the case against me withdrawn, but that was beginning to look increasingly unlikely. There were two possible ways of finding the money. One was to initiate court cases for damages, in the hope that someone might be persuaded into settling out of court, and the other was to sell the farm, although I had been trying unsuccessfully for some time to do that. The mortgage on the land, and the building work that had been done, meant it was only really sellable to someone who wanted to take over the business and continue to build the pig farm, and then it was only just viable. In a discussion with the Socialist Group of the European Parliament and myself my lawyer Erich Diefenbacher listed the following cases as a possibility:

1) Re-opening the Criminal Proceedings for violation of *Art. 273* Criminal Code ('Economic Espionage') for not taking in consideration the *Swiss Constitution Art. 113 last chapter and Art. 6 of the European Convention on Human Rights*.
2) *Civil Proceedings* against *Hoffmann-La Roche and Co.* and *jointly* against *Roche* and the *Swiss Confederation* for damages.
3) *Criminal Proceedings* against *Willi Schlieder* and others, and *Civil Proceedings jointly* against *Schlieder* and the *E.E.C. Commission*.

The first two proceedings were palatable to the Socialist Group, but the last one clearly caused problems as Willi Schlieder was a German Socialist and German Socialist M.E.P.s were scarcely likely to support legal action against him. I think too there was a feeling that a lawsuit against the E.E.C. Commission at this stage was like admitting defeat. The European Parliament wanted a little more time to see what they could do behind the scenes. In Diefenbacher's eyes the most important case to start with was the re-opening of my trial in Switzerland. If I won that, then the road would be clear to claiming civil damages later. But of course, there were so far no funds to pay for court cases, Diefenbacher had not yet been paid for anything and, according to the European Commission, was not going to be. The Socialist Group were considering the possibility of paying for Erich Diefenbacher to prepare the first case in Switzerland, but they needed convincing that I really was totally without funds. I think some of the allegations about my investments in real estate were still floating around and it disturbed people, even if they didn't really believe them. (I wish I knew who started that rumour. It must have been started deliberately to discredit me, but I don't know precisely where it came from.) It was also difficult for people to understand how I could be in the situation I was in when I owned land worth over £100,000, if you counted the value of the work and building done so far. It just didn't make sense. I agreed with them. It didn't make sense, but that was the way it was. On November 2nd I wrote to John Prescott and Richard Caborn. (John Prescott had been making enquiries for me in Britain about the possibility of my getting a British passport if I came to the U.K.)

Dear Friends,
From the telephone conversation of last night with Richard I was able to learn of the various difficulties both in the Euro-Socialist Group regarding providing me with funds to start the case in Switzerland for my rehabilitation, and the U.K. regarding the possibility of your obtaining a British passport for me soon, and getting me into the U.K., and after that finding a job.
  Seeing this I feel it will help if I gave you at this stage some clarification on the various points, and especially on my present status in Italy. I will therefore go in order:
1) *The farm* Nobody should doubt for one moment that I do

want to sell the farm soonest possible. However, it is very difficult. I have been trying for over two years now without success. As time goes on, it will become more difficult because interests on pending debts increase, and thus the farm becomes more expensive for the prospective buyer. At this moment we are at an even stage of debts/farm value. I am dealing with two men and they have come to Latina twice already; but they have not yet managed to find the finance it takes. I must say that I am rather pessimistic about the result. Evidently if I sell I will settle every debt and would then get my passport back and leave Italy with my head high.

If I do not manage to sell then the only way out is to let the Company (owner of the farm) go bankrupt. In this case the creditors (Mediocredito, Cassa etc. etc.) would be authorized to sell 'at best' and the farm would fetch a price which would cover only part (say half) of the debts. I would be held always responsible for the balance of debts and would not get back my passport to leave Italy. In this case, even if I left Italy on the quiet (I have another travelling document) I would not ever be permitted to enter Italy without being arrested. But this does not worry me, for if I do leave Italy I would not wish to visit this country again. And once in the U.K. I would get a new British passport, presumably . . .

In accordance with Richard's guidance I will not at this stage start court cases against the E.E.C. Commission and against Willi Schlieder himself. Even though it is likely that I will secure the necessary funds and barristers available in London and Brussels for these two cases, hand in hand with Erich Diefenbacher. So I will not upset the apple cart; I will certainly wait until the Socialist Group grants what is necessary for the Swiss rehabilitation case, and Diefenbacher starts things in Switzerland in this respect, before I do anything in the other cases. And naturally, if (as Richard hopes) we manage to get Roche and E.E.C. Commission with the Swiss authorities all in the same room and settle damages humanely and privately, then I certainly will not give any trouble to Schlieder, a Socialist, who belongs to the S.P.D. of Germany; and that although the German Socialist Group Members of the Euro-Parliament would not support me in anything if I take action against their friend Schlieder, I feel sure that you two

could not possibly approve of Schlieder's action against
me . . .

I feel equally certain that you agree with my view that, if we
do not manage to settle things in a humane way privately soon
with the E.E.C. Commission and Schlieder, then with funds
obtained outside the Euro-Socialist Group I should take legal
action against the mentioned people. However I am always
ready and willing to listen to you both, for I know that you have
both always looked after my best interest.

I went on to explain that the cat was really out of the bag now as far
as Schlieder was concerned, since Diefenbacher had already
talked to several journalists about it and given them the evidence,
but I would do what I could to try and stuff it back in and suppress
the information in the hope of being able to reach an amicable
solution with the E.E.C. and refrain from embarrassing everyone.
I wasn't sure how successful I would be. I was expecting a visit
from B.B.C. *Nationwide* in a few days, and I promised that at least
I would say nothing to them about it.

On November 6th the Socialist Group decided formally to
finance the re-opening of my case in Switzerland and handed Sfr.
30,000 to Erich Diefenbacher to begin preparing the necessary
papers. Meanwhile I continued making enquiries into the possibility of fighting the other cases, without actually starting anything,
looking for lawyers who might be prepared to help me and for ways
of financing the cases which depended more on good will and an
expectation of damages than on ready cash. It looked as if there
might be ways, but there were legal difficulties as well. There was
no point, for instance, in starting a case against Roche in Switzerland because I would be certain to lose, but I had to find a way of
fighting it in Europe somewhere. I wanted to fight it in the U.K.
but I wasn't sure it was possible. On the continent there is a Law
of Attachments which means you can start a case against someone
you believe owes you damages by laying claim to some of their
property in payment of those damages. They then have to take the
initiative by going to court to get the claim removed. Sir John
Foster, K.B.E., Q.C., Chairman of Justice, had declared himself
willing to act for me, but he didn't think the U.K. had any such law
and therefore it would be difficult to bring a case in Britain, so I
had to start looking at other possibilities. I still hoped all the time

that somehow a friendly solution could be found. Going to court is a long and expensive business and I didn't want to do it unless I had to, except in the case of Switzerland. That was different. That was a matter of principle, of getting my name cleared and seeing justice done. I was determined to achieve that, even if it meant going to the European Commission of Human Rights (and from there to the Court of Human Rights), and even if it took the rest of my life.

By now I had had several letters from the children and had spoken to them on the phone. They were settling in well and seemed cheerful and happy, if occasionally a little homesick. They had made friends and were beginning to speak a little English. Several well-wishers wrote to them, giving them warmth and encouragement. One of those who wrote was Mrs Jill Lyle, wife of John Lyle of Aims of Industry and Tate & Lyle Ltd.

> Dearest Nathalie, Sandy and Stephanie,
> We are the Lyles and John Lyle runs Aims of Industry with Michael Ivens – I am Jill his wife and mother of Timothy who is 19 and working in an office and Juliet who is 17 and still at school. We first heard all about you on the radio and were very sad to know all your father had suffered and you three as well. However I am sure that is all behind you and you will be very happy in the future.
> With lots of love,
>
> The Lyles

(If Mrs Lyle had not been listening to the radio on the crucial morning, the Appeal Committee to help me would never have been set up . . .) Michael Ivens wrote to my children too, enclosing some chocolate to stave off the pangs of homesickness. Nathalie's English was now good enough to attempt a thank you letter.

> Dear Mr Ivens,
> Thank you for the three packets of chocolate. We like chocolate very much. Today I received your letter; my father told me before that he has a good friend in England, but he did not tell me that you are so very, very kind. I hope, and my two sisters Sandy and Stephanie (she is eight years old), if we can we

would like to meet you and your family. I am here from about three months; when I came here I didn't speak English, now my English is much better and I can write to you (and to my father) in English. Sandy can also a little, but she is sick, just coughs and now she rests. When your packet arrived we opened it on Sandy's bed very quickly because we were anxious to look what it contains. Now Sandy hopes to recover for the week-end when we can eat chocolate.

Thank you. Thank you very much . . . Say Goodbye to all your family.

Yours,

Nathalie and sisters

They spent their first half-term partly with friends in North Wales, and partly with friends Rod and Eunice Trotman at 'Silver Beach' on the River Dee in Hoylake. The three Trotman children (Nicky, Pip and Jeremy) and their parents quickly gave my daughters love and confidence and a feeling of belonging; they really made them feel at home. Even the Trotmans' dog 'Nelson' helped, and soon became my daughters' favourite pet.

So I had plenty of reports of how they were. I still have photos of them taken on the Welsh hillsides in the snow, a novelty for them coming as they did from the warmth of middle Italy. I was relieved to know that all was well with them, and secretly I was rather proud of the way they were coping, though I pretended to take it all for granted. They were coming home for Christmas and I was looking forward to seeing them and hearing all about their new life in Britain. A friend had lent me the money to pay for their tickets so we could be together for Christmas. After last Christmas I was determined that we should celebrate this Christmas together at all costs, and this time whatever might happen to me, I knew the children would be going back to school in Britain where they would be safe and well looked after. God willing, I intended to follow the children out of Italy as soon as possible.

On December 10th Erich Diefenbacher presented my case for re-opening in writing to the Basle Appeals Court. It was then up to the court to set a date for the hearing. The case was based on three new pieces of evidence. These were the judgment of the European Court of Justice against Roche in 1979, the report of the Legal Affairs Committee (the Donnez report) and the resolution following this adopted by the European Parliament on May 23rd. The main tenor of the argument was that my conviction had been against the Swiss Constitution as Article 113 stated that international law took precedence over national law, and my previous conviction had not sufficiently taken this into consideration. Diefenbacher also argued that under Swiss law, and under Article 6 of the European Convention of Human Rights, to which Switzerland was a signatory, the trials should not have been held in secret, since the matters being discussed were not matters of defence, nor matters too obscene for a public hearing. I was quite hopeful that this time the Swiss courts might find for me. There had been so much diplomatic manoeuvring since the last case in early 1978 that I thought, and others thought as well, that the Swiss might take this as a way out and remove a rather thorny diplomatic problem.

Christmas 1980 came and went, this time without event. The children spent their holidays with me and were full of their new life and friends, and questions as to when I was coming over to join them. 'Soon' I promised them, 'soon'. And I meant it. My situation in Italy was such that I could no longer wait for a legal solution to my problems. It was clear that any damages claim would probably take several years to process, and there had been no sign of any move within the Commission to show they were about to change their mind and offer me further compensation. The potential buyers for my pig farm had not been able to raise the necessary finance so the farm was still unsold and looked like remaining so. I would shortly be forced to go voluntarily bankrupt and there was the risk that when I did so one of my creditors' lawyers, considering the charge already outstanding against me, might add the word 'fraudulent' to the bankruptcy, thereby making it a penal case and possibly leading to my arrest again. I had no intention of waiting around to see that happen . . . On January 2nd, 1981 I wrote again to John Prescott, Richard Caborn and Erich Diefenbacher.

Dear Friends,
The storm is now gathering so fast against me, that I have decided to leave this country as soon as possible, and come to the United Kingdom, as has been suggested by you on many occasions. My Latina lawyers have to take certain steps during

January '81 with regard to the bankruptcy of my farm (company) and to avoid possible arrest I should be out of Italy before then. I will therefore travel by road (car) from here, via France and come to London, probably towards the end of January '81. I will use the travel document in my possession now, obtained from Malta. Temporary accommodation has already been arranged for me in London.

I will enter the U.K. probably through Dover customs, where I trust not to meet with any difficulties. Perhaps it would help me if I had a letter (invitation) from you, to show that I am entering the U.K. for some purpose . . .

It is evident that the contents of this letter must remain secret, since if this information was to fall into Italian hands I would be arrested immediately. This matter should not be discussed on the telephone in my house, as this is very likely under control. When necessary I could be asked to call you from another number . . .

I will travel by a car which has a Belgian number plate, and which I am authorized to drive. I will telephone you three from the Italian–French border as soon as I am out of Italy, to furnish you with full details of my whereabouts and my further travelling plans, en route to the U.K.

I wish you all a Happy New Year, and thank you in advance for your help in this matter. Kindly simply acknowledge receipt of this letter, so that I am sure it has reached its destination safely . . .

As soon as I had seen the children to Rome airport on their way back to school I started making detailed plans. I had already been offered a place to stay when I arrived in England by Michael Ivens and his wife Katherine, so I didn't have that to worry about. My brand new Maltese passport was hidden away waiting for the journey. I had a 1972 Opel Manta car with Belgian number plates to travel in. All I had to do was pack everything up without arousing suspicion and choose a date to travel. I had previously redeemed my furniture and household possessions with the money given me by the E.E.C. Commission, so now I sold the bulkier bits and packed the rest into crates ready to be railed to England after me. Arrangements were made very quietly. The last thing I wanted was to be arrested now on the eve of freedom.

When the B.B.C. *Nationwide* team had filmed me in November 1980 I had told the producer (Bernard Clark) privately of my plans and he had expressed a wish to return and film me leaving when I knew when I was going. We had arranged a codeword which I could use over the phone to him when I knew the date on which I was going. Finally I settled on Saturday January 24th, 1981, as the best day on which to travel. On the Thursday the *Nationwide* team came out and spent that day and the next filming me doing my last packing and asking me how I felt about the coming trip and the thought of arriving in England. I was too busy packing to have many thoughts of anything (those I did have were of possible arrest, and I was trying to suppress them), but I did my best to answer their questions. Early on Saturday morning, at six o'clock while it was still dark, the film crew arrived on my doorstep again. It was cold but I couldn't even offer them a cup of coffee to warm themselves up because everything was cleared away. I loaded the last suitcases into the car. It was crammed to bursting point. At seven o'clock, when the first light came, they filmed me driving the car out of the garage and on to the road outside. The road was deserted. There was no one else about at this hour on a Saturday morning, which was why I had chosen it.

I gave a last look at the house that Mariléne and I had chosen together and that had been my home for seven years, six of them without her, and then I put the memories aside and set off on the road to Rome. The B.B.C. crew followed, filming the first stages of my departure. At Rome we parted company and they flew back to England with the film. All being well we had arranged to meet again at Calais in two days' time, for the filming of the final Channel crossing into Britain.

I was on my own now. I had decided to cross the border at Ventimiglia near Nice, a route I had never taken before and where my face was unknown. It was a long drive, and I didn't arrive at the border until five that night. I hadn't stopped at all. I was too nervous to eat. I just prayed all the way that I would be able to cross the border safely.

When I reached it I pulled the car into a lay-by for a rest a little distance back, to give myself time to pull myself together and to make sure that there was a long queue of cars building up before I attempted to go through. I had dressed carefully, with suit and tie and briefcase beside me on the seat. I was in a car with Belgian number plates and I wanted to look as much like a businessman returning from a trip as possible. When quite a queue of cars had built up I nosed out of the lay-by and joined the stream of traffic moving towards the customs post. It was six o'clock on a Saturday evening and the road was busy. Foreign registration numbers were common and there were cars from Italy, Britain, America, France, Monte Carlo and myself in a Belgian car all heading for the border. The queue moved slowly. Sometimes a car would be stopped and the passports checked, sometimes the customs men simply waved cars through. I knew that if I was stopped and arrested I faced at least three years in prison. I noticed that most of the cars that were stopped had Italian number plates and I breathed a quick thank you to my Belgian benefactors. Of course, if I were stopped, I still had my passport, which was perfectly valid, and there was no reason to suspect that I would be recognized and arrested, but still, on the whole, I thought I would prefer not to be stopped. My experience in Switzerland had made me uneasy about customs posts. When my turn came it was all over very quickly. I was lucky. The Italian guard glanced casually at the Belgian number plates and waved me through. I nodded a thank you at him and drove on to the French checkpoint. Here they looked at my passport, I chatted to the guard in French, asking him the most direct route to Nice, and they handed me back my passport and pointed me on to the right road. As soon as I was through I stopped the car. I parked it up against a wall, and sat there trembling with reaction. I was free. I was safe. I was out of Italy, and I was completely incapable of driving anywhere.

After about half an hour I had recovered sufficiently to find my legs again and I drove slowly into Nice which was only thirty minutes away. The lights were coming on and the town looked gay and welcoming. I knew it well from previous occasions and I drove to an hotel I had stayed in before on the Promenade des Anglais and booked a room for the night. I had a long, luxurious bath, changed into clean clothes, and then started phoning the good news to all my friends who were waiting anxiously to hear if I had crossed the border safely or not. When everyone had been assured that all was well, I suddenly realized that I was starving and hadn't eaten anything all day, not even breakfast. I celebrated my freedom in the hotel bar with a few drinks, and then went down to the restaurant and ordered a large dinner. That night I slept well for the first time in weeks. The next morning, Sunday, I left early to drive to Calais.

Arrivals are always messier in real life than they are in the imagination. My children were being brought to Dover to meet me when I arrived on Monday morning. The B.B.C. *Nationwide* crew were supposed to pick me up in Calais early Monday morning and follow me across on the morning boat to film the crossing and glad reunion. Unfortunately, for some reason they arrived on Monday afternoon and landed up in Boulogne, so instead of travelling Calais to Dover I had to join them in Boulogne and travel Boulogne to Folkestone, where my children weren't. I passed through Folkestone customs without too much difficulty, and my passport was stamped with a six-month temporary-stay permit. Eventually I reached Dover around 9 p.m., where the children had been waiting for me in an hotel since lunchtime and were trying bravely to keep awake to give me a welcome. They'd been brought down by Michael Ivens, accompanied by Mrs Jean Bawtree, their headmaster's wife. They had both been having terrible visions of my being arrested at the last moment and wondering what on earth they would tell the children.

But all was well. I was really there. We all spent that night at the Holiday Inn Hotel in Dover which Michael Ivens had kindly organized. I had kept my promise to my daughters and I had followed them to England. All I had to do now was get permission to stay there. The next morning at breakfast, my daughters were full of it. Where were we going to live? What was I going to do? When would they be able to see their new home? None of these questions I had any answers to yet. I promised them that we would have somewhere by the end of term, in a couple of months and as soon as I had found a place for us to live I would let them know exactly what it was like. And with that they had to be content. I found their questions quite unnerving. I had no money, no job, and no permission yet to stay in Britain for longer than six months. I could not return to Italy, nor did I want to, and I was going to be totally dependent on the good will of friends for the next few months to help me find employment and accommodation, and employment would only be possible when I had permanent residence. My conditions of stay at the moment forbade it. When

I told my children that we would have somewhere to live soon, I had no idea at all how I was going to achieve that. I hoped I was definite enough in my answers to reassure them. They caught the train back to school from Dover, escorted by Jean Bawtree, and I accompanied Michael Ivens in my car back to his house in St John's Wood, London, where I was to stay as a guest for the next two months. My first lunch in the U.K. was with Katherine Ivens and Carla Dobson of the *Standard*, who was the first journalist to interview me in London on arrival at the Ivenses' house.

Michael and Katherine Ivens were very good to me. They made me welcome and included me in their family so I felt as if I belonged and was totally at home. Never once did they make me feel as if I was intruding on their family life. They had two charming sons, Mark who was seven, and Paul who was five. I enjoyed being in a family with children around, and the company of the boys and their friends gave me a lot of pleasure. At weekends we often went together to the swimming pool at Swiss Cottage or played football in the children's school grounds, having first enjoyed Katherine's delicious cooking.

Michael not only opened his home to me, but he also gave me the facilities to help me pursue my cases, and in the meantime the Stanley Adams Appeal Committee continued its work on my behalf.

On the morning of Wednesday January 28th, 1981, two days after I had arrived in Britain, the Appeal Committee had arranged a press conference for me (in the Churchill Room at the Press Centre) as the start of the campaign to gain me permanent residence in Britain. Michael Ivens and Eric Moonman jointly chaired the conference, which was extremely well attended. The next day the morning papers carried my story, stating my desire for British nationality, my feelings about Willi Schlieder and detailing my hopes of suing Hoffmann-La Roche, Switzerland and the European Commission. The British papers were not the first to carry the details about Schlieder's involvement. I talked about it at my press conference because the story had already been broken two weeks earlier by the German magazine *Der Spiegel*. In an article entitled 'Like the Dreyfus scandal' (a quote from Ernest Glinne), *Der Spiegel* gave a comprehensive account of all that had happened to me to date, Schlieder's involvement in it, and the subsequent relations between the E.E.C. and Switzerland. The journalist had talked to my lawyer, Erich Diefenbacher, at length, and the *Spiegel* story contained a number of details from the court records, including those about Willi Schlieder's phone call to Dr Claudius Alder, Roche's lawyer, in which he was said to have given my name as the informant. Diefenbacher was quoted:

'Impossible and completely incomprehensible' ... is what Adams' lawyer Diefenbacher calls what E.E.C. Director-General Schlieder is alleged to have done.

The person at whom Diefenbacher's abuse is directed is still responsible for ensuring that trading practices throughout the whole Common Market are kept under control. He squarely rejects the allegations that he betrayed his own informer to the other side.

On the note in the files of the Basle State Prosecutor's office compromising him, the German E.E.C. official last week protested to *Der Spiegel*. 'I do not recall any telephone conversation with Alder and even if Alder did speak to me on the telephone, I certainly did not name Adams to him as the informer.'

Then he recollects an even better version: 'I dispute that I ever spoke to Alder on the telephone. Alder must first prove this.'

So it is one man's word against another's ...

Two days after this article appeared in *Der Spiegel* the European Commission issued a press statement. It read:

Press reports on the Adams case have mentioned by name Herr Willi Schlieder, the Director-General for Competition, alleging that he disclosed at the time to the Hoffmann-La Roche company's legal adviser the identity of the Commission's informant in the action brought by it against Hoffmann-La Roche over its vitamin products. In this connection the Commission would set the record straight as follows.

The Commission was informed in an anonymous letter asking for its help which reached it on 25 January 1975 that Mr Adams had been arrested in Switzerland on 31 December.

The Commission at once endeavoured to verify this, inter alia by a telephone call from Director-General Schlieder to

Hoffmann-La Roche's legal adviser, C. Alder. Herr Schlieder asked whether it was true that at Hoffmann-La Roche's request someone had been arrested in Switzerland for economic espionage on the Commission's behalf, and if so on what legal grounds.

The Commission would add that it and its staff have consistently refused both then and on other occasions, to divulge the source of its information with respect to Hoffmann-La Roche. With the same end in view, its verbal note of 5 February 1975 to the Head of the Swiss Delegation to the European Communities asked whether criminal proceedings had been instituted by the competent Swiss authorities against a person on the charge of breaching Article 273 of the Swiss Criminal Code.

The Commission moreover made use of all the means at its disposal to help Mr Adams both during his trial and after his conviction, thus it paid his defence costs and bail, and later in addition made him a special ex gratia payment of 50 million lire.

Despite the Commission's denial the press reports continued. On March 5th, 1981 a written question was put down to the Commission in the European Parliament by Mrs Bodil Kathrine Boserup, a Danish M.E.P.

Subject : The Adams Affair

According to recent reports it was in all probability a Director General in the Commission who, in 1975, denounced Stanley Adams to the Swiss authorities as 'thanks' for confidential information he had given to the Commission about Hoffmann-La Roche.

I am aware that the Director-General concerned has denied this accusation, but does not the Commission consider that this fairly well substantiated accusation itself throws doubt on the Commission's discretion and this will inhibit any further disclosures of confidential information? Will the Commission therefore take steps to remove all doubt about its Director-General's complicity in Adams' denunciation? If so, how will it do this?

The new Commissioner for Competition, the Dutchman Frans Andriessen, replied, somewhat tartly.

> . . . the Commission and its staff have consistently refused to divulge the source of confidential information in their possession.
>
> In these circumstances the Commission firmly insists that the allegations made in the Adams affair, which are both ill founded and tendentious in their presentation, and cast doubt on the strict compliance by Commission officials with the fundamental rules relating to the protection of confidential information, should cease.

But it was too late to matter any longer to Willi Schlieder. On January 27th, 1981 the *Daily Mirror* reported his resignation. Schlieder denied it had anything to do with the 'Adams Affair' and said his resignation was under discussion before the *Der Spiegel* article. On January 29th, two days later, in the *Daily Telegraph*, the Commission denied any connection, and said, 'With the change of the Commission there will also be a change of some Director-Generals, but these changes have not yet been decided and will not be decided for a couple of weeks . . . ' The Commission changed once every four years, at least most of the fourteen Commissioners and the President did. The bureaucracy that served them remained intact, apart from the occasional shuffle, as is the case with the British Civil Service. Schlieder had been Director-General of Competition since November 1970 and he had served in the Cabinet of Commissioner Haferkamp before. There seemed to be some confusion all round now as to whether he had already resigned, if so, why. The only certain fact is that he did resign in early 1981 and disappeared from Europe on a year's lecture tour of the United States.

Remarkably, the press conference following my arrival in Britain finally stirred Hoffmann-La Roche into comment. For the last few years they had habitually refused to comment on anything that was said about my arrest, imprisonment and subsequent life. They had refused to be interviewed by B.B.C. Radio Four saying first that it was an old case and best forgotten, and then that it was too fresh to talk about and would need a historical perspective. They refused to talk to the *World in Action* television team as well, stating simply, 'We are not involved in this case.' Not that their line had changed much since then, but they did expand a little, pointing out that 'the practice (fidelity contracts) objected to by the E.E.C. had ceased before the case came to court,' and that 'At no stage has Roche sought to impede or frustrate Mr Adams in his plans to set up a farming project. Nor has it any intention of hindering his attempts to make a new life for himself.'

I was glad to hear it. My energies were concentrated on two things, bringing pressure to bear on the new Commission in the hope that they might change their mind and award me proper compensation, and persuading the British authorities to give me permanent residence in Britain. What I really wanted was to have my British nationality restored, but permission to stay would at least be the first step. With the change of Commission from January 1st, 1981 there was a new President, Gaston Thorn. The Stanley Adams Appeal Committee began to plan the submission to him of a dossier on my case, in the hope that the new Commission might be more humane than the old one. (This dossier, signed by two Q.C.s and sent to Mr Thorn on March 31st, 1982, unfortunately brought no satisfactory results.) On February 3rd, 1981 a question was asked in the House of Lords by Lord Orr-Ewing. He wanted to know whether Her Majesty's Government 'will make strong representations to the European Economic Commission to ensure that justice is done to Stanley Adams, who suffered imprisonment, bankruptcy, the suicide of his wife, and received only derisory compensation after he had drawn the Commission's attention to the illegal practices of drug companies.' Her Majesty's Government, in the shape of Lord Trefgarne, the Foreign Office Minister, returned the usual bland replies about the British Government having no formal right to intervene, though 'Our permanent representation in Brussels have discussed the case informally with the Commission, with whom prime responsibility lies. We understand that the Commission are seized of the issues involved.'

Lord Orr-Ewing, Lord Fletcher, Lord Elwyn-Jones (a former Attorney-General), Lord Monson and Lord Waddon all spoke in my favour, urging the Government to make representations to the European Commission on my behalf, but the debate was chiefly remarkable for the views of Lord Paget of Northampton, once a Labour M.P. and prominent Q.C. He wanted to know:

Is it quite clear that there was no question at all of Mr Adams' employers Roche marketing any drug which had been insufficiently tested, or anything of that sort, the offences committed being purely commercial; that he was an executive of Roche, enjoying their confidence, and that, without warning them or protesting to them he went and sneaked to the European Commission; that the Swiss, who in my view are certainly a very highly civilized country, regard this kind of private treachery as criminal, that on a charge of this private criminal nature he was tried and sentenced; and that, so far as the European Commission are concerned, what they do to compensate their 'grasses' is their business and not ours.

Clearly, as far as Lord Paget was concerned, 'commercial' offences were unimportant, regardless of the effect they might have on ordinary people. The only excuse, ever, for 'sneaking' or 'grassing' could be a life-and-death situation, and then I rather fear it might have been frowned upon if one hadn't first nobly owned up to the multinational concerned about what one was about to do . . . Lord Paget and Roche were of one mind in this, though Roche disdained the use of quite such schoolboy terms. They complained that I had not reported any of my misgivings to my superiors before leaving Roche. It's true. I hadn't. I had a fine sense of self-preservation at the time which seems since then to have been justified.

I had come into Britain on a six-month temporary-stay permit, and it was essential that I change this into permanent residence as quickly as possible. I didn't want to find myself back in the Italian situation, fearing that each knock on the door meant that I was going to be deported, and it was well known that in Britain the immigration procedures had been tightened up lately and there had been a number of deportations of people who had 'overstayed' their welcome. If I was deported, the most likely country would be Italy, where I had come from, and that would have been completely disastrous for me and for my children. John Prescott, who had helped me so much in the past in Europe, was working for me again within the House of Commons, making representations about the possibility of getting British nationality, and initially of gaining me the right to live permanently in Britain. On March 5th he received a letter from Timothy Raison, the minister responsible for Immigration, saying that so far I had not made a formal application for residence, and that though he was happy to see John Prescott there wouldn't be much point in a meeting at this stage.

Peter Archer, P.C., Q.C., M.P., who had also been making representations on my behalf, received a similar reply and both he and John Prescott advised me to put in an application for residence. I had held back so far to give time for various representations to be made to the Home Office on my behalf. I had not wanted to risk being refused residence by an official unaware of my situation, as I knew from experience that it is always much more difficult for decisions to be reversed once they have been taken, than it is simply to give a favourable decision.

Once I had applied for residence (and I was helped in drafting my application by Ivor Walker, a member of the Appeal Committee and a Labour lawyer), letters in my support were sent to the Home Secretary and to Timothy Raison, minister at the Home Office. They were written by Labour and Conservative M.P.s in the House of Commons and by representatives of both parties in the House of Lords. Some had been supporters of mine for some time and others were contacted by the Appeal Committee after my arrival in the U.K. and asked for help, which they gave freely. I have copies of letters written by Ken Baker, Peter Bottomley, Sir Peter Emery, Sir Hugh Fraser, Anthony Steen, Geoffrey Finsberg, Peter Archer, John Prescott, Lord Orr-Ewing, Lord Chitnis, Lord Fletcher, Lord Fenner Brockway and Lord Belstead, and there were many more, including several bishops, who made either written or verbal representations to the Home Office asking that I be allowed to stay in Britain. All in all, I think about twenty M.P.s and a similar number of peers backed my case, as well as many people from outside Parliament, such as Sir John Foster, K.B.E., Q.C., Eric Moonman, Ivor Walker, Michael Ivens and John Lyle.

In June the Home Office replied to the various M.P.s and peers who had written to them on my behalf. For example, a letter to Anthony Steen on June 12th read:

You wrote to Mr Raison on 16th May on behalf of Mr Stanley Adams who wishes to be allowed to remain permanently in the United Kingdom.

This is to let you know that an application on this basis has now been received from Mr Adams and is being considered. As this is a complex and unusual case it will be necessary for some enquiries to be made. I am afraid that it may be some time before the results are known but Mr Raison will write to you as soon as possible.

The other replies said the same thing.

My permit was due to expire on July 27th. On July 2nd I was called for interview at the Immigration Department, but by July 15th I still had not heard anything and was becoming worried. That day, a Wednesday, Paul Foot ran a piece in the *Daily Mirror* saying I could be thrown out by the end of the month and asking why the Home Office had not yet done anything. In the course of writing the article he contacted the Home Office and was assured that I would not be thrown out until a decision had been reached. The next day, Thursday, I received my passport back with a six-month extension of stay stamped in it. The stamp said: 'Leave to remain in the United Kingdom, on condition that the holder does not engage in employment paid or unpaid, and does not engage in any business or profession, is hereby given until 12th January 82.'

This left me in a very difficult situation. The Home Office were obviously still considering my application for permanent residence. I wasn't sure if this was a good or a bad sign, but whichever it was I felt very insecure. I was also increasingly anxious to find a job so I could start paying my way again, and the conditions of my stay made that impossible. If I attempted to take a job then I would be in breach of the conditions, which even prevented me doing unpaid voluntary work. I had now left Michael and Katherine Ivens and with money provided by the Appeal Fund found a flat in London where I could be with my daughters during the school holidays. (I moved in the day before their term ended in April.) On October 22nd, 1981, I wrote a very depressed letter to Richard Caborn.

As I informed you on the telephone I am in a pretty mess at the moment. All things which I had expected to happen once I entered the U.K. have not happened at all. I am now on a six-months extension which expires 12.1.82. I am not allowed to work and earn a living; no funds come in any longer from the Stanley Adams Appeal, yet I am supposed to live on. But how? I do not even dream of mentioning my Nationality problem, knowing that if the U.K. government did not give me even Residence, they are even less likely to grant me British nationality. I feel quite let down.

A fortnight later, on November 5th, all the M.P.s and Peers who had written to Timothy Raison on my behalf received the following letter from him.

... I have given very careful consideration to all the facts of this case, in the knowledge that neither Mr Adams nor his children qualify for settlement under any part of the Immigration Rules. You will be pleased to know that I have decided, in view of the wholly exceptional circumstances of the case, to allow Mr Adams and his children to remain here permanently.

My children and I had a home, finally. We had a country we could call our own and we had the right to live and work in Britain for the rest of our lives without fear of being deported, whatever might happen in the future.

It was a security we hadn't had for a very long time.

17 A Story without an Ending

Today, as I write, it is November 5th, 1983. I can see the fireworks cascading down outside my window. It is nearly three years since I came to Britain, and two years to the day since my family and I were given British residence. I still live in a flat in London. It has two bedrooms and when my daughters are home with me the three of them share one small bedroom. Most of the year, though, they are away at school. Their fees have been met partly by the good will of the schools, and partly by educational trusts. In September 1981, on becoming thirteen, Nathalie moved on from Kingsmead, the school where she and her two sisters started, to King Edward's, a secondary school in Witley, Surrey. Sandy and Stephanie joined her at King Edward's in September 1983. By the time I finally got my residence and was entitled to move them to state schools they were well settled where they were and arrangements had been made to cover the fees. I am still unemployed, although I have applied for many, many jobs. Once or twice I have even made it to the interview stage. We now exist entirely on supplementary benefit. Even so, I still worry about what would happen to my children if they were at home and I did get a job. Who would look after them when I was at work and who would be in the house when they came back from school? So for the moment I have left them where they are, where I know they are happy, and secure.

It is over ten years since I first reported Roche to the E.E.C. for illegal trading practices, and I am forced to ask myself whether it was really worth it, and whether it achieved anything at all. To answer that question I need to know whether Switzerland has changed its attitude to secrecy, or its relationship with the big multinationals. I need to know whether Roche is still the same company I worked for, or whether it has reformed, or whether those who speak out, inside or outside Roche, are still likely to be put under pressure. I need to look at the wider context of the pharmaceutical companies and their activities in the world and see if they have changed at all. I need to examine the role of the European Commission, and the European Parliament, and assess how they have behaved, and why. And when I have done all that, I don't expect to find, in a chart of pluses and minuses, that there will be many pluses.

The Swiss government have never admitted that they were at fault in arresting me and charging me with spying. They didn't admit it at the time, and they don't admit it now. They have consistently argued that the Agreement they signed with the E.E.C. was to be applied within the framework of their own domestic law, and that my prosecution did not contravene any part of that agreement. Urged on by the European Parliament, the Commission eventually took the matter to the Joint Swiss/E.E.C. Committee, and tried time and again to persuade the Swiss to change that position. They could not even produce an expression of regret.

A statement about the final position came from a diplomatic meeting on October 28th, 1980 between Wilhelm Haferkamp (Vice-President of the European Commission and Foreign Affairs spokesman) and Mr Jolles (Secretary of State at the Swiss Foreign and Economic Affairs Ministry). As Haferkamp explained to the Legal Affairs Committee, it was 'not of course a legally binding obligation on the part of Switzerland since the agreement was and could only be reached at a political level'.

1) The parties agreed that the existing machinery for information and consultation between Switzerland and the Community should be used where information from Switzerland or the Community is involved which concerns the application of the principles relating to competition contained in the Free Trade Agreement between Switzerland and the European Economic Community.

2) The parties stated moreover that under the Swiss Federal Code of Criminal Procedure the Federal Council has a margin of discretion in deciding whether to bring criminal proceedings for any breach of Article 273 of the Swiss Penal Code. They also stated that in this connection *inter alia* the

close relationship and the Free Trade Agreement between Switzerland and the Community will naturally be taken into due consideration when weighing up the interests of the parties concerned.

Haferkamp concluded his explanation cheerfully: 'I wish finally to say that the Commission takes the view that an important step has been taken towards doing justice to the concern of the Parliament ... The Commission will follow closely the practical application of the political solution indicated. If, contrary to expectations, difficulties arise in this connection, this arrangement will be re-examined.' Such as when the Swiss decide again that despite the E.E.C.'s concern it is still in their interests to prosecute? After all, Article 273 is a powerful deterrent to would-be informers. Big business does not want it removed, and in Switzerland big business and the State are virtually inseparable. Their law says so.

If Wilhelm Haferkamp is right, and there is no possibility of another me being prosecuted in the future, then you would expect the Swiss to show their good will retrospectively. But they didn't. On November 25th, 1981, after two postponements, the case I had filed the previous year for a re-opening of my trial came to court. It was heard at Basle Appeals Court, where it was again held partly *in camera*. This time three Parliamentarians from the Socialist Group attended the proceedings; Professor Mauro Ferri, Chairman of the Legal Affairs Committee, Tom Megahy, member of the Legal Affairs Committee and Richard Caborn. With them was Jean-Pierre Simon, Deputy General-Secretary of the Group. Like everyone else from the general public, including the press, they had to leave the courtroom while the 'sensitive' areas were discussed. Because parts of the case were held *in camera*, I did not attend, as before.

The judge refused to re-open my case or rehabilitate me. He agreed with the State prosecutor that there was no new evidence that could justify a re-opening. Erich Diefenbacher had claimed that the European Court of Justice judgment against Roche in February 1979, the Legal Affairs Committee Report in March 1980 and the European Parliament's resolution of May 23rd, 1980 calling on the Swiss to re-open my case had all happened since my final appeal had been heard in 1978 and justified a re-opening. The judge agreed that the European Court of Justice had produced its judgment on Roche after my appeal, but said that as the European Commission had already produced its decision in 1976 the issues had been hypothetically considered and rejected as being irrelevant by the previous hearings. Diefenbacher had also claimed that by holding my trials *in camera* they had broken Article 6 of the European Convention of Human Rights, which was part of Swiss law. This was dismissed as being irrelevant to whether they re-opened the case or not.

When we failed to get my case re-opened in Basle, Diefenbacher appealed on my behalf to the Federal Supreme Court in Lausanne. This time he was not even called to a hearing. Out of the blue he received a letter saying that on February 17th, 1982 the appeal had been considered in private, with no public hearing, on the written petition only, and dismissed.

Whatever the politicians might be saying to each other, the courts maintained the *status quo*. I was convicted, I remained convicted, and the case was not going to be re-examined whatever the legal experts in the European Parliament might say. The case was being held in Switzerland, not in the E.E.C., and the Swiss would operate their law alone. No one could ever accuse the Swiss of not being consistent. Looking back, I don't know why we were all so disappointed at the result. There had never really been much evidence that the Swiss courts would change their position. I suppose we just found it hard to believe that so much diplomatic pressure could be resisted for so long without having some effect.

In June 1981 I appeared on a B.B.C. television *Man Alive* programme about Switzerland, 'Trouble in Paradise'. My story took up about twelve minutes of the hour-long programme. Nothing was said that had not been said before many times in the press or in other interviews. But the Swiss government were still moved to protest. On December 31st, 1981, the editor of *Man Alive* had a memorandum passed on to him which had been sent to the Vice-Chairman by the Swiss Ambassador. The memorandum was headed 'The cases of Roche and European Community cartel law and of Adams and Swiss Criminal Law, as represented in the programme "Trouble in Paradise" broadcast on BBC 2 on 24th June, 1981 and the true facts.' It was set out in two columns with quotes from the programme on one side, and 'the facts' on the other. The facts were the arguments used both by Roche and the Swiss government in the past and were fairly predictable but to me the most remarkable thing about this memorandum from the Swiss Ambassador is that it was ever sent at all. Besides my story, the programme contained references to the Swiss banking system, riots in the streets of Zurich, the Swiss parliament, multinational policies, and the sale of useless and dangerous drugs in the third world, and contained allegations not only about Roche's aggressive marketing strategies but about the sales policies of Ciba-Geigy and Nestlé as well. Yet it was three specific references to Hoffmann-La Roche and the Swiss government which provoked the Swiss Ambassador into complaining 'about the treatment given to Hoffmann-La Roche'. In a previous B.B.C. radio programme on my story the Swiss government had first said the case was nothing to do with them and, on being reminded that it was, had refused to comment. In the *World in Action* programme the Swiss government equally declined to comment, and to the best of my knowledge made no complaints either. To my mind this raises four questions. Firstly, the E.E.C. think they have a 'gentleman's agreement' with the Swiss that no one in my position would be prosecuted again. Just what is that agreement worth when the Swiss government are still claiming that my case had nothing to do with the Free Trade Agreement with the E.E.C.? Secondly, just how close is the relationship between Switzerland and Hoffmann-La Roche when nine years after Roche was first reported to the E.E.C. for illegal trading practices, and three years after they were finally convicted by the European Court of Justice, the Swiss government is still prepared to take up the cudgels on their behalf and plead they were not really guilty, only ignorant? Thirdly, it is obvious that this memorandum was never written to be made public, and the pressure was applied to the B.B.C. through the old boy network, involving the Swiss Ambassador and the B.B.C. Vice-Chairman. Where the network was not available then it appears that the pressure has not been applied, otherwise other independent television programmes would have received complaints. How much of this kind of pressure has been applied by Hoffmann-La Roche and the Swiss government privately in the past, with no one knowing about it? Or by Hoffmann-La Roche and other willing spokesmen? Fourthly, why is my case still, after all this time, such a sensitive issue? I can only conclude that it really does touch on Switzerland's most tender nerve, her secrecy laws, and she is determined at all costs to protect them, even if it means there have to be a hundred more Stanley Adamses to serve as examples to others who might be tempted to follow suit and report the illicit practices of their employers.

If it was Switzerland who prosecuted me, it was Roche who first lodged the complaint that led to my prosecution, and it was Roche's lawyers who worked in close co-operation with the State Prosecutor's office when the Prosecutor was preparing the case against me. As far as Roche were concerned, I was a spy. In a rare interview given in November 1981 in Zurich by Dr Adolf Jann, former president of Roche, to a foreign journalist, Dr Jann said of me, 'He was a spy . . . I mean a spy, there is an expression, you can say he was a traitor.' To Roche, and the people who worked there, what I did was totally incomprehensible. On the B.B.C. *Man Alive* programme a Roche spokesman was asked what the company view on me was, and replied, 'We think that Stanley Adams was misguided. It is very difficult for me to understand why he didn't do what would be the natural thing, to go to his bosses and tell them what his misgivings were about what the company were doing.'

Dr Jann was more forthright, 'Look here – I told you that I haven't known Mr Adams. I don't know his mentality. I do not know if he is normal or not. I do not know if he is satisfied with his career – or let's say salary or career – in Hoffmann-La Roche, I do not know.' (We did know each other, but only in business terms.)

The implication of what Dr Jann was saying is quite clear. To do what I did I must either have been mentally unhinged or else have held a grudge against the company and reported them to the E.E.C. out of revenge. The sad thing is that he probably believes that. No other motive would be credible to him, and he is not the only one. Ever since I wrote that fateful letter in February of 1973 to the European Commission people have said to me, 'Why? Why did you do it?' And it's hard to give a reply that they can understand. There was no blinding revelation, no sudden appalling experience, no bitter argument with a colleague or superior. I was paid well, I lived well, the company were good to me in many ways, so how do I explain what I did? How do I explain the cumulative sense of unease that finally pushed me into action?

I was a foreigner, which probably helped. I had not been brought up under the Swiss system with the belief that corporate loyalty is inviolable at all times, and that what the company does must be good, because your welfare is dependent on the company's welfare, and the company's welfare is dependent on the State's welfare, and the State's welfare is dependent on the welfare of all the companies put together, and the chain may not and cannot be broken without grave consequences to all concerned. To me, business was just business. It could be moral or immoral, depending on the way individuals chose to conduct it, and if the good of the company demanded the ruthless suppression of the individual or of smaller businesses, then there was something wrong. I had been brought up to question the *status quo*, not to take things for granted, to explore other ways of doing things. It was second nature to me to ask why something was done this way, and not that way. Ironically, it was just this quality that helped my advance in Roche. Applied to everyday problems it was creative and useful. Applied to the ethics of business it was embarrassing and challenging and had to be suppressed immediately.

From the moment I was arrested and charged in Switzerland I was an officially declared outcast. I had had hundreds of friends in Roche at headquarters and around the world. Once I had left and it was known that I had been in contact with the European Commission not one friend phoned or invited me for a drink, or wrote to me, or asked how I was despite all that had happened to me. I discovered later that Dr Jann had sent a circular to all Roche employees everywhere, from top management to the cleaning staff, to say that no one was to have any contact with me. There were one or two friends who made initial contact with the Stücklins when I was arrested to find out what had happened, but once the circular went round their questions and phone calls stopped abruptly. If the company said I didn't exist, I didn't exist.

As a foreigner, I had also had experience of what happened when power was uncontrolled. As a young boy in Malta I had stood and watched the bombs dropping day and night on the island. I can remember vividly even now the rage I felt at my helplessness and the belief that grew in me that it could not be right for one group of people to treat another group of people like this, simply because they were bigger and more powerful. Perhaps an echo of this was awakened in me later by the ruthlessness of Roche's business practices, in which the individual simply didn't count, and by the arrogance that assumed that size and power automatically bestowed the right to do whatever one chose and to crush any opposition that was unfortunate enough to get in the way. Dr Jann complained in the interview he gave that 'The press was always against us' and that the newspapers were only interested in sensation and not in reporting what Roche were doing for the good of mankind. But if Roche were getting a bad press, they had only themselves to blame. Their history over the last twenty years shows clearly the lengths to which they were prepared to go in order to suppress competition and ensure that their profits remained high, even at the expense of the individual.

There are few of the big companies who have not been accused at some time in their career of suppressing individuals in an attempt to maximize profits. The drug industries do have one particular problem in common. On the ethical side (medicines) they are protected from competition to some extent by the use of patents, which guarantee them the sole use of a drug for the lifetime of its patent (unless specific licences are granted for others to produce it). This is enough to help the companies keep their prices high (they would say, to pay off their research costs . . .) but in turn it creates another problem, because it means that the companies' key profits are usually based on comparatively few products. In the early 1970s Roche were making 80 per cent of their profit on just ten major items. If any one of the key products is then threatened, whether by doubts about safety, or pricing, or proper usage, then there is a vast amount of money at stake. It is understandable in these circumstances that the drug companies do not welcome 'scares' of any kind. The problem has always been in defining where the line of natural caution ends, and unscrupulous protection of profits begins. There is a long history of occasions when critics have accused the drug industry of crossing that barrier: whole books have been written on the subject (such as *Bitter Pills* by Dianna Melrose, published by Oxfam in November 1982). Thalidomide, Entero-Vioform, powdered baby milk in the Third World . . . a list of them only goes to show that whatever the pharmaceutical companies may say, it is not enough simply to allow them to police themselves. There is too much money, and too much self-interest at stake for any such policing to be totally reliable. As I see it now, and possibly my experience has made me cynical, the companies are not there to add to the good of human kind, they are unfortunately there to make a profit. If a lot less money were spent on producing parallel drugs to compete with other firms in the most profitable areas, where there are already sufficient drugs on the market, then far greater sums could be freed for research into cures for rare diseases.

The multinational companies can act across national frontiers which means that the Third World may find not only that several of its drugs are suspect, or simply unnecessary, but that it may be paying much higher prices for them than it should. This is made easier for the drug companies by the fact that local pharmaceutical industries (if they exist) are still in their infancy and provide little competition. The majority of drugs are still imported. By using the system known as transfer pricing, in which the parent company sells materials to its subsidiaries, sometimes through other subsidiaries, at prices calculated on the maximum the market will bear, and adapted to the tax demands of various countries, companies can make huge profits while declaring only a minimum profit, or even a loss in individual countries. Government economists in Colombia were puzzled to find in 1973 that the pharmaceutical companies were very keen to expand their operations, while at the same time they were reporting very low profits. An investigation revealed that the average over-pricing of ingredients by foreign-owned subsidiaries of the drug companies was 155 per cent. Librium, manufactured by Roche, was over-priced by a staggering 6,478 per cent. The general overcharging meant that in reality the profit rate being earned by the foreign-owned drug companies was not the 6 per cent reported to the Colombian government, but 79 per cent.

In moral terms this amounts to exploitation, either in charging excessively high prices which might deprive individuals and medical services of the drugs or vitamins they need, or in denying a true level of tax to the host country, which may well have offered very generous development grants to enable the company to set up shop in the hope of tax and employment returns, or in many cases both. (It is not only the Third World that suffers, of course, the British Monopolies Commission report demonstrated how it worked with Librium and Valium in Britain, but the Third World is generally more susceptible because of the lack of competition.)

When, in the November 1981 interview, Dr Adolf Jann was challenged about Roche International Ltd in Motevideo, Uruguay, he first said, 'I do not know, I do not know about these details,' and later, when pressed by the interviewer replied:

My dear friend, I can only tell you one thing. In the U.S.A. most of the American pharmaceutical firms have their daughter companies in Puerto Rico . . . that means they are free in importing their products into the United States and they can make all the profits in Puerto Rico . . . I mean that is human, humanly understandable that you try, if it is legal you know, to make some money there where you don't have to pay 50, 60, 70, 90% of the profit in tax, because we need that again for other purposes especially reserves and investments . . .

Do you think that somebody is considered a criminal because he is using the loopholes in the United States tax system to avoid taxes?

Huh? Why?

He then denied any connection between the Puerto Rican analogy and Roche International Ltd in Montevideo. But his answer is indicative of the way that the big companies think, and certainly the way that Roche thought as I knew it when I worked there. If something is technically legal, then it is permissible.

I never set out to be a martyr. I never wanted to suffer for any cause. All I ever intended to do was pass information quietly to the relevant authorities to help them exert a tighter control over the multinational pharmaceutical companies in the area in which I worked. I expected to tell the Competition department of the E.E.C. what I knew, help them in any way I could, and preserve my anonymity so that no one would ever know what I had done. It didn't work out that way. As far as the European Commission were concerned I rapidly changed from being a valuable informer who was going to help them control the multinationals, to a diplomatic incident when I was imprisoned, to an embarrassment who had to be helped out of problems in Italy when the banks and agencies refused credit, to an irritant who still appeared to be unemployed and who was causing a stir in the European Parliament, to a downright nuisance who wouldn't accept the payment offered by them following the Donnez report and wouldn't keep quiet about it either. The Commission has always refused to acknowledge any link or 'causal effect' between what had happened to me in Switzerland and what happened to me in Italy. Of course, once you refuse that link then I must appear merely as an incredibly incompetent businessman, who is incapable of making good, and blames the European Commission for not helping him out. It was not how the elected European Parliament viewed me, but increasingly I suspected it was the way the appointed European Commission viewed me. They were simply not prepared to accept that the results of my giving them information could be so long-term or so devastating or that they had any legal responsibility to protect me from those results. Their position has still not changed. Despite endless letters on my behalf, from politicians and peers of all different political colours, my file remains firmly closed and they have no intention at all of re-opening it.

On July 7th, 1982 I presented a complaint against Switzerland to the European Commission of Human Rights in Strasbourg. It followed the final rejection of my application to re-open proceedings in Switzerland on February 17th, 1982. (This time I was within the six-month period necessary.) I presented the application myself without legal expenses. On July 8th the Socialist Group in the European Parliament presented a motion for a resolution which stated:

The European Parliament, A. having regard to its resolution on the Adams case and the trade agreement between the E.E.C. and the Swiss Confederation (Donnez report Doc.1–44/80); B. having regard to the decision of the Swiss Federal Court in the Adams case of 17 February 1982,

1) Again reminds the Commission of its moral obligation to support Mr Adams both financially and by the release of evidence, in any proceedings before the Commission and Court of Human Rights in Strasbourg designed to rectify the injustices of legal proceedings resulting from his actions which were instrumental in halting the illegal business practices of the company Hoffmann-La Roche.

2) Instructs its President to forward this resolution to the President of the Commission.

As with all other resolutions presented to the European Parliament on my case, this one was adopted without difficulty. The European Parliament was beginning to get very tired of reminding the Commission of their 'moral obligation' to me. They had hoped that the Donnez report and resolution adopted in May 1980 would have solved my problems for once and for all, but had reckoned without the obstinacy of the E.E.C. Commission.

My application to the European Commission of Human Rights has been accepted for registration, and a *rapporteur* named. The preliminary hearing to determine whether the application will be forwarded to the complete session of the Commission of Human Rights for consideration is due to take place shortly. It should have taken place in October 1982, but I had problems.

To help me in my application I had written to the Competition department of the E.E.C. Commission reminding them of the European Parliament's latest resolution and asking them to send me copies of the documents which I originally sent to them about Roche's activities, and which they used to help obtain a conviction against Roche. I stressed that I was not asking for any copies of papers belonging to the E.E.C., but only copies of those papers which I gave to the E.E.C. during 1973.

The letter was addressed to Mr Hans Andriessen, the new Dutch Commissioner for Competition, and was sent on September 24th, 1982. On October 23rd I had still had no reply from Mr Andriessen, despite two telexes. I needed the papers urgently as my application was due to be heard at the end of October. On the 23rd I wrote to Mr Pieter Dankert, the Dutch Socialist President of the European Parliament, asking him to intervene for me and persuade the Competition department to reply. Finally, on November 4th (after I had had to postpone the hearing till the next session in December) the Commission sent their reply. My letter had been passed from the Competition department to Mr Ehlermann, my old acquaintance the German Director-General of Legal Services. Mr Ehlermann wrote,

I am instructed to inform you that the E.E.C. Commission is prepared to assist you in your case within the limits of its own regulations. To that end you may convey the following to the Commission on Human Rights.

1) The E.E.C. Commission accepts that it received from you certain documents originating in Switzerland which permitted it to take a decision against Hoffmann-La Roche for an infringement of E.E.C. competition law.

2) This decision was published in the Journal of the European Communities no.L223/27 of 6 August 1976 and was largely confirmed by a judgment of the Court of Justice of the European Communities of 13 February 1979, Case 85/76/ 1979/2 European Court Reports, 461.

3) Having regard to the nature of the documents in question, and in particular to the fact that they may contain business secrets, the Commission is not at liberty to make disclosure of them as such to you. However, if requested to do so by the Commission on Human Rights, the Commission is prepared to have the appropriate official appear before it to speak about the events surrounding your case and in particular the fact that the documents you provided did indeed enable the decision to be taken. In the same circumstances the Commission is prepared to examine how far it might be possible to release the documents in question to the Commission on Human Rights, and under what conditions . . .

There's a kind of Alice in Wonderland logic to all this that defeats me.

I give the E.E.C. documents, secretly.

The fact that it was me who gave the documents is a secret, but the documents are not.

The E.E.C. Commission gives away the secret that it was me who gave them the documents.

The E.E.C. Commission uses the documents, which are not secret, to convict Roche.

Roche tell the Swiss government it was me who told the E.E.C. and the Swiss put me in prison for giving away secrets.

The Commission say they are not secrets and pay to get me out again.

I say they are not secrets.

The Swiss say they are secrets and convict me.

I say they aren't and appeal to the European Commission of Human Rights.

The E.E.C. Commission says they are.(??)

I can't have them back, in case I give away what I gave them in the first place.

But they might let the European Commission of Human Rights have them, if they ask nicely and promise not to tell anyone the secrets that are not secrets that are secrets.

But they are not sure.

It would be funny if it wasn't so crazy and didn't have such far-reaching implications. My story has no ending. There is no victorious triumph, no 'individual beats the system', no 'Adams wins out at last', just an endless grey struggle and a dogged determination on my part to keep going for reasons I am sometimes no longer sure of. In September 1982 my lawyer, Erich Diefenbacher, resigned his mandate in despair. Despite repeated letters and statements from him that on February 13th, 1979 he was assured verbally, in the presence of Roy Jenkins, then President of the Commission, Wilhelm Haferkamp, Commissioner, and John Prescott, M.P., that his fees would be paid as Dr Bollag's were, the European Commission has consistently refused any liability, denied any such guarantees were made, and refused to pay him. In addition to this he has been subjected to considerable harassment from the Swiss authorities. He tells me that his chambers have been raided by the police, and he has been reprimanded by the Swiss Bar Association for 'unethical publicity' following the article in *Der Spiegel* which named Schlieder and referred to Court documents. If it happens again he says he will lose his licence to practise as a lawyer. Finally, he has had enough. In June 1983 I sent him £3,300 (money which I was forced to borrow) to secure the return of some of my documents. I have managed to find other lawyers in Britain, Germany and Switzerland to help me.

I do not have any money at all. I left Roche in 1973 earning Sfr. 97,500 gross a year (£32,500 – the exchange rate by then was Sfr.3 to £1). Since then I have had no income. I have had to live on the kindness of friends, and now on the minimum benefit I am entitled to. And yet there has been no shortage of publicity, no shortage of people prepared to campaign for me. Nobody could argue that what happened to me happened only because no one knew what was happening and if people had known it would have been stopped. To me that's the most frightening element of this story. I have had the whole of the European Parliament on my side. I have had politicians of all colours, businessmen, newspapers, radio, television, old age pensioners, young children, married couples – all trying to help or tell my story. And still little has changed since I came out of prison in Switzerland in 1975. Is the opposition to me really so powerful? And if it is, what would have happened if I had not been articulate, not been used to dealing with people at all levels of society, not been a linguist, not been someone trained never to take no for an answer? If I had been someone less aggressive, less articulate, and yet with an equally tender conscience? Would my children and I have starved to death quietly somewhere, unnoticed and unheard of? Would there have been an initial splash of publicity when I was released from Basle prison, only for my case to be forgotten once it had left the public eye? If I had stopped phoning when secretaries told me that people were not in, if I had stopped writing when my first letters received no answer, if I had stopped being a nuisance and gone away when people wanted me to go away, would I have been allowed to rot to death in some prison somewhere or end up broken in some psychiatric hospital, or would I have committed suicide? I know it sounds melodramatic, but there were times during my last two years in Italy when I was very close to that, and that was when I had friends at least trying to help me, even if in material terms they weren't very successful. I had many people helping me in Britain, people in positions of power. If there had been no one, would I have been deported back to Italy by the immigration officials to face a further prison sentence? After all, the Home Office itself said I had no claims to stay under the immigration rules, and I wouldn't be the first or the last person to be deported from Britain to face prison elsewhere.

All this is speculation, but I wonder sometimes when I measure the power that was used against me, whether there aren't other individuals, many of them, who have followed their consciences but, unlike me, have never been heard of again. I acted according to my conscience in a way that I thought was both moral and legal. Mine was not a mercurial and impetuous act. It was planned and calculated, and never intended as a gesture of defiance. It was not a quixotic act of individualism nor a petition for martyrdom. I wanted to help the European Community control the power of giant firms who laughed at national borders and fixed the market between them with impunity, leaving the small man to go to the wall, and I wanted to help the millions of ordinary people around the world who suffer because the power of the multinationals goes unchecked. The result was that the company I worked for was fined £150,000, a tiny drop in its ocean of profits. I was imprisoned. My wife hanged herself. I was banished from Switzerland. My reputation was ruined. My business went bankrupt. I was imprisoned a second time in Italy. My children were forced to live away from home and eventually I fled to Britain, homeless and penniless. Today I live in London with my three daughters. I do not know what the future holds for us.

In 1980 Ernest Glinne wrote an article in a Belgian newspaper in which he referred to me as Europe's 'Dreyfus'. My case, he said, 'like Dreyfus . . . has deservedly become a *cause célèbre* in Europe'. The article was published immediately after the European Parliament had voted unanimously to accept the Donnez report. 'It is indispensable', said Glinne, 'that Stanley Adams, a fifty-year-old who is now almost a broken man, be acquitted of all the charges brought against him, and that the iniquitous judgments made on this case be annulled.' But if I was Europe's Dreyfus, Europe's 'test case', then Europe has failed the test. Switzerland has failed because I remain convicted. The judgments against me have never been annulled. The European Commission has failed because it refused to protect an individual against the power of the multinationals, and because it failed to stand by its principles and force Switzerland either to abide by an agreement signed with the E.E.C. or withdraw from that agreement. The European Parliament, for all the efforts on my behalf, and in spite of the adoption of the Donnez report, also failed, ultimately because it simply did not have the power to force the Commission to accede to its wishes, despite repeated attempts to do so. Of what use is an elected European Parliament if it has no say on a matter even when it presents a totally united front? It does have one power, the power to pass a motion of no confidence in the Commission and force the Commission to resign, but this power was never used.

I shall continue as best I am able, without funds, to fight. I am pursuing my case against the Swiss Confederation at the European Commission of Human Rights. On July 18th, 1983 I issued a writ against the E.E.C. Commission at the European Court of Justice (case no. 145/83) for breach of confidentiality and negligence, and I have claimed considerable damages. I shall also sue Hoffmann-La Roche for damages. How, I do not know, but I will do it. And I shall do it not only for me, but for all those other potential whistle-blowers who now look at me and think, as they are meant to think, 'It's not worth it,' and keep silent.

Because we need them. The world needs them if it is to survive. The fiercer the pressures to keep silent, the more urgent the need is for people to speak out.

Friends ask me now, 'Would you have done it, if you had known everything that was going to happen?' That is an impossible question to answer. But, if you leave aside the death of my wife, then I would say without hesitation Yes, and mean it. Because if I answer No, and other people answer No, then what hope will there be for my children? and my children's children?

If you have a tale to tell, then I say, tell it.

It is better to die standing upright, than to live on your knees.

Index